Lives, Letters, and Quilts

Lives, Letters, and Quilts

Women and Everyday Rhetorics of Resistance

Vanessa Kraemer Sohan

The University of Alabama Press
Tuscaloosa

The University of Alabama Press
Tuscaloosa, Alabama 35487-0380
uapress.ua.edu

Typeface: Minion and Scala Sans
Cover image: Gee's Bend, Alabama, photograph by Carol M. Highsmith; courtesy of the George F. Landegger Collection of Alabama Photographs in Carol M. Highsmith's America, Library of Congress, Prints and Photographs Division
Cover design: Michele Myatt Quinn

Cataloging-in-Publication data is available from the Library of Congress.
ISBN: 978-0-8173-2038-6
E-ISBN: 978-0-8173-9267-3

For Mike, Preston, and Madeleine

Contents

Figures

Acknowledgments

Thank you to my family and friends for making the seemingly impossible possible, each and every day. Thank you to my husband, Mike, for the invisible-to-most-but-not-to-me hours of labor you have put into keeping our lives intact while I write: you're amazing, you make me laugh, I love you. Thank you to Preston and Madeleine for letting me work and for interrupting my work; I promise my next book will have more pictures. Thank you to my mom and dad, Mark and Jayne Kraemer, for serving as models of artistic and intellectual engagement throughout my life and for supporting me always. Thank you to my inimitable in-laws, Jim and Peggy Sohan, for the care and support you've given so selflessly over the years. Thank you to Laura for believing in me as only a little sister can, and to your crew, Daniel, Leo, Julia, and baby Dan, for your love and laughter. Thank you to my brothers-in-law, Jim and Pat, and to my nephew Nicholas, for your encouragement and support over the years. Thank you to Grandmom Helen Kraemer, for my love of books, and to Grandmom and Grandpop Pilong for my love of the word, and to the (many) Pilongs and Kraemers for their support from afar.

Thank you to Samantha NeCamp for providing comments in record time, and encouragement at the right time—you've read more drafts of this project than anyone, and I can't thank you enough for your guidance and model stoicism throughout this process. Thank you to Bruce Horner, Min-Zhan Lu, Carol Mattingly, Susan Ryan, Karen Kopelson, Tom Byers, A. Suresh Canagarajah, Lisa Arnold, Brice Nordquist, Carrie Kilfoil, Kelly Blewett, Alicia Brazeau, and the numerous other teachers, mentors, writing group members, and collaborators I was blessed to work with during my time at the University of Louisville, many of whom continue to support me today.

Thank you to the J. B. Speed Art Museum for hosting the exhibition *Gee's Bend: The Architecture of the Quilt*, which captured my imagination as a graduate student.

Thank you to my colleague Paul Feigenbaum for your encouragement, for keeping me accountable, and also for brainstorming the phrase "everyday rhetorics of resistance." Thank you to Martha Schoolman, Heather Blatt, Wanda Raiford, and Nandini Dhar for providing a productive, safe space for commenting, collaboration, and commiseration. Thank you to my department chairs, Heather Russell and James Sutton, and my colleagues in the writing program, Kimberly Harrison, Jackie Amorim, Maheba Pedroso, Andrew Golden, Ming Fang, Luke Thominet, and too many others to name. Thank you to my students for making academia matter, and for inspiring me with your recontextualization of languages, genres, media, and modes.

Thank you to the Oregon Historical Society, Portland, including Scott Daniels and the other amazing librarians who helped me retrieve files during spring 2016. Thank you to the Wolfsonian–Florida International University Museum and Object Collection and its staff of dedicated researchers and librarians for permission to include the image of the Townsend Plan quilt. Thanks particularly to Amy Silverman for your help finding the image of the quilt, as well as your work with me and my students in Material/Cultural Rhetorics and Writing, during the spring of 2015, made possible through an Andrew W. Mellon Foundation course infusion grant. Thank you to Kelly Ritter and the reviewers at *College English* for your feedback and support in the publication of a previous version of chapter 3, portions of which were published as "'But a Quilt Is More': Recontextualizing the Discourse(s) of the Gee's Bend Quilts," *College English* 77, no. 4 (2015): 294–316 (copyright 2015 by the National Council of Teachers of English; used with permission).

Finally, thank you to Dan Waterman and his team at the University of Alabama Press for your amazingly efficient and effective feedback and support on this project, and thank you to the reviewers of my manuscript for your thorough and helpful feedback and support.

Abbreviations

ARYE	Aged Retirement Youth Employment, Inc.
FQB	Freedom Quilting Bee
OHS	Oregon Historical Society
*SAE	*Standard American English
SL/MN	Single Language / Modal Norm
SRTOL	"Students' Right to Their Own Language" (1972)
SSA	Social Security Act
SWE	Standard Written English
TNW	*Townsend National Weekly*

INTRODUCTION

(Un)Conventional Means

Recontextualizing Everyday Rhetorics of Resistance

It appears you leave no sympathy for the living elderly people, the house just passed #B552—now I wonder if you will have respect for the dead and use your influence in getting this bill passed. You sure are a joke. You leave broken your promise with us.

—From a letter by Townsend Club president Pearl S. Burkhalter to Oregon state senator Howard C. Belton, chastising him for not supporting a pension bill to help the elderly, Oregon City, Oregon, c. 1938–45

Nothing short of the constraining love of Christ, nothing short of a positive sense of religious duty could induce me to make this request, and trusting the President will kindly excuse the liberty I have taken. . . . I may add that I believe I should not occupy more than fifteen minutes of the President's time, which I am well aware is exceedingly valuable.

—From a letter by Quaker traveling minister E. P. Gurney to President Abraham Lincoln, requesting a meeting with him after she and her delegation were turned away from the White House, Washington, DC, September–October 1862

When I piece quilts, I take my material off the shelf and lay it out on the bed. I see which materials I want to match with the other pieces. Sometimes I don't know my color. Sometimes it don't matter what color it is, I just feel that it will fit. When I hold it up and look at it, if it don't look right in there, I take it out. Sometimes it looks good, and sometimes it don't look right or it don't look the way I want it to be, so I take it out. Sometimes I let it stay in there. If I let it stay in there, it is a challenge to me. Then I try another piece to get it to work out. And then it come out right. When I finish it and lay it on the bed, I see all them pieces that I

didn't believe would work, but I made it work. And it looks good to me. And that's what matters.
—Quiltmaker Mary Lee Bendolph, explaining her quiltmaking process to art collector Matt Arnett, Gee's Bend, Alabama, 2006

God Decrees "Youth Work for Work, Age for Leisure." Townsend.
—Embroidered inscription on Townsend quilt, Mitchell, South Dakota, c. 1940

In the above scenes, we hear from a diverse set of composers differently situated by their race, gender, class, region, and religion, who are connected by their ability to see, engage, adopt, and adapt the most effective means of persuasion available to them in a particular time, place, and space, for specific purposes and audiences.[1] Pearl Burkhalter's draft letter is one of many such missives found in the archives of the Oregon Historical Society (OHS) documenting her tireless work as a local leader in support of the Townsend Old Age Revolving Pension Plan, a $200 monthly pension scheme developed by a California medical doctor to rescue the impoverished elderly during the Great Depression. Burkhalter and thousands of elderly women and men proselytized and raised funds for Dr. Francis Everett Townsend's monthly pension plan in the hope of lifting themselves out of penury and into the working or middle class. Though the plan itself never succeeded, their work established the elderly as a political constituency and paved the way for Social Security as we know it today. Quaker minister E. P. Gurney sought to meet President Abraham Lincoln during a turning point in the Civil War, intending to console and encourage him and also, potentially, to take the opportunity to address the issue of Quaker conscientious objectors. Gurney did eventually secure a meeting with Lincoln, and their interview and subsequent correspondence made such an impression on him that one of her letters was rumored to be in his pocket on the night of his assassination.[2] In describing her quiltmaking process, Mary Lee Bendolph highlights the intentionality of her improvisational quiltmaking choices. The abstract quilts created by Bendolph and other women in the Gee's Bend, Alabama, community have been praised by quiltmakers and art historians as some of the finest pieces of abstract art created during the twentieth and twenty-first centuries; they also demonstrate the power of material objects to engage viewers in confronting injustice and social inequality.[3] The quilt created by Club No. 1 of Mitchell, South Dakota, boldly proclaims Townsend mottos, offering a snapshot of the diverse ways Townsendites offered their support and fought for pension reform.

This book examines how writers and composers without traditional forms of power resist dominant social, cultural, and political structures by engaging in what I term *everyday rhetorics of resistance*: the conscious, purposeful recontextualization of the seemingly ordinary means and materials available in order to mediate thought and action, and to persuade others.[4] To address the question of how composers across history have gained agency over their words and work to find creative and productive ways of making meaning, speaking back to power, and gaining a hearing, I make use of a translingual and transmodal framework informed by feminist rhetorical practice. I apply this framework to three case studies: the letter-writing campaigns of the Townsendites, particularly club president Pearl Burkhalter; the ministry of nineteenth-century Quaker E. P. Gurney; and the abstract work-clothes quilts created by the Gee's Bend quiltmakers and a fundraising quilt created by quiltmakers associated with the Townsend Movement. Everyday rhetorics of resistance matter because they are at the core of grassroots political and social movements. Through recontextualization, composers engage in what Paul Feigenbaum identifies as *collaborative imagination*, working together to envision and enact a better future for themselves and their communities.[5]

To identify and understand the rhetorical facility at work in such texts, I draw on a translingual approach, which builds upon and revises previous interdisciplinary discussions of the intersections of language, agency, and power by redefining difference as the norm, rather than a deviation from or alternative to the norm. The translingual approach seeks to disrupt the dominance of standard language ideology and draw attention to the diverse ways in which *all* composers—whether ostensibly monolingual or multilingual—engage in difference and repetition within and across languages, genres, and discourses (*translinguality*), as well as modes and media (*transmodality*). As Lu and Horner have argued extensively, understanding difference as the norm requires looking at sites of less obvious difference, including *difference-in-similarity* (texts that might appear standard, conventional, or normal).[6] In this book, I look to examples of composers, compositions, or contexts we might otherwise term *everyday* in a pejorative sense (generic complaint letters, conformist prayer and preaching, utilitarian quilts) to consider how the case studies provide instances of *recontextualization*: the process by which composers deliberately reform, reinvent, and reconstruct the languages, media, and modes available to them in light of the time, place, and space of their particular practice (their temporal, spatial, and material contexts). Through recontextualization, the composers I study draw attention to and seek to improve the material conditions of their own lives and the lives of people in and beyond their communities.

The case studies help to test the premise, forwarded by A. Suresh Canagarajah and others who promote a translingual approach to literacy practice, that the field should "treat cross-language interactions and contact relationships as fundamental to *all* acts of communication and relevant for *all* of us."[7] I argue that if translingual literacy practices are relevant for all and apply to seemingly monolingual and monomodal as well as multilingual and multimodal practices, and if these practices are not new, but can be applied to contemporary and historical contexts, then the translingual and transmodal approach can also be applied to a necessarily disparate set of cases in which composers engage in everyday forms of resistance and represent an intersection of positionalities by virtue of their age, gender, class, status, race, ethnicity, religion, and ability. Important scholarship considers the translingual practices at work in transnational sites with more obviously multilingual histories; fewer studies, however, take up the call by Lu and Horner to engage with sites of less obvious forms of difference.[8] And while Bruce Horner, Cynthia Selfe, and Tim Lockridge have called for transmodality as a way to disrupt the ideology of a "single, uniform ('standard') language or modal norm" (SL/MN), more scholarship is needed for the field "to recognize the degree to which existing (and past) practices are at odds with the ideology of SL/MN (e.g., the mythic English monolingual character of the U.S.) and to recuperate the full array of practices occluded by dispositions advanced by that ideology," including newer and older technologies, such as letters and quilts.[9] My project thus forwards current conversations on translingual and transmodal literacy practices by offering historical examples of the "full array of practices" composers have used, and by applying translinguality and transmodality beyond classroom walls.[10]

Without an understanding of how ordinary composers have engaged in extraordinary everyday rhetorics of resistance, we might perpetuate the historical tendency to overlook the important contributions to politics, art, history, and culture made by individuals outside the mainstream—a tendency that feminist rhetorical scholarship has worked against for years. This project therefore responds to the call by feminist rhetoricians to reconceive of rhetorical practice and to "relativiz[e] rather than universaliz[e] what Aristotle identified as 'the available means of persuasion'" in order to consider how women (and men) have composed across time and space, "often in very different channels and genres than the public discourse of the male establishment."[11] As feminist historiographer Carol Mattingly has convincingly argued, the field needs to "redefine what counts as evidence in evaluating rhetoric and rhetoricians," a move that requires scholars to "consider evidence not typically considered in determining rhetorical acumen—evidence essential to a worthy reshaping of our tradition. We must immerse ourselves in a broad range of historical texts, across genres, including but not limited to texts of speeches, to gain a clearer understanding of both the politically active women in our history and the evidence that demonstrates their facility with rhetorical matters."[12] By drawing attention to the life and letters of local Townsend activist Pearl Burkhalter, by exploring how E. P. Gurney adapted her religious rhetorical practice to effectively engage her interlocutors, and by studying women quiltmakers in rural Alabama and in the Townsend Movement, I immerse myself in a "broad range of historical texts" created by women—texts whose import has often been overlooked because they "do not fit neatly" into "traditional definitions of rhetoric . . . constructed around notions of masculine rhetoric."[13] Such texts, I argue, demonstrate women's "facility with rhetorical matters," though with means and materials not always recognized as important or understood as rhetorical or discursive. My project thus answers Mattingly's call for feminist rhetoricians to "continue to question the stories handed down to us . . . even those we helped to create."[14] Though I, by necessity, single out particular women for analysis, I am aware of the potentially problematic repercussions of celebrating individual women rhetors as part of recovery work (a move Barbara Biesecker warns might perpetuate the trends inherent to patriarchal canon formation).[15] Instead, I aim to demonstrate how the individual women in these studies engage in recontextualization in ways that are representative of the strategies of innumerable other unrecognized women whose words and work have been lost to history, in part because their contributions were considered everyday, ordinary, and, therefore, unworthy of notice or preservation.

The case studies allow for new insights into women's rhetorical practice by asking and answering some of the simple, yet groundbreaking questions Royster and Kirsch identify as central to feminist rhetorical practice: "Where were the spaces in which women chose / were permitted to speak? What were their fora, their platforms, the contexts of their rhetorical performances? Who were their audiences? What were their concerns? What tools for interaction did they use? How did they construct their arguments? What were the impacts and consequences of their rhetorical performances? How were they trained? How did they convey legacies of action?"[16] In examining the spaces, places, platforms, concerns, arguments, and audiences represented by these case studies, we can better understand recontextualization as a flexible strategy employed by female rhetors who sought to make their voices heard in spite of the asymmetrical power relations that worked to silence them. The work of the case studies therefore moves beyond "mere" recovery and points to rhetoric as a social, not just a "public" phenomenon. In this way it helps us to break the false binary between public and private that feminist rhetorical practice has long sought to disrupt.[17]

In the first case study, I examine the Townsend Plan letter-writing campaigns as detailed in its national newspaper, the *Townsend National Weekly (TNW)*, and the archives of Oregon City, Oregon, Townsend Club president Pearl S. Burkhalter. The newspaper's reporting and Burkhalter's own letters suggest that the plan circulated in complex ways across time, place, and space (including local, regional, and national contexts via the Townsendites' letters to their political representatives). I argue that the Townsendites recontextualized the plan's message within and across language, genre, mode, and media in ways that often subverted the attempts by Townsend leaders to control the Townsendites' messaging to their political representatives. Though her passion for the movement was extraordinary, Burkhalter's commitment to the movement and her rhetorical choices were typical of the thousands of Townsend activists working in clubs across the country. Burkhalter's particular rhetorical strategies are representative of the choices made by many Townsendites at the time; however, unlike her fellow Townsendites, whose often transitory activist work was lost to history, Burkhalter's words have been meticulously preserved in the archives. Everyday rhetorics of resistance are usually ephemeral: letters are sent and received, but not necessarily copied or saved; interviews and speeches are conducted, but not recorded; quilts get worn out, recycled, or discarded. Through these case studies, we are able to uncover the everyday that so often remains hidden and fades from sight. By studying Burkhalter's letters, poems, songs, meeting minutes, and memos, we can better understand how she and other similarly dedicated Townsend activists across the country supported their cause and, at the same time, reworked the Townsend message to more accurately reflect their desperate desire for a better life.

In the second case study, I turn to the letters, speeches, and interviews documented in Quaker traveling minister E. P. Gurney's *Memoir and Correspondence* (published posthumously in 1884). I seek to reclaim her as more than a mere footnote to, or lens through which to consider, the powerful men with whom she came into contact, including her husband, the Quaker minister and activist Joseph John Gurney, and the president she came to call her friend, Abraham Lincoln. Throughout her travels, Gurney recontextualized modes, including speech and writing, to make her voice heard in a variety of contexts characterized by asymmetrical relations of power. Gurney drew upon Quaker religious practice, recontextualizing for more activist purposes the ordinarily passive forms of silence, prayer, consolation, and praise. I situate her work within recent conversations pluralizing *ethos* (as feminist *ethē*), valuing rhetorical silence, and recovering epideictic rhetoric to argue that the everyday rhetorics of resistance Gurney engaged in throughout her life constitute feminist rhetorical practices well worth recovering. As in the cases of the Townsendite letter writers and the Gee's Bend and Townsendite quiltmakers, Gurney's everyday rhetorics of resistance could easily be overlooked: her words and work were not flashy, and much of her speech and writing could be seen as merely repeating Quaker religious norms and narratives. But I argue that Gurney should be recognized as a feminist rhetor who engaged in "difference-in-similarity," recontextualizing form and meaning by drawing on the means available to resist the status quo.

In the third case study, I rhetorically listen to the words and work of two sets of quiltmakers—the Gee's Bend quiltmakers and the quiltmakers associated with the Townsend Plan—in order to examine how quilts represent a transmodal literacy practice whereby the quiltmakers recontextualize "the available means for a creative text."[18] Historically, women have engaged in everyday rhetorics of resistance by using modes and media that have often been devalued and overlooked as "women's work," such as dressmaking, the weaving of textiles and the making of samplers, quiltmaking, scrapbooking, and the writing of cookbooks. In line with recent feminist scholarship on needlework, textiles, and material culture—including work by scholars such as Carol Mattingly, Maureen Daly Goggin, Beth Fowkes Tobin, Elaine Showalter, Rosalyn Collings Eves, Elaine Hedges, and others—my work participates in the recovery and reclamation of women's material rhetorical practices. It thus suggests, as Goggin argues, that the field has "moved far beyond language as the sole, or at least only worthy, epistemic practice."[19] As Goggin suggests, work on women's material rhetorical practices "redirects attention to the power of the needle as an epistemic tool that exceeds the limits of an ocular focus."[20] And as Heather Pristash, Inez Schaechterle, and Sue Carter Wood have argued, needlework has functioned as a "vehicle through which women have constructed discourses of their own, ones offering a broader range of positions from which to engage dominant culture."[21] The Gee's Bend and Townsend Plan quiltmakers take up the "needle as the pen," engaging with quiltmaking as a form of composing.[22] In their compositions, they recontextualize pattern, stitches, and design for particular social, political, aesthetic, economic, and material purposes. Both sets of quiltmakers subjugate form to meaning and engage difference and difference-in-similarity in order to communicate the material conditions of their lives to others in and beyond their community, and to seek change.

As Paul Feigenbaum argues in *Collaborative Imagination: Earning Activism through Literacy Education*, instead of focusing on the individualist narratives of more familiar, extraordinary activist heroes like Rosa Parks, we need to recognize as well the collaborative labor of the unsung heroes who could just as easily have become icons. By moving toward a collaborative framework, we can "broaden our imaginations about what it means to become an activist," for no one can earn activism alone: "we must earn (and *re*earn) *our* activism in alliance with others."[23] Fortunately, there has been an increased recognition of the importance of "adding the stories of other remarkable people" to the dominant narratives that circulate in popular culture. See, for example, Oprah Winfrey's speech at the Golden Globe awards citing the life of the less well-known civil rights activist Recy Taylor.[24] Or the "Overlooked" series in the *New York Times,* which publishes obituaries of the (extra)ordinary "others who left indelible marks but were nonetheless overlooked" in the paper's pages.[25] The move to reclaim the overlooked and everyday prompts us to rethink what counts as effective activism, how we can earn our activism, and what kind of activism is seen as valued and valuable.

Rethinking "what counts as evidence" also necessarily involves examining and acknowledging our own scholarly prejudices. Unfortunately, as Biesecker, Mattingly, and others have pointed out, the field has tended to problematically hold up a few feminist rhetorical figures who align with more familiar, contemporary understandings of effective rhetorical work (often defined according to a more aggressive masculinist or liberal feminist *ethos*).[26] This has created blind spots in our scholarship and has led us to ignore the thousands of ordinary women who were rhetorically active in their communities, or whose political beliefs or religious training may have pushed against contemporary understandings of effective rhetorical work. Our biases may blind us to the excellence of the work engaged in by the elderly Townsendites because Burkhalter and her fellow club members could easily be viewed as dupes repeating the propaganda of an appealing populist figure. Our understanding of what fits within rhetorical tradition(s) may blind us to the rhetorical sophistication involved in Gurney's recontextualization of language, genre, mode, and media, because much of her life's work could easily be written off as missionary work and her activism reduced to a discussion of how Lincoln's letters to Gurney presaged his second inaugural address. Our prejudices about what counts as activism may limit our ability to see, for example, quiltmakers as artists, composers, and activists who employed quiltmaking as an effective rhetorical means for African American women and the elderly to engage in activist literacy practices that reflected and refracted their experiences in and beyond their communities. And yet, each of these everyday rhetors earned their activism by not going it alone and by innovatively reworking the resources immediately available to them.[27] The framework I provide in this book seeks to rhetorically listen to the ways composers inside and outside the classroom recontextualize the resources at their disposal to "collaboratively imagine" the work necessary to improve the conditions of their lives.[28]

A Translingual and Transmodal Framework

In outlining, developing, and applying a translingual and transmodal framework to the case studies in this book, my goal is fourfold. First, I want to avoid the tendency to oversimplify or objectify the concepts of language, discourse, and practice, especially as they relate to our understanding of conventions, standards, and traditions. As applied linguist Alastair Pennycook argues, "language, discourse and practices are always too complex to be all about themselves," and so throughout this book, I consider language as a practice situated within temporal, spatial, and material contexts.[29] To this end, I draw on Jacqueline Jones Royster's definition of discourse as "language in particular use," an embodied, "people-centered enterprise" endowed "insidiously with the workings of social, political, and cultural processes."[30] Second, as mentioned earlier, I seek to understand difference as the standard and the norm—instead of the alternative, exceptional, or abnormal—in part so I can also understand repetition (what I call, throughout, difference-in-similarity) as a site for creativity and meaning-making. This move enables me to recognize the contributions of women across history whose work may have been devalued because, for some reason, it has been categorized as everyday or "ordinary." As Jennifer Sinor argues, "ordinariness is not a quality intrinsic to a text but rather one afforded to it."[31] Adopting such an approach to language practices "make[s] visible the typically indiscernible action and agency on the part of the writer," an aim in line with my third goal: to recover and reclaim the ways individual composers recontextualize within and across languages, genres, modes, and media.[32] I view language as a performative practice, actively shaped and reshaped in both form and meaning by composers in ways for which it may or may not have been "traditionally" used. As we will see in the case studies, individual composers' recontextualizations are shaped by multiple, competing economic, social, cultural, and political processes.[33] My fourth and final goal is to show how a translingual and transmodal framework reiterates the importance of adopting more democratic and descriptive approaches to language and modal practices (as opposed to the prescriptive approaches that have dominated for so long).[34]

The move to adopt a translingual and transmodal approach to writing is not unprecedented. Since the publication of the "Students' Right to Their Own Language" (SRTOL) document in 1972, the field of rhetoric and composition has increasingly recognized the need to understand and promote the legitimacy of diverse language varieties and language speakers in our teaching, writing, and research. Many of our students and research subjects (and many of us, as well) have been "othered" within and outside academic contexts by virtue of the intersection of our gender, language, culture, ethnicity, sexual identity, class, status, religion, ability, and/or immigration status, among other positionalities.[35] Scholars study the intersection of language, culture, and identity in order to reveal the workings of monolingual ideologies in and beyond colleges and universities, and to develop theories and practices to counter those ideologies, including the predominance of *Standard Academic English (*SAE) as the only legitimate way to write in the academy.[36] Such scholarship includes theorizations of linguistic difference and "alternative" discourse practices (see the work of scholars such as Bizzell, Dobrin, Mao, Matsuda, Royster, and Wallace); theories and practices for teaching monolingual and multilingual students to work with and against discourse conventions in academic writing (see the work of Canagarajah, Elbow, Kynard, Lu, and Royster); and scholarship employing explicit forms of linguistic, stylistic, or generic hybridity and "difference" in order to reflect the lived identities and experiences of diverse writers and researchers (see the work of Gilyard, Powell, Smitherman, Villanueva, Wallace, and Young).[37]

The translingual approach adds to and revises previous scholarly discussions of language, power, and agency inspired by the SRTOL resolution by emphasizing the fluidity of language and the need to see language practice both as a resource and as a right.[38] As defined by Horner and colleagues, the translingual approach asks rhetoric and composition scholars to adopt a "disposition of openness and inquiry" toward language and language difference—one that willingly takes the time to examine how composers translate and negotiate within and across language and genre in light of their temporal-spatial location.[39] The translingual approach "sees difference in language not as a barrier to overcome or as a problem to manage, but as a resource for producing meaning in writing, speaking, reading, and listening."[40] Translingualism actively works against the monolingual paradigm, which posits language(s) as "static, discrete, and defined by specific norms" and perpetuates "myths of unchanging universal standards for language."[41] Instead, the translingual approach works to understand languages, discourses, and standards as multiple, contingent, and constantly in flux.[42] Such a disposition carefully considers language acts that might previously have been identified and eradicated as deviation or error within the contexts of their production, consumption, and reception, including a consideration of the multiple, sometimes conflicting, ways a reader's expectations intersect with the intentions of the writer: conventions are "contingent and negotiable," not fixed and uniform.[43] Some might argue that translingualism treats all writing as error-free or allows composers a free pass to write however they want regardless of the standards against which they may be judged. Horner and colleagues disagree, arguing that a translingual disposition toward writing requires a careful consideration of the limits and possibilities (conventional and otherwise) inherent to the particular time, place, and space of the composing situation, and so requires "more responsibility, not less from writers and readers."[44] In the case studies throughout this book, I adopt a translingual "*orientation* to writing and literacy," while also focusing more specifically on "the practices that constitute translingual literacies," which Canagarajah identifies as a narrower approach that enables scholars to "start asking what strategies characterize the construction and negotiation of meaning in such forms of literacy"—strategies such as recontextualization.[45]

Advocates of the translingual approach thus participate in the well-established move in rhetoric and composition to attend to process, not product, in writing. As Min-Zhan Lu writes, translingual literacy practice requires readers and writers to "shift attention from what one produces to how one explores options and makes decisions when writing and learning."[46] If agents have the power to change and transform the conditions of their lives through writing, we need to recognize the ways we all recontextualize difference *and* sameness in our compositions, negotiating across time, place, and space. This requires a listening approach to difference, an approach to language practice that moves the focus away from highlighting the more extreme forms of difference, and instead approaches all rhetorical choices and language acts as moments of potentially disruptive meaning-making exchanges.[47] In this way, translingualism aligns with *rhetorical listening*, defined by Krista Ratcliffe as a "stance of openness . . . in relation to any person, text, or culture" that requires adopting "a code of cross-cultural conduct" in "cross-cultural exchanges."[48] In my analysis of the three case studies, I rhetorically listen across time, place, and space to how composers communicate across asymmetrical lines of power from different positions of (dis)privilege, recontextualizing language, media, and mode in diverse ways so as to engage in the kind of everyday activism that is often overlooked but should never be underestimated.[49] Instead of focusing on the product and defining the difference and difference-in-similarity at work in these texts as *code-meshing*, I rhetorically listen to how translingual composers recontextualize in terms of both form (*glossodiversity*) and meaning (*semiodiversity*). Instead of labeling or categorizing the work of the composers in these studies as "alternative" or traditional, mainstream or nonmainstream, I choose to focus on the processes of recontextualization at work in their language practice.

When understood in their temporal, spatial, and material contexts, individual acts of reading and writing represent recontextualizations that can change how we understand and appreciate the writing and agency of all composers, no matter their relative position of (dis)privilege. The translingual framework reveals the power of the everyday rhetorics of resistance engaged in by composers who, at first glance, might not look as if they are engaging in groundbreaking activist work due to the nature of the language, modes, or medium with which they compose, or the rhetorical choices they make in those compositions. Paying attention to both the more and less obvious forms of difference in the case studies enables us to see the complex ways everyday rhetorics of resistance contribute to the disruption of the status quo.

The "trans-" prefix enables the field to better understand the ways composers work across language and genre, as well as modes and media. One of the main proponents of the translingual approach, A. Suresh Canagarajah, points this out in his discussion of how the "trans-" prefix operates: "Firstly, the term moves us beyond a consideration of individual or monolithic languages to life between and across languages. . . . Secondly, the prefix encourages us to treat acts of communication as involving more than words" (that is, other semiotic resources, including symbol systems, modalities of communication, and ecologies).[50] Canagarajah's point that communication constitutes "more than words" has been echoed by Bruce Horner, Cynthia Selfe, and Tim Lockridge, who call for writers and scholars to take what might previously have been identified as multimodality and instead think of it as *transmodality*.[51] Just as the translingual approach views language standards and norms as fluid, the transmodal approach defines the working of modes and media as fluid, and shifts the focus to the "design resources" employed by author/designers/composers.[52] For Horner, Selfe, and Lockridge, the implication of the move away from a monomodal and monolingual norm is threefold:

> (1) these relatively recent changes bring into awareness features of all communicative practice that ideologies posing the "norm" of a single, uniform ("standard") language or mode (hereafter referenced as "SL/MN") elide, (2) these same changes bring to awareness the presence of communicative practices in the past that SL/MN ideology has suppressed, and (3) currently emergent communicative practices are themselves materially different from past, and other, communicative prac-

> tices in ways that challenge both "SL/MN" ideologies and the practices now identified (ideologically) as "SL/MN." . . . We resist, in short, any understanding that statistically standard language practices are singular either in their linguistic or modal forms, and we resist the understanding that *statistically standard* is the linguistic or modal equivalent of *normal*. This ideological formation is two sided and doubly dangerous.[53]

In short, transmodality, as a term and as a frame of reference, allows for an increased awareness of the ways composers across history have always already worked across language and modes (defined as fluid and dynamic). Moreover, normalcy should not be defined according to whether a text is viewed as "statistically standard," when all language and modal practices are multiple, transitory, and contingent. Transmodality pushes scholars to investigate what we can learn from past communicative practices that SL/MN ideology may have suppressed, such as quiltmaking or letter writing. Though past communicative practices may be materially different from "currently emergent communicative practice," these past practices have long contributed to the ongoing evolution of language and the disruption of SL/MN ideology.

Subsequent scholarship on translingualism has both expanded upon and pointed out ways to revise and focus the field's responses to language difference: further theorizing the translingual approach as initially outlined by Horner and colleagues; supplementing theoretical discussions with more practical discussions of how language can be reworked by students and teachers in classrooms and in undergraduate and graduate writing programs; applying the translingual approach to, and differentiating it from, transnational texts and contexts; and critiquing how translingualism intervenes in past, present, and future language studies scholarship.[54] Thus, translingualism as a concept is constantly being worked and reworked, as editors Min-Zhan Lu and Bruce Horner argue in a *College English* symposium on "Translingual Work," which reiterates the unfinished and ongoing nature of defining, understanding, and applying the translingual approach. Translingualism cannot be pinned down as something to be transmitted to students or teachers of writing; moreover, the aim of the translingual approach is not the product-oriented goal of getting students to code-mesh or demonstrate difference, but instead the goal of understanding the complex choices all composers make when writing, even choices that lead them to align more closely with what might be viewed as the so-called standard. The focus is on difference *as* the norm, not difference *from* the norm. As the participants in the symposium suggest, translingualism can be seen in a variety of everyday interactions and language practices, and can shape the field's current and future discussions of transfer, writing assessment, second-language pedagogy, and genre, among other issues pertinent to rhetoric and composition.[55] More work needs to be done to understand how composers outside of university contexts engage in such translingual work, which is why I look to these contexts in this book.

A better understanding of how a translingual orientation might be applied to genre can be particularly useful when applying the translingual framework to these three case studies. In the same symposium mentioned above, Anis Bawarshi extends the translingual orientation to genre difference, proposing a view of "genre difference not as a deviation from a patterned or recurrent norm, but rather as the norm of all genre performance."[56] Although the field has come to recognize genre as social action (see Carolyn Miller's work), Bawarshi argues that pedagogical approaches to genre still largely depend on "genre explication," identifying and relating conventions to their social functions and purposes, as well as (sometimes) their ideological implications.[57] To move beyond an understanding of genres as tools, things, or sites of access, Bawarshi focuses on *genre performances*, arguing that "we need to extend genre agency to include knowledge of strategic genre performances in space and time, within asymmetrical relations of power."[58] Bawarshi's approach to genre agency hinges upon the idea of *uptake*, defined by Anne Freedman as "situated and strategic genre performances . . . the bidirectional relation that holds between . . . a relational force or interplay that operates between genres and that accounts for the interconnections, translations, and movements of actions and meanings across genres."[59] Bawarshi's work requires scholars to rhetorically listen to "the historical-material conditions and dynamics of agency and power that function between, hold together, and shape genre performances."[60] Even though Bawarshi's discussion (in this particular article) centers on pedagogical understandings of genre inside the classroom, his discussion of a translingual approach to genre can be applied to nonacademic contexts as well.

As we will see in this book, the composers in these studies were able to strategically and purposefully recontextualize genre, and with a translingual framework we can better understand some of the specific choices they made. Recontextualization enables us to better understand the idea of uptake as it relates to the movement of action and meaning within and across genres. For example, in order to understand fully the intricacies at work in Burkhalter's and Gurney's letters, we need to view the letters not as static objects to be circulated, but as strategic *genre performances*, shaped by the women's historical-material conditions and understanding of their own agency and power (or relative lack thereof). As Bawarshi writes, a translingual approach to genre views agency in horizontal terms, "shift[ing] our attention from genre conventions to the interplays between genres—the complex performances that take place between and around genres where agency is very much in constant play in relation to myriad forces and factors."[61] How and why Gurney and Burkhalter choose to open and close their letters becomes more than the straightforward application (or rejection) of genre conventions. Both women recontextualize the letter-writing genre across temporal, spatial, and material contexts in relation to "myriad forces and factors," and so make choices that relate to their positionality, which affords each of them agency in contexts where they are at a power disadvantage. Gurney's decision to address Abraham Lincoln using the Quaker term "friend" in the opening and closing of her letters enables her to situate herself in relation to the president and, to a certain extent, level the playing field (notably, he echoes this move, though from a differently situated position, in his letter to her). Burkhalter's decision to sign one of her letters with her own name and the names of her father and husband highlights both her family's support of her political beliefs and an earlier threat to wield the power of their votes to "ax" the intended audience in the upcoming election.[62]

As Bawarshi's work illustrates, more and more scholars have taken up the call to expand the theoretical and practical contexts in which we connect and apply translingual and transmodal research. Laura Gonzales's scholarship on the rhetorical dexterity, translation, and design choices of multilingual college students represents another expansion of the translingual orientation. Gonzalez puts translingual and transmodal theories into conversation, and her work has been praised by Bawarshi (and other scholars) for its contribution to our understanding of how translingual composers draw from diverse semiotic resources in their writing.[63] As Gonzales's scholarship demonstrates, student composers have an amazing ability "to utilize a variety of semiotic resources when attempting to communicate [their] ideas," and "students who have a history of broad linguistic transitions may be especially adept at generating cues across languages and modes based on their extensive experiences code-switching (both linguistically, culturally, and often times transnationally) in order to adapt to 'the whole new system' of writing in English-dominant American classrooms."[64] Adaptation requires students to draw on all the resources at their disposal in creative and productive ways. In the case studies that follow, I am interested in how composers outside university contexts, and across history, engage in such work—albeit by using more obviously monolingual resources—and how they adapt to and change the system as a result.

Jody Shipka's scholarship also pushes the field to consider transmodal approaches to language practice, while reminding us of the need to recognize multimodality as not always wholly or partially digital, onscreen, or composed with *new* media.[65] Shipka's scholarship offers an important caveat to the push to realize how "new production tools and environments offer different potentials for accomplishing multimodality than print-based, alphabetic texts allow."[66] She writes, "It is important to avoid equating 'new' or 'newness' with digitally-based or new media texts and practices. In so doing, we neglect to consider how the uptake of older, and perhaps more familiar, varieties of language (both verbal and nonverbal, English and non-English), tools, techniques, and environments might be used in new ways, remixed, transformed and put to new, creative purposes."[67] Such work includes, Shipka notes, studies of "older," more familiar technologies (such as my study of the Gee's Bend and Townsend quiltmakers). Numerous examples exist of composers and designers inside and outside the classroom context who engage in language practice that is familiar, but no less creative or transmodal than work that engages "new production tools or environments."[68] Shipka's call provides further justification for studying how the uptake of older modes, media, materials, tools, and genres—such as quiltmaking or letter writing—contribute to the ongoing recontextualization of language, media, and modes.

As this brief, and by no means comprehensive, review of recent trends in translingual scholarship suggests, context matters, and scholars are increasingly engaging in important discussions of how composers draw on difference and difference-in-similarity within, across, and between languages and cultures, including in transnational texts and contexts. For example, Nancy Bou Ayash's work engages with the idea that, as Lu and Horner suggest, "representations of language are language practices themselves."[69] Ayash draws on translingualism to understand the linguistic representations of multilingual Lebanese English education students in Beirut, Lebanon—a transnational context also explored by Lisa Arnold, who has sought to situate translingual approaches historically. Arnold's discussion of the consequences of the globalization of English education paradigms in Beirut underlines the need for the field to situate itself in a transnational context (see also the work of Christiane Donahue), so that we can avoid import/export models for understanding international texts, contexts, and histories of composition and composition research.[70] To ignore these transnational, historical sites would (blindly) define translingual approaches to writing as US-based and contemporary.[71]

And yet, Lu and Horner argue that the field needs to avoid framing the translingual as a panacea. The translingual approach is not a substitute for, but part and parcel of, approaches to language practice that scholars in the field and associated fields, such as linguistics and second-language studies, have been advocating for years.[72] When considering difference as the norm, I therefore heed Keith Gilyard, who cautions against the trap of "sameness-of-difference," the idea that if we are all translingual, we all differ from the standard in the same way. As Gilyard argues and I would agree, we are punished for our languages and language choices differently by virtue of our identities and contexts. As Victor Villanueva writes, "language is also race in America. Spanish is color."[73] And as he and many others have argued, the English Only movement and the move to reinforce the idea that there is a single, unified, or "correct" way to speak and write academic English reveal the nationalism, racism, and anti-immigrant rhetoric underlying these discussions.[74]

In understanding all language users as translingual, I do not want to suggest that a white Quaker woman composing in the nineteenth century faces the same challenges as an African American woman making a quilt in the twentieth century, or the Latinx student who draws upon the multilingual resources at her disposal in the twenty-first century writing classroom of a Hispanic-serving institution such as my own. Composers recontextualize the means available to them for diverse purposes and ends, and also suffer different consequences as a result of their positionalities and temporal, spatial, and material contexts. The prejudices and biases we confront may limit our freedom to experiment in writing, and our own and others' perception of our (in)ability to work with and against the conventions and standards at play are always connected to language, power, and positionality. However, by recovering and reclaiming the overlooked contributions and workarounds engaged in by differently situated composers, we can gain inspiration from their choices and better understand how to navigate and engage in our own everyday rhetorics of resistance today.

Instead of looking to the classroom or the university as the site for translingual research, this book turns the focus to historical case studies of everyday texts and contexts in order to reveal how composers have always already been engaged in disruptive work that recontextualizes the materials, media, and modes available to them—"those acts of writing that are ordinarily recognized as producing simply 'more of the same': conventional, unoriginal, ordinary, conformist."[75] I reconsider our understanding of what counts as different, so that we can understand and recognize how so-called everyday, ordinary composing practices and contexts are potential opportunities to challenge the status quo. Rather than viewing the women in these studies as unsung heroes, I prefer to think of them as antiheroes. Like other antiheroes, they could be seen as lacking the "conventional heroic attributes" more readily available to those in power.[76] And yet, like other antiheroes (who often come from underrepresented groups), the women in these studies saw their seeming lack of agency as an opportunity to engage in resistance from below. Their choices speak to the power of patience and persistence over more flashy, brute force. The women expressed their agency by remaking and reshaping the (un)conventional means available to claim the right to speak for and represent themselves and their communities.

The Practice and Art of Recontextualization

Adopting a translingual approach to the recontextualization of language, media, and mode across three disparate case studies addresses one of the questions at the heart of a translingual orientation, which asks students "what kind of difference to attempt to make through their work with and on conventions in their writing, how, and why."[77] As I demonstrate in the case studies that follow, such questions are just as pertinent when reading non-academic contexts and compositions. I turn to the practice of recontextualization in order to move away from an evaluative or enumerative approach to difference and toward an investigation of how "language is the achieved outcome of the everyday doing of language by ordinary people."[78] In what follows, I explore the theoretical underpinnings of my approach to recontextualization throughout this book.

The concept of recontextualization has been employed by scholars across disciplines, and though each scholar defines the term slightly differently, most agree on a basic definition: recontextualization draws attention to the limits and possibilities of moving from one context to another, whether within or across language, genre, mode, media, or discipline. In particular, scholars in the fields of linguistics, education, and rhetoric and composition have drawn on the idea of recontextualization to emphasize the importance of considering how teachers and students move and re-present themselves within and across contexts, and how students as composers make meaning by drawing on the particular contexts of their writing, which include their understanding of previous iterations of the languages, genres, and conventions at work in their communicative practices. For example, in a study of the linguistic patterns of bilingual language users, applied linguist Lilia Bartolomae uses the term "recontextualized language" to refer to "language (both oral and written) that is used to communicate information to others with little reliance on the immediate physically present situation to which reference can be made."[79] Bartolomae draws on recontextualization as an alternative to *de*contextualization to emphasize how "no language can be completely without cultural context and that what is referred to as decontextualized refers to mainstream or macrocultural practices of contextualizing language."[80] (As I will discuss further below, Judith Butler also draws on the relationship between decontextualization and recontextualization.)

Genre theorist Carol Berkenkotter also argues for the importance of context, suggesting that "studying institutional genres requires the investigator to examine the ways in which they *recontextualize* prior texts and discourses," since "actors' situated, meaning-making activities . . . are densely contextual."[81] The ways composers move within and across contexts matter, and recontextualization provides one way to make such movement visible.

Jeff Bezemer and Gunther Kress's scholarship employs the concept of recontextualization to understand the range of semiotic resources composers employ for the purposes of teaching and learning, and, I would add, social action.[82] Their social-semiotic framework for studying multimodality, learning, and communication draws on educational sociologist Basil Bernstein's definition of *recontextualization* to understand the circulation of meaning in learning environments: "Recontextualization is, literally, moving 'meaning-material' from one context with its social organization of participants and its modal ensembles, to another, with its different social organization and modal ensembles. Meaning-material always has a modal/semiotic realization, so recontextualization involves *the re-presentation of the meaning materials in a mode apt for the new context, in the light of the available modal resources*."[83] Their definition focuses on how users re-present semiotic meaning-making materials in light of new contexts. Bezemer and Kress argue that designers (whom I refer to throughout as composers) make meaning by drawing on multiple modes, defined as "socially and culturally shaped resource[s] for making meaning," all of which have "differing modal resources" (speech, writing, images, moving images, layout, and so on).[84] Modes and *media*—defined materially as "the substance in and through which meaning is instantiated/realized and through which meaning becomes available to others (cf. 'oil on canvas')" and socially as "(the result of) semiotic, sociocultural, and technological practices (cf. film, newspaper, billboard, radio, television, theater, a classroom, and so on)" have different *affordances*, "potentials and constraints for making meaning," depending on the complex, contradictory relationship between composer, audience, and context.[85] The *site of display*, "the space that becomes available as medium for the display of text as complex sign," can change, even if the medium does not.[86] To understand how and why composers recontextualize, Bezemer and Kress explore four principles: *framing* establishes the internal coherence of the semiotic, meaning-making text both in relation to and as distinct from other, similar texts; *selection* helps to explain "what is to be signified, what is to be brought into the frame, and how"; the *arrangement* of the selection has meaning and is made in relation to audience, purpose, and context; what is *foregrounded*, backgrounded, how, why, and to what effect differs according to the particular social and cultural environment.[87]

Bezemer and Kress's work aligns with the goal of recovering and reclaiming multimodal practices that might otherwise remain invisible, "the seemingly 'banal' examples we have encountered in our everyday lives."[88] Though they employ the prefix *multi-* instead of *trans-* to describe their approach to modality, their goals are in line with a translingual, transmodal, and feminist framework: they view meaning-making (and learning) as "constantly transformative and innovative" and seek to recognize the range and resourcefulness of the means employed by composers by establishing creativity and innovation as "the ordinary, banal, constant processes and phenomena that they are."[89] Bezemer and Kress's work helps to break down more clearly how the composers in my three case studies draw on the semiotic resources available by employing a variety of modes (speech, writing, design/layout, images) and media (letters, quilts, and "speaker-as-body-and-voice") by recontextualizing, or re-presenting, the everyday rhetorics of resistance available to them.[90] For example, when writing her letter to Lincoln after their interview, Gurney recontextualizes the modal resources available in writing, including word choice, grammar, and syntax, to persuade; she recontextualizes the material and social dimensions of the medium of the letter, since letter writing operated in the nineteenth century as a familiar sociocultural practice for communicating, particularly with audiences at some remove (both physically and in terms of power) from the composer. The genre/frame of the letter enables her to recontextualize the work she had begun during her in-person interview with Lincoln, and she arranges her letters' contents according to the affordances available and her particular social position and rhetorical purpose.[91] In speaking with Lincoln, Gurney uses the framing of rhetorical silence to establish an *ethē* of relation-relating; in her letters, Gurney establishes her *ethē* of relation-relating in a different way, by foregrounding their "memorable" meeting, citing Lincoln's request that she write to him (and so situating her letter as a response), and quoting scripture to establish her purpose for writing as, in part, religious consolation.

Although Bezemer and Kress's social semiotic framework points to innovation and creativity as the norm in multimodal learning environments, they admit they do not spend a great deal of time exploring issues related to identity and socialization.[92] Moreover, their focus on multimodal learning environments may not fully address the significance or subtlety of the rhetorical and linguistic choices being made by composers, like those in my case studies, who are more firmly situated in everyday spaces and places that are not focused on learning (though, of course, learning does take place in these spaces). I therefore find it helpful to supplement their approach to recontextualization with scholarship from the translingual approach in order to better understand and acknowledge the innovative (and often quite subtle) ways all language users recontextualize language and modal practice for the purposes of rhetorical resistance.

Translingualism's approach to recontextualization draws in large part on work by linguists Claire Kramsch and Alastair Pennycook, which provides a theoretical foundation for the translingual orientation to language diversity—locating diversity not within language but within the social acts that produce language. Kramsch critiques those who would have us move to a multilingual framework that celebrates and forwards *glossodiversity* (diversity of languages, conventions, and fixed forms) without an attendant focus on *semiodiversity* (diversity in meaning).[93] Therefore, she argues, "language teaching should strive to retain the diversity of meanings that can be and have been expressed in a given language."[94] In the process of doing language, individual writers can create different meanings out of practices that, on the surface, appear to be instances of similarity and repetition. Kramsch suggests language teachers focus on teaching students to "learn to mean in another language" and so work to avoid essentializing the means by which difference can be produced. Diversifying meanings (versus languages) can promote better cross-cultural understandings, enabling composers to focus on the processes, the when and why of languaging, not merely on what is being produced. Kramsch's considerations are echoed in the questions with which this section began, regarding how composers engage with the question of what kinds of difference to make, how, and why.

Pennycook picks up on the argument for semiodiversity versus glossodiversity, adding to it by countering the view of language as an entity, and repetition and repetitive discourse as examples and instances of a fixed instantiation of that entity: for Pennycook, the very existence and fixity of the language norm itself should be challenged.[95] He uses the term "recontextualization" to describe "occurrences of the same things in different contexts."[96] Acts of repetition, when recontextualized in place, time, and space, produce difference; repetition and repetitive discourse become "a central meaning-making resource."[97] This means focusing on the flow of language—its "fertile mimesis"—instead of the stability of language, for "it is sameness, not difference, that needs to account for itself."[98] Difference, creativity, and flow, therefore, become the norm, and repetition becomes "the key to understanding difference."[99] Pennycook argues that language scholars should take a second look at repetition as a site of meaning-making and difference, a point he makes by turning to Charles Kahn's translation of Heraclitus, "who insisted that change was real and stability only illusory, famously proclaiming that . . . [w]e both step and do not step in the same river. We are and are not."[100] Just as we can never step in the same river twice, so we can never produce identical forms or acts of languaging twice because language practices are recontextualized; they will always be informed by multiple local perspectives informed by the time, place, and space in which they were produced. This necessarily shifts where and how we look for differences, drawing attention away from immediately recognizable difference and toward similarity as a site of difference (repetition recontextualized).

Pennycook's discussion hearkens back to the quotation from quiltmaker Mary Lee Bendolph in the epigraphs to this chapter. In describing her process, Bendolph outlines a process that "takes change and flow as the norm," depending on what she feels "works" or not. Bendolph engages with color, pattern, and design differently each time she sits down to make a quilt; what remains the same is the fluidity of her creative process, and what we notice in her description is the intentionality of her choices as part of that process (a counter to those who might see the design choices as "errors" or as evidence of poor quilting). In their quiltmaking, the Gee's Bend quiltmakers engage in recontextualization of form and meaning, and so contribute to the ongoing redefinition of what counts as "good" quiltmaking and also provide a way to understand the kinds of differences that composers engage in, how, and why.

In redefining what counts as "good writing," the translingual approach also redefines creativity as the norm, "the common stuff of everyday language use," instead of the rarified work of the genius acting alone, and so asks language scholars to "consider creativity in terms of repeated sameness rather than observable difference."[101] If language users are constantly breaking the rules, then perhaps the so-called rules and conventions that are said to govern language and discourse are a function of sedimentation, not something inherent to language. In this framework, the idea of a single language and modal norm as representative of stability and convention is replaced by the idea of sedimented practices governed by flow: structure and agency become mutually interdependent.[102] If we agree that difference emerges from the recontextualized repetitions found in everyday language use, then we need to better understand the workings of such "everyday language use," and these case studies provide examples to that end.

Lu and Horner further theorize the agentive possibility of so-called iterations of convention by drawing on and supplementing Pennycook's approach to language, creativity, and difference with the work of Homi Babha (on mimicry and fertile mimesis), Anthony Giddens (on structuration and agency), Pierre Bourdieu (on recognition/misrecognition), and Judith Butler (on the performative). For Lu and Horner, translingual literacy practice enables *all* users to have agency over their language practices: "From this perspective, difference is an inevitable product of all language acts."[103] When engaging with the problem of what kinds of difference to make, how, and why, writers engage in recontextualization, or "'rehearsals' that try out or practice conventional formulae in different temporal-spatial contexts."[104] Butler situates all linguistic practice as recontextualization, and Lu and Horner argue that her work "highlights the potential of all acts of recontextualization to create nonconventional ways of rehearsing the very convention being iterated by dislodging (164) or 'unmooring' (165) the convention from its ostensible 'originary' or authoring context (or, the prior territory of its operation)."[105] In order to apply their temporal-spatial theory in practice, Lu and Horner turn to the infamous (in the field of rhetoric and composition) "White Shoes" essay discussed by David Bartholomae as an example of a student who has failed to "invent the university" in the ways privileged in the context of a composition placement essay. Instead, Lu and Horner see the essay as a site of iteration-recontextualization, and so they "examin[e] the small, ordinarily unrecognized, often unintended shifts in meaning, function, and context [the student] produced through iterating-recontextualizing a certain convention"—in the student's case, the convention of what constitutes creativity.[106] In this book, I look for the "small . . . shifts in meaning, function, and context" at work in everyday language practice, particularly in nonacademic contexts and communities, such as the Townsend Clubs, the Society of Friends, and the quiltmaking community of Gee's Bend, Alabama.

While Canagarajah focuses mainly on multilingual writers, the composers in my case studies might identify as monolingual, and yet I would argue their work engages in the recontextualization, or reconfiguration, of semiotic resources from their languages, cultures, and communities in diverse ways. For Canagarajah, translingual literacy is "intrinsically rhetorical," and he argues that in order to negotiate difference, multilingual writers draw on a variety of negotiation strategies for reception, interpretation, and production.[107] Canagarajah associates recontextualization with the production of such negotiation strategies, defining it as the process "whereby semiotic resources from diverse languages and cultures are reconfigured for one's purposes."[108] Like Bartolomae and Pennycook, Canagarajah suggests a way of moving beyond mainstream, macrocultural practices and toward a more recontextualized approach: "As these are rhetorical processes, we are compelled to treat translingual literacy beyond the narrow bounds of language norms or textual structures and situate them in larger contexts of history, culture, and social relations."[109] The case studies both offer up and require a consideration of such larger contexts, cultures, and social relations.

In another important iteration of the term "recontextualization" within translingual scholarship and research, LuMing Mao uses the "art of recontextualization" as a necessary way to describe the process of engaging in ethical transcultural work, since "studying another culture or tradition almost always dictates the dialectical process of moving between the external and the internal, between the familiar and the unfamiliar."[110] The art of recontextualization "calls for an appreciation of the relationship between the external and the internal as coterminous and interconnected rather than binary and hierarchical. The external is bound to impinge upon the internal, and the internal cannot help but find ways to dialogue with or speak back to the external."[111] Rachel Griffo takes up Mao's work in her study of Chinese scholars' contributions to composition studies.[112] She situates Mao's "art of recontextualization" beside Canagarajah's discussions of recontextualization as a translingual practice in order to employ recontextualization as a rhetorical lens through which to view and compare diverse writing histories and rhetorical traditions. Her work enables us to see the potential application of recontextualization as a prism for understanding transnational contexts. In rhetorically listening to the recontextualization of the composers, texts, and contexts in these case studies, I also want to consider the ethical imperative of the art of recontextualization, as Mao and Griffo do in their work.

Situating recontextualization within a translingual, transmodal, and feminist framework connects the diverse composers in these studies, all of whom seek change by employing difference and difference-in-similarity in diverse times, places, and spaces, using diverse means and materials. If we look closely at Burkhalter's letters and Gurney's speeches and letters, we can see the complexity of the women's recontextualization of languages, genres, modes, and media, and the particular challenges they faced when choosing how to present themselves and their messages to their audiences—challenges related to their particular historical-material and social conditions. Some of the case studies present examples of composers engaging in the kinds of difference that stand out—the ordinary made more obviously extraordinary—as in the work of the Gee's Bend quiltmakers, who use recycled materials to, in the words of Mary Lee Bendolph, "make a way outa no way," and in the process disrupt the conventions of quiltmaking.[113] Other examples, such as the Townsend Plan quilt, might seem less obviously different in terms of the quiltmaking practices at work; yet, we can also see how the composers recontextualize a standard pattern, the "signature" quilt, to reflect the particular aims and purposes of the Townsend Movement. Each case study provides examples of how "individual language users fashion and refashion standardized conventions, subjectivity, the world, and their relations to others and the world" in their work.[114] Recontextualization helps us to see the power and agency of composers whose words and work we might otherwise dismiss as "everyday."

Everyday Rhetorics of Resistance as Feminist Rhetorical Practice

In my inquiry into the translingual and transmodal literacy practices of the women in the case studies, I adopt the feminist rhetorical practices identified by Jacqueline Jones Royster and Gesa Kirsch, including *critical imagination*, *social circulation*, *strategic contemplation*, and *globalization*. Throughout my research, I have drawn on the archives and materials available, adopting *critical imagination* as "an inquiry tool, a mechanism for seeing the noticed, rethinking what is there and not there, and speculating about what could be there instead."[115] Because of the necessarily ephemeral and fragmentary nature of everyday rhetorics of resistance, I have to look for the "traces in the stream" in places people usually wouldn't, including in texts and contexts that have been overlooked.[116] I seek simultaneously to fill the gaps and also remain mindful of them—imagining the lives of the women I am studying in relation to those gaps.

In my work on the Townsend Plan quilt, for example, I participate in what Royster and Kirsch frame as "educated guessing" about the ways the Townsend quilt circulated in and beyond the local community, based on how similar quilts and handmade artifacts are described in the *TNW*, and based on the evidence available on the quilt itself, which includes the names and places of the community leaders and businesses from across the country. As part of this critical imaginative work, I have to "think between, above, around, and beyond this evidence to speculate methodically about probabilities, that is, what might likely be true based on what [I] have in hand."[117] I necessarily engage in some speculation about the contexts, purposes, and audiences for the quilt, drawing in part on my research on contemporary quilt practices, some of which have changed, some of which have not. Royster and Kirsch would describe this as tacking in and out, moving "back and forth between past and present, their worlds and ours, their priorities and our own, local analyses and more-global ones, doing all with the cautionary tale that a core value is an ethos of humility, respect, and care" in order to create a vision of hope for the future.[118] I engage in these practices not to be disrespectful of the past, but to engage in "critical imagination as a dialectical and dialogical analytical tool" in order to "enhance our capacity to account more substantially and respectfully for the performances of women."[119]

I also employ *strategic contemplation* as a way of mindfully and meditatively engaging with the composers I am studying, including "recognizing—and learning to listen to—silence as a rhetorically powerful act."[120] I draw on critical imagination and strategic contemplation to better listen to and understand the words and silence of Gurney, including the silences she actively engages in her work as a minister. *Social circulation* "focuses on where women's writing and speaking take place, where the work goes and what it does, who encounters it and how they respond, and more," shifting attention to the neglected and undervalued spaces of women's activities, such as clubs.[121] For example, the local Townsend Clubs often established Ladies' Auxiliaries, whose more socially oriented activist work enabled the women to engage in important, yet easily overlooked, everyday rhetorics of resistance. The social spaces and contexts of quilters and quiltmaking also represent "neglected and undervalued" spaces; fortunately, as Royster and Kirsch note, Goggin's scholarship has made important strides toward revaluing and reclaiming the power of needlework.[122] Social circulation therefore helps to reframe quiltmaking as a rhetorical, meaning-making activity, and draws attention to the women, what they do, how, and why. Finally, my analysis of the translingual and transmodal framework as applied to these case studies *globalizes the point of view*, so as to see the connections between and among transnational and international rhetorical work. For example, though Gurney is best known for her relationship with Abraham Lincoln, she lived much of her life abroad in the United Kingdom, and engaged in missionary work across Europe both before and after her husband's death.

The work of Burkhalter, Gurney, and the Gee's Bend and Townsend quiltmakers underlines the need for a revised understanding of *ethos*, one that works against what Suzanne Bordelon identifies as the "tend[ency] to view *ethos* primarily in terms of texts instead of considering it more broadly in terms of social and material practices, locations, and relations."[123] As Bordelon notes, feminist scholars such as Nedra Reynolds, Carolyn Skinner, and Risa Applegarth forward a broader consideration of *ethos* as co-constructed—influenced and constrained by—the speaker and his or her social, material, and spatial contexts.[124] Bordelon's work builds upon the feminist, ecological approach to *ethos* as *ethē* proposed by Kathleen Ryan, Nancy Myers, and Rebecca Jones: a more pluralistic understanding that highlights the diverse ways composers have sought to establish *ethē* as relation-relating, interruption-interrupting, and advocacy-advocating.[125] While Burkhalter employs the *ethē* of interruption-interrupting in her letters, embracing a more pugilistic tone to insert herself into the conversation, Gurney adopts the less abrasive, but no less powerful, *ethē* of relation-relating in her letters and exchanges, which enables her to connect with her audiences. In their quilts, the Gee's Bend women engage in *ethē* as advocacy-advocating by adopting and adapting the conventions and values of more traditional quiltmaking for their own particular purposes, "negotiat[ing] a perceived lack of authority and identification with the normative expectations of dominant publics" by both claiming their expertise and rejecting outsiders' characterizations of that expertise.[126] The Townsend quilt presents an example of *ethē* as advocacy-advocating composed in response to the "power, relationships, experiences, and imagined versus real needs" of its makers' translocal contexts.[127] In each of these examples, women found innovative ways to work within and against the dictates of the standard and conventional frameworks in which they were composing to make sense of and represent their particular context by adapting *ethē* that worked for them.

The turn to everyday rhetorics of resistance necessarily problematizes the distinctions often made between the public and private and the domestic and academic—binaries that feminist rhetorical practices seek to disrupt. As Royster and Kirsch point out, unsettling these long-standing binaries is not enough: feminist investigations of women's activities and social networks suggest the need for "a more intense interrogation of the whole concept of social space."[128] Concepts such as social circulation work toward that goal by demonstrating the "fluidity" of women's language practices and the complexity of their social networks, which are "often civic in nature, rhetorical in function, and both activist and community building in outcome, such that the circles of ideas created within such discourses have the capacity to compound effects across time and across space."[129] The work of the Gee's Bend and the Townsend Plan quiltmakers illustrates how women's social networks operate at the interstices of civic, activist, and community-building practices.

The everyday rhetorics of resistance in these case studies also unsettle distinctions between the domestic and the academic, between writing for the classroom and writing in and for the world. In the case studies, I pay attention to what Anne Ruggles Gere calls the *extracurriculum* of composition, "listen[ing] to the signals that come through the walls of our classrooms from the world outside," including the "self-sponsored pedagogically oriented writing activities outside of the academy."[130] Gere's work has challenged the field "to take a wider view of composition" and so "acknowledge the extracurriculum as a legitimate and autonomous cultural formation that undertakes its own projects."[131] I ask questions about who and what sponsored the everyday rhetorics of resistance in each of these case studies, including "the publications and groups that sustained the extracurriculum of composition in the past."[132] Where and how did these composers come to know what they knew about writing and persuasion? How, for example, did the Townsend Clubs encourage and discourage their members from particular forms and genres of writing, and how did the members' work for the clubs shape their literate practices (and their understanding of themselves)?[133] All three case studies illustrate particular and complementary ways of unsettling such distinctions by drawing attention to the places and spaces where composers sought to engage themselves and others through the translingual and transmodal literacy practices available (writing letters, participating in meetings, and quiltmaking)—practices that sustained them and their communities over the course of their ongoing struggle to improve their lives.

By looking at historical examples of how writers—particularly writers occupying positions outside the dominant power structure—composed themselves within and against particular communities and social networks, we can better understand how individuals gain agency, and "how writing effects changes, both tangible and intangible."[134] Why did the aged in the 1930s turn to the Townsend Plan to improve their lives, what hope did the Townsend Plan give these women and men, and, most important, what did the Townsend Plan teach them about how to make their voices heard? Answering these questions requires moving away from a view of "rhetoric as a specialized *techne*—the property of a small economic and political elite—to understanding and teaching rhetoric as a *mass, popular art*—the practice of *ordinary* people who make up our country's multiethnic, working-class majority, in their press for relief, reform, and radical change."[135] I argue that there is value in looking at such "ordinary" work, and that, in order to listen fully, we also have to seek out such work in the archives, to see whether, where, and how such work has been preserved, so that we can rhetorically listen to the stories the archives tell and see the gaps that are revealed. The process of writing about the "everyday" and the extracurricular elevates the writing in such a way that the point about its ordinariness may be lost in translation. As Jennifer Sinor points out, "one of the ironies found in studying ordinary writing is the fact that as soon as you mark it as ordinary writing, lift it from the stream of the everyday, you make it remarkable and, therefore, no longer ordinary. I fail before I even begin."[136] In labeling the composers' work as ordinary, I am, in a sense, courting failure: drawing attention to and commenting on their everyday rhetorics of resistance proves that their work is anything but ordinary.

On the one hand, many of the composers could be seen as failing to get the response they wanted, as in the case of Burkhalter, who writes letter after letter to no avail. However, I do not want to suggest that what we may see as the lack of significant public response means that their work did not have value at the time. The everyday rhetorics of resistance these composers engaged in must have had an impact on their understanding of themselves as writers, composers, and agents of their own futures. The clubs provided the framework for, and the plan itself inspired, a variety of everyday rhetorics of resistance: consider the diversity of modes, media, materials, and genres employed by the Townsendites in support of the movement, including letters, poems, plays, and songs; banners and billboards; or quilts and pillowcases, to name a few.

On the other hand, some of the composers in the case studies were, at least briefly, singled out as extraordinary, and some of their work did receive notice by the larger public, as in the case of Gurney's interview with Lincoln and the rising fame of the Gee's Bend quiltmakers. Lincoln's exchange with Gurney was noted in newspapers at the time, and her memoir was published posthumously to be read by other women (and men) in the Society of Friends; the Gee's Bend quiltmakers did experience an initial wave of interest from the broader public in the 1970s and later in the 2000s that cemented their status as artists. In these cases, the women's recontextualization of the means available might be seen as more obviously successful because their work has been more widely acknowledged, but I want to resist resorting to such public/private distinctions to confer value. Yes, Gurney's rhetoric was notable for its influence on Lincoln; however, as I argue in my analysis of her *Memoir and Correspondence*, her life's work encompasses so much more: she proved herself an effective rhetor whose ministry, letters, and mentorship inspired many of the women and men with whom she came into contact, both inside and outside the Quaker community, and I hope she continues to inspire others today. And though the Gee's Bend quiltmakers present an example of the ordinary made extraordinary, their interviews suggest they are comfortable with who they are in spite of, not because of, the attempts by the public to label what they do as art.

The feminist rhetorical practices I adopt contribute to the recovery of the Townsendites' grassroots contributions to pension reform in the United States, to the appreciation of the value of the writing and speech of a Quaker woman rhetor whose ministry actively engaged the powerful and the less powerful through a message of peace and justice, and to the recognition of quiltmaking as a complex semiotic practice. The case studies move us toward understanding and recognizing the disruptive potential of instances of difference and sameness, the extraordinary and the ordinary. As a result, we can see the thousands of Townsendites as actively shaping the world around them, and redefining their identities through the community-engaged literacy practices of the Townsend Clubs. We can see Gurney as an active participant in, not just a witness to, history—a mind at work shaping Lincoln's perspective and priorities and also shaping the hearts and minds of others in the Society of Friends. And we can see the Gee's Bend and Townsendite quiltmakers as agents who define the terms of their own aesthetic and political practices and beliefs, not according to the outside world, but according to their own particular values. The case studies provide further evidence that writing comes out of networks of people *not* going it alone, but instead working together with the "complex delivery systems through which writing circulates."[137] The individuals in these case studies matter to all of us. Their stories contribute to the ongoing work of rewriting the history of rhetoric to be more inclusive of those outside of the mainstream. Recontextualization functions as a terministic screen through which to view the everyday rhetorics of resistance used by women and men across history to act upon and change the material conditions of their lives.

The forms of rhetorical resistance employed by the composers in this book—making quilts, participating in local clubs, writing letters to political representatives—might appear outdated. And yet, even as technology, social media, and political, social, and cultural contexts change, composers continue to recontextualize within and across diverse materials, media, modes, and genres toward activist ends. The models provided by the case studies open up the possibility for uncovering and recovering many more such examples of everyday rhetorics of resistance. As I discuss further in my conclusion, the case studies in this book provide historical context for the grassroots activism of hashtag movements like #blacklivesmatter, #metoo, and #neveragain, as well as earlier movements led by individuals engaging in everyday forms of activism in their local communities. I draw hope from recognizing the long history of social, political, and rhetorical activism ordinary Americans have engaged in by using the means available to work for change.

Do everyday rhetorics of resistance make a difference? And if so, to whom? I would answer yes. This book provides an entry point for those who want to work against injustice but feel overwhelmed and so may resort to throwing up their hands, as if to say, what good can one person possibly do? If we uncover more examples of everyday rhetorics of resistance that work against the "perfect standard," we will better understand the reality of activist labor on the ground, including, as Feigenbaum argues, "starting humbly and making mistakes as part of a learning process, finding allies and gradually coming to understand the broader complexity of these issues," and understanding the local circumstances in which women and men have sought to collaboratively imagine and earn activism across history.[138] As I argue throughout the book, composers have always employed strategies that blur the lines between the mainstream and the margins, and have always already recontextualized multiple media and modes when working for social change. It is simply up to us to recognize the power of their words and work.

CHAPTER ONE

The Pen as Sword

The Townsend Letter-Writing Campaigns and the Case of Pearl Burkhalter

It all began with a letter. In September 1933, Francis Everett Townsend, a sixty-seven-year-old unemployed doctor with an eccentric work history who had lost most of his savings in the 1929 stock market crash, wrote a letter to the editor of California's *Long Beach Press-Telegram* titled "Cure for Depressions."[1] He called for a 2 percent sales tax to fund a pension of $150 a month (later changed to $200) for all Americans over sixty, with the caveat that in order to qualify, all pensioners must retire and spend their allotment within thirty days.[2] The plan, he argued in his letter, "will insure an even distribution throughout the nation of two or three billions of fresh money each month. Thereby assuring a healthy and brisk state of business, comparable to that we enjoyed during war times."[3] While other, similar pension plans had been proposed (as pointed out by Townsend's contemporary critics who accused him of plagiarism), Townsend's plan took off as no others had. His radically simple solution appealed to many elderly Americans who, like Townsend, had lost their retirement and financial security, and were suffering enormously during the Great Depression. The newspapers that reported on and reprinted Townsend's editorial received an overwhelming number of letters and petitions in response, and on January 24, 1934, Townsend and real-estate entrepreneur Robert Earl Clements co-founded Old Age Revolving Pensions, Ltd., to promote the "Townsend Plan."[4]

Townsend and Clements quickly set to work promoting their pension plan as a solution to the nation's economic crisis and a way to provide dignity and a better quality of life to the aged.[5] They encouraged followers to form and join Townsend Clubs, where members could elect officers, publicize the plan, recruit other members, socialize with like-minded people, and raise funds for the movement and themselves on a real-estate-commission-based model (Clements's profession). Within a year, Townsend and Clements had made enough money from their efforts to pay off their own debts, and by the mid to late 1930s, at least a thousand Townsend Clubs had been organized across California and the West.[6] Though exact figures are difficult to come by, between 1934 and 1954, thousands more Townsend Clubs were established across the United States.[7] What came to be known as the Townsend Movement continued for years (even through the 1950s), well after it had become clear that its often-incoherent political proposals, contradictory ideological underpinnings, and inept leadership would prevent the plan as originally imagined from ever reaching fruition.[8]

Political scientists, historians, and political sociologists continue to debate the Townsend Plan's impact on the subsequent development and evolution of Social Security legislation. In this study, I am less interested in debating the plan's relative success or failure than in understanding the plan from the ground up. What impact did the movement have on the Townsendites themselves—on their lives and literacy practices? What resources did the Townsendites bring to their work for the movement? Instead of accepting the more prevalent narrative that the men and women supporting the movement were the unthinking pawns of a charismatic leader who promised them the world but delivered nothing, I examine the everyday rhetorics of resistance the Townsendites engaged in, to determine how the plan enabled them to speak back to power and gain some agency over their lives.

As I argue throughout this book, composers with less power often engage in activism in unexpected places and spaces by using ordinary materials to disrupt dominant political, social, and cultural practices. In their work for the movement at the local, regional, and national levels, the Townsendites used whatever means they had at their disposal to fight for pension reform, and what they had the most of was free time.[9] They donated their hard-earned pennies, nickels, and dimes, and spent innumerable hours recruiting, canvassing, and fundraising for the plan. The Townsendites exploited every opportunity to make their voices heard, by taking up the pen, needle, ladle, paintbrush, guitar, or washboard to promote their cause. Much of the Townsendites' advocacy took recognizable, officially sanctioned forms, such as attending conventions, meetings, and rallies; signing petitions; participating in membership and voter-registration drives; and writing letters to their local newspaper editors and elected state and national political representatives. However, the Townsendites also adopted less familiar and less explicitly political—but, I would argue, no less persuasive—forms of activism. They created pillows and tablecloths; put up yard signs and highway billboards; wrote and produced plays, poems, and songs; designed parade floats to use in protests and small-town celebrations; performed in kitchen bands; organized potlucks, raffles, auctions, and readings; and designed quilts.

Whatever the chosen genres, modes, or media, the Townsendites' activities blurred the line between politics and entertainment, fundraising and entrepreneurship. Their work provided a social and political outlet and a moral and civic purpose during dark times, and at the same time enabled them to see themselves as a political constituency with the power to shape national political and economic policy debates. The movement thus served as what Deborah Brandt has called a *literacy sponsor*, supporting the development of the Townsendites' translingual and transmodal literacy practices by providing a political, economic, and social network that fostered and, at times, suppressed the development of their everyday rhetorics of resistance.[10] Both in spite and because of the close sponsorship and regulation of the clubs' activities by movement headquarters, the Townsendites innovatively recontextualized the languages, genres, modes, and media available, working with and against the standards and conventions established by headquarters in order to openly and honestly explain their circumstances and vent their frustration to those in power, and passionately fight for pension reform.

In this chapter, I begin by providing a brief background of the movement and how scholars evaluate its long-term impact. I then turn to the evidence available in the archives of the Oregon Historical Society (OHS) to understand one of the most prevalent forms of resistance engaged in by the Townsendites, letter writing.[11] I describe the push-pull dynamic between the directives provided by national headquarters (as detailed in the national newspaper and official bulletins) and the letters drafted, written, and sent by Townsendites in local clubs. To move beyond the officially sanctioned narratives of the movement, I look to the records of Oregon City, Oregon, Townsend Club No. 1, and its president Pearl S. Burkhalter, whose archives provide detailed evidence for a representative account of how she and other Townsendites cleverly reworked the movement's message in relation to their particular temporal, spatial, and material contexts. I consider the *ethē* of interruption-interrupting that Burkhalter developed in her often angry, *pathos*-filled letters and op-eds; the playful creative work of her poems, songs, and journals, which inspired her and other members' loyalty to one another and the movement; and the receipts, minutes, budgets, and memos she preserved as the administrator and organizer of her club's activities. Although Burkhalter's experiences cannot stand in for those of all Townsendites, her work for and dedication to the movement were typical of Townsendites across the nation: the materials in her archive, along with the evidence provided in the *TNW*, demonstrate the great demands made on the movement's most loyal members, the multiple roles the Townsendites played as part of the Townsend Clubs, the multiple resources and literacies the Townsendites drew on in these roles, and the Townsendites' dedication to communicating the reality of their material conditions in order to fight for a better life for themselves and their communities.[12]

The case of the Townsendites suggests that in order to move forward current conversations about rhetorics of resistance, change, and difference, we need to look back, to recover and reclaim the (extra)ordinary ways rhetors throughout history have employed everyday rhetorics of resistance toward disruptive ends. Even when social movements fail, they contribute to ongoing sedimented change, enabling composers to redefine how they identify and position themselves in relation to dominant structures. The Townsend Plan provides an illustrative historical example of composers engaging in translingual and transmodal literacy practices to collaboratively imagine and work toward a better future.

The "Old Folks' Crusade": A Populist Movement for Pension Reform

Historian Arthur Schlesinger establishes the exigence for the Townsend "Old Folks' Crusade" by citing the dire situation faced by elderly Americans during the Great Depression. He writes, "No group of Americans, except [African Americans], was harder hit by depression than the aged," who constituted a larger portion of the overall population than ever before, and were less able to get jobs than younger workers, in part because they were more likely to be sick and disabled.[13] At the time, old-age pensions were nonexistent in almost half of the states, and where they did exist, "pensions averaged around twelve or fifteen dollars a month and were hopelessly inadequate."[14] Schlesinger clarifies that the elderly were not "a rabble of paupers," but that the Depression "had brought so-called solid folk into their ranks—men and women who had faithfully worked and saved according to the precepts of the capitalist system and who, in reward for their virtue, had nothing now to keep them in their old age, no savings, no jobs, nothing but relief or charity. Such people were proud and bitter. Their despair was rendered the more poignant by their memories of the America of their youth—a rugged, self-reliant, optimistic land where men always looked ahead to new frontiers."[15] The aged, particularly the "old-lower middle classes," felt betrayed and frustrated by a system and government they had believed in for so many years, and by President Roosevelt's Social Security system, including the Social Security Act of 1935, which they believed made them "paupers."[16] The context was therefore ripe for a figure like Townsend to tap into the despair and discontent of America's elderly; it is no wonder that the elderly themselves clung desperately to the promise of a monthly pension and the hope that comes with dreaming about what they might do with their large pensions.[17]

The populist impulse that led to the rise of Townsendism echoes, to a certain extent, recent sociopolitical trends. As *New York Times* writer Sam Tanenhaus notes, the rise of populism that led to the election of President Donald J. Trump has deep historical roots. Depression-era demagogues, including "'radio priest' Father Charles Coughlin," "minister of hate" Gerald L. K. Smith, and Huey Long with his "Share Our Wealth Society," gained large followings among underrepresented sectors of the population, who were "jolted from apathy into near-hysteria by the shock of economic collapse" and were open to "millennial" solutions.[18] Unsurprisingly, given the overall lack of attention given to the Townsend Movement in popular media and history books, Tanenhaus leaves Townsend off his list of better known populist figures of the Great Depression. However, following Schlesinger and other scholars in political science, history, and political sociology, I would argue that we need to continue to wrestle with and attempt to understand the Townsend Movement, which has a complicated legacy. The populist figures of the 1930s became the vehicles of an existential protest, a "revolt against both contemporary politics and contemporary economics."[19] Theirs was a fight of "the guardians of the political order against those whom that order was holding back or keeping down"—a fight that resonates with our current political and social reality, as I discuss further in the conclusion. However, rather than focus on the populist figure of Townsend, I turn to the population that supported him, in order to understand how, why, and to what ends they engaged in everyday rhetorics of resistance to support the Townsend Plan during the 1930s, 1940s, and even the 1950s, in spite of its failure to produce any significant legislative or policy victories.

The Townsend Plan's allure came largely from its straightforward approach to alleviating the financial problems of the elderly. As one congressional representative, Hon. Ralph O. Brewster of Maine, described the plan to delegates at the third national Townsend convention: "The idea is amazingly simple and in that lies its chief charm."[20] Historian Abraham Holtzman identifies four factors contributing to the Townsend Plan's popularity: first, it spoke to the aged population's dissatisfaction with the status quo; second, it was uncomplicated, concrete, and made "common sense" (though detractors called it senseless); third, it offered a "positive program of hope and earthly salvation for all"; and, finally, it provided a way to accept the machine economy (which had rendered many of the elderly jobless) by "establish[ing] man as [the machine economy's] master, never again to fall victim to technological unemployment and business cycles."[21] Instead of laying the blame for the Great Depression on the individual, the plan blamed "the complexity of the economic system."[22] Most important, the plan "was phrased in terms of *everyday* hopes and ambitions for jobs, higher wages and profits, comfort in old age. . . . In place of confusion the plan offered order and direction; for despair it substituted faith and certainty."[23] It made sense, then, that the "everyday" folks who made up the Townsend faithful would draw on equally "everyday" means and materials to express their "everyday hopes and ambitions," which were simple: the ability to retire in comfort and peace, and to hand off their jobs (and a better economy) to the younger generation.

Perhaps because of its origins as an unexpectedly popular letter to the editor—the 1930s-era equivalent of a viral video—Townsend's plan could be described (nicely) as lacking sound reasoning. As Holtzman notes, it offered a curious blend of "economic naiveté and irresponsibility" and "shrewd insight into the dynamics of political psychology."[24] Somehow, its mix of conservative and radical ideology appealed to its base: Marxist, but only to a certain extent, the movement proffered a belief in the government and free market capitalism as the solution to American workers' problems.[25] Political sociologist Edwin Amenta writes that the plan tried to appeal to everyone, all at once, and so "to sell its image of the future, the Townsend Plan amassed Americanism, Protestant religiosity, received economic wisdom, California utopianism, mass consumption, and populist appeals."[26] (As I discuss in chapter 3, the Townsend quilt brings together many of these contradictory appeals in one material object.) According to official Townsend literature (which was plentiful), the plan would save the elderly and the entire US economy through its focus on "consumer-purchasing power": the elderly would be required to spend (rather than save) the annuity provided by the plan and so would stimulate the financial system and bring the nation out of depression.[27] At the same time as the movement proposed a radical economic plan, it forwarded conservative social values that echoed those of its mostly conservative and moderate elderly members.[28] The movement was heavily invested in reestablishing an idealized version of the American family, in which men were heads of household, women were homemakers, and the elderly of both sexes were given the dignity long overdue them.[29] And though many critics viewed the plan as ill-advised and thrown together, one of the plan's greatest strengths was its well-designed public relations and marketing plan, which was "state of the art" and revolutionary, according to historian Steven Burg, who identifies the old-age crusade as the first "corporate grassroots movement."[30]

In the pages of the *TNW*, movement leaders continually sought to educate Townsendites across the nation on the economic, political, and social justifications for and ideological underpinnings of the plan, often in great detail. Townsendites were exposed to the Townsend "philosophy" through featured columnists and authors, as well as numerous question-and-answer columns about the movement. Of course, as a news source, the *TNW* was heavily biased, particularly in its coverage of the Townsend Plan's progress in Congress: no matter how many setbacks the Townsend leadership faced in Washington, the newspaper reframed their failures as successes for its readers. Because the plan billed itself as nonpartisan (even as it repeatedly attacked President Franklin Delano Roosevelt and many Democrats for their version of Social Security legislation), a great deal of space in the newspaper was dedicated to parsing out which candidates Townsendites should endorse in the elections and publishing lists of the politicians who voted for and against Townsend-friendly legislation. The plan itself was constantly changing, and particularly during the latter days of the movement, Townsend and the plan's leadership made a number of politically motivated compromises to its policies, sometimes even to its most basic platforms, as with the $200 monthly pension.[31] Though the plan was simple in theory, in practice both the plan and its sponsors were plagued by an unfortunate inability to explain its proposals when called upon to do so in congressional committee hearings and other national venues. Multiple attempts to pass a bill, or even allow debate in congressional committees or on the floor of the House or Senate, failed (Townsend-related bills were considered by Congress in 1935 and 1939), after which the plan "ceased to be a meaningful alternative in the field of social security reform."[32]

Though its opponents pronounced the plan doomed from the start, the movement maintained a fairly active following. Even its harshest critics acknowledged how deeply the movement resonated with the elderly who had been struggling since before the Great Depression. For example, in *An Army of the Aged*, a 1936 critique of the Townsend Plan, Richard Neuberger and Kelley Loe described with horrified amazement the religious zealotry of the Townsend Plan's adherents, perpetuated by the *TNW* and other propaganda tools of Townsend and his partner Clements. Neuberger and Loe detailed the difficult situation faced by members of Congress who saw the impracticality of the plan and who at the same time had many constituents who believed in it wholeheartedly. They describe the "utopia-chasing movement" as more fantastic than even Benito Mussolini or Adolf Hitler's plans, and the control exercised over the Townsendites by Townsend and Clements as antidemocratic at best, autocratic at worst. In this and many other critiques of the plan, Townsend and Clements come off as slimy hucksters, personally benefiting from the plan and its poor elderly supporters, who gave their hard-earned money to a movement that many others saw as impractical and ill-fated. To an extent, the critics were right: the co-founders initially owned and profited from the plan's publications, though later Townsend claimed the weekly's profits went mostly to the support of the plan.[33] Townsend and his family lived off the plan for many years, and the elderly did give a great deal of money and time to a movement that failed to produce any real legislative success.

However, in spite of its dubious founder, questionable policy proposals, and contradictory ideological underpinnings, I argue, following recent scholarship on the movement, that the plan transformed the elderly from a "demographic group with generic problems and issues" into a powerful political constituency by providing a "mass organizational vehicle that identified injustices, expressed specific grievances, and made demands for the group as a whole."[34] Through the plan, the elderly found their voice, demanding a better life, and as my discussion of the letter-writing campaigns and the work of Pearl Burkhalter will show, the plan provided a great deal of organizational and logistical support meant to both support and regulate the Townsendites' translingual and transmodal literacy practices.

If the movement was a "mass organizational vehicle," the Townsend Clubs were its engine. Although no exact records were kept, scholars estimate the movement had seven thousand clubs and approximately two million members in 1936, which would account for more than 10 percent of the elderly population in the United States at the time.[35] Headquarters touted the movement's widespread national appeal, but contemporary scholars point to the highly regionalized nature of its network. In a comparison of the number of clubs to the number of elderly in each region, Holtzman finds the movement was most successful in the far West where it began, as well as in the Northeast where the elderly were traditionally more politically active; while there was club representation in the Midwest, very few clubs existed in the South.[36] Townsend leaders claimed that membership continued to grow steadily over the years, but Townsend membership records suggest the movement flagged after 1936, entering a rapid decline with the entry of the United States into World War II in 1941. Notably, women were more active during this latter period, which points to why clubs took up political and fundraising efforts that may have centered upon women's work, such as quilts.[37]

Though the demographic makeup of the clubs fluctuated slightly over the years, the majority of Townsend Club members were native-born, white Protestants, described in one popular rendering among scholars as "just folks" and "Methodist picnic people."[38] Over the years, the movement included middle-class, low-income, newly poor, and working-poor Americans; scholars have generally come to agree that the movement was more heavily middle-class during its early years, and included more poor members after 1935–36.[39] Just as many of today's Americans might claim middle-class status despite evidence to the contrary, many Townsendites also saw themselves as part of the middle class "in identity and outlook."[40] Followers with the most social capital—particularly the well-connected, better off members of local communities—made up the club leadership, directing local club activities.[41] Pearl Burkhalter offers an example of a member who directed activities in spite of a lack of financial capital and so suggests that the club leaders were not always the most well-established people in their local communities; that said, her records suggest she developed social (and perhaps financial) capital as a result of her role as club president.

The Townsend Movement saw itself as a proper and positive educational force for change, though its leaders had very particular ideas about how its followers should seek change. The Townsend Movement cultivated its followers' political and economic literacies, encouraging them to participate in door-to-door activism, to canvass for Townsend-endorsed candidates, and to gather signatures for petitions in support of Townsend legislation to be forwarded to their congressional representatives (the instructions for these petitions were provided in the *TNW*).[42] However, the movement's leadership was ultimately unable to control the diverse means and materials members employed to make their voices heard, in part because the Townsendites chose to recontextualize officially sanctioned modes and media, cleverly using (un)conventional means for radical, disruptive ends.

Scholars are thus left to debate the long-term impact of the movement and how it should be remembered today. Most now acknowledge that the Townsendites developed into a viable political constituency, making themselves heard by signing enough petitions, holding enough rallies, and writing enough letters to their representatives to have an impact on national and state-level Social Security and pension legislation.[43] The Townsendites' continued fight for a more dignified pension for years after the passage of President Roosevelt's Social Security Act of 1935 enabled a speedier, more widespread implementation well beyond what the president and his committee had initially imagined (see, for example, Burkhalter's letters to the head of the Social Security Administration, discussed below).[44] In large part because of the Townsend Movement's strength and appeal, the federal government could no longer ignore the elderly, who now saw pensions as a basic right—what today might be labeled an "entitlement." As Amenta argues in *When Movements Matter*, the Townsend Movement can teach us a great deal about the history and future of Social Security, as well as the difficulty of determining the impact of social movements—especially when such movements appear (at least on the surface) to be unsuccessful in obtaining their demands or effecting their particular version of social change. Moreover, as Burg points out, the "business social movement" was one of the most successful of its time, a prototype for postwar public advocacy organizations like the AARP and NRA. Even the plan's contemporary critics acknowledged its potential long-term impact on the American political scene: writing at the height of interest in the plan, Neuberger and Loe admitted that "if the Townsend Plan were to die tomorrow . . . it would still have left some sedimented flood marks on the national consciousness."[45]

The Townsend Movement demonstrates the power of sedimentation: slow, incremental change to the status quo through everyday rhetorics of resistance that, while not always visible, provide an important foundation for long-term change. At its core, the Townsend Plan resonated with millions of Americans because its adherents recognized the inequality of the entire system. Neuberger and Loe were right to suggest that the plan would leave a mark, but the plan has not always been given credit for its influence, and even more important, its supporters' work has largely been devalued, overlooked, and lost to history. The challenge for scholars interested in how the movement influenced and affected its followers comes from finding ways to recover the work of, and listen directly to, the Townsendites. The national letter-writing campaigns as reported in the *TNW* offer us one opportunity to rhetorically listen to the complex and sometimes contradictory ways Townsendites recontextualized the means available to speak out in support of the Townsend Movement.

"Be Plain But Positive": Townsend Letter-Writing Campaigns

As the movement developed under the watchful eye of Francis E. Townsend, national headquarters strongly emphasized letter writing as a form of advocacy, organizing letter-writing campaigns in which Townsendites were asked to write their congressional representatives to voice their support for the movement in general and for pro-Townsend legislation in particular. The Townsend leadership attempted to educate followers about the best, most persuasive practices for letter writing, and at the same time to standardize the style, form, content, and delivery of the Townsendites' letters, including specifying exactly when, where, and how the Townsendites should circulate their missives. However, when we compare the instructions found in the direct appeals published in official outlets—such as the *TNW* and official club bulletins—with reports of Townsendites' letters from the *TNW* and Pearl Burkhalter's archives, we can see their letters as strategic genre performances. The Townsendites' uptake of the complaint letter reformed and revised the genre in relation to their particular temporal, spatial, and material contexts so as to more accurately and passionately explain to those in power why they, the elderly, mattered.[46] In spite of the frustration Townsendites must have felt at the plan's repeated failures in Congress, they persisted in writing (often angry) letters in the face of repeated disappointments. I argue that this was because they got something else from the process of writing: the act of writing to their political representatives and local newspapers empowered the Townsendites to identify as a political constituency. In the letters, the elderly put their newfound activist literacies to work; their words—both polite and angry, on message and off—contributed something essential to the collective effort to "collaboratively imagine" a better future for elderly Americans.

Letter writing and the multitude of other forms of advocacy engaged in by the Townsendites could be tedious and labor- and cost-intensive, and so the Townsend Clubs served as community centers, offering educational, financial, and social support for translingual and transmodal activist literacy practices. Club meetings included public readings and discussions of official bulletins and communications; group listening parties for Townsend radio programs; the writing and staging of Townsend poems, plays, and pantomimes; the recitation of pledges; and the composition and singing of Townsend-themed hymns and anthems.[47] According to headquarters, clubs and their members were meant to focus their political activism solely on Townsend-related matters, and the Townsend leadership sought to control the messages that were being circulated in the club halls and meeting spaces. They did this by keeping local politicians out of the clubs; providing a wealth of Townsend literature, such as the *TNW*, pamphlets, books, and other audio, visual, and written materials; requiring members to buy, sell, and circulate Townsend materials within and outside the club; certifying accredited Townsend speakers (whose speaker cards could be revoked at any time); and asking members to regularly report on club activities. In addition to these more official functions, the clubs also provided a space for the Townsendites to connect and socialize with similarly situated and like-minded elderly members of their community—a space to rehearse and perform their political activism. Editorials asked members to discuss their letters with one another before sending—a way to "workshop" the letters, and also a way to identify the club members guilty of writing threatening, vindictive letters and offer them help (or persuade them to stop writing altogether).[48] As we will see in the case of Burkhalter, club members often provided their own letters as models to be copied by others in their clubs. Unfortunately for the Townsend leadership, these models were often not as courteous or polite as the leadership might have liked, and so perpetuated, rather than solved, the problem. In their letters, the Townsendites felt empowered to exercise their agency and were not satisfied to simply let the Townsend leadership speak through or for them; they wanted to speak for themselves, which often meant recontextualizing the affordances of the letter—including tone, style, and content—to express their anger at their desperate socioeconomic situation.

Given the oft-repeated origin story of the Townsend Plan—Townsend's letter to a local newspaper, prompted by the "distress, pain, and horror" he witnessed serving the elderly as a medical doctor for the Long Beach county health department—it makes sense that the movement foregrounded the activist possibility of letter writing, including letters to politicians and local newspapers.[49] In its official literature, the movement leaders repeatedly attempted to encourage Townsendites to follow in Townsend's footsteps and at the same time dictate their letter-writing practices from afar.[50] In order to embolden *all* Townsendites to write, the paper also highlighted letters written by women and young people—a reflection of its ongoing efforts to encourage the younger generation to support the plan and to maintain its support among women (who made up the majority of Townsendite supporters during the latter years of the movement).[51] In the earliest official bulletin available in the OHS, published on February 7, 1936, we find a direct appeal for club members to write to their congressional representative. After a warning to stay out of local and state politics and remain united in the face of opposition, the bulletin includes in bold letters: "**Write your Senators and Congressman**; courteously tell them you are for the Plan and ask them to study and let us here in Washington discuss the merits of the Townsend Plan with them individually."[52] The notice positions the letter writers as supporters of, but not experts on, the plan, who should courteously ask their members of Congress to study the plan, direct questions related to the plan to its Washington office, and thank loyal congressional representatives. Two weeks later, members are reminded once again: "Don't Threaten—Don't Use Form Letters—Don't Use Postal Cards."[53]

Headquarters put Townsendite letter writers in a tricky position: be polite, original, knowledgeable, and supportive of the movement's message without straying from the official message or getting into great detail about the movement itself (let the Townsend leadership do that work). And yet, while consideration, civility, and controlled timing are stressed in most of the instructions regarding letter-writing campaigns, the *TNW* sent mixed messages: reporting delightedly on the cheeky rhetorical choices of its supporters and offering contradictory messages about when, where, how, and to whom to write letters. The paper praised its members' sarcastic responses to critics of the plan, and during the effort to pass H.R. 2 in 1939, club members were asked specifically *not* to write, for "national headquarters will tell you when to do so."[54] And though club members were asked to "write or wire" Townsend to report on their local successes, their letters must have quickly overwhelmed Townsend headquarters staff members, as less than a month later Townsend asked them to stop writing him with so many questions.[55]

In spite of these inconsistencies, the most common message Townsendites received was simply to write as many letters as possible, as seen in a February 28, 1936, official bulletin in which club members are informed of a commonly held belief on the Hill that the Townsendites *cannot* keep up their "drive on Congressmen and Senators" in support of the McGroarty Bill—the first sustained attempt to adopt Townsend-friendly legislation. The Townsendites must increase the volume of their letters by writing their members of Congress weekly, with the goal of no less than one million letters reaching Congress. The bulletin provides details about how to approach those in power and make changes depending on their intended audience's position on the Townsend Plan: if their representative is opposed to the plan, they should ask him to change his mind; if he is unsure, they should ask him to take a stand; if he supports the plan, they should be encouraging. Most important, they should "write letters—courteous letters—expressing your definite desires as their constituents;—tell them why you want the Plan enacted, and what you expect them to do. DON'T THREATEN. DON'T BE VINDICTIVE. Be plain but POSITIVE. WRITE; write often; write one Senator and one Congressman at least each week."[56] Despite leadership's repeated requests that, no matter the context, the letters maintain a level of courtesy and avoid threatening their audience, Amenta notes that Townsendites still sent a "flood of hectoring letters" to Congress that, he argues, hurt rather than helped the plan's support.[57] The fact that editorial correctives are included in *TNW* issues spanning several years (and at the height of the Townsend Plan's legislative efforts in Congress) supports the assertion that the Townsendites did not fully buy in to the approach to letter writing taken by Townsend leadership.[58] Ultimately, the McGroarty bill, H.R. 2, and the other Townsend bills and amendments failed.

Thus, in spite of the repeated instructions issued by headquarters, the style, tone, and content of members' letters continued to be an issue, and headquarters often used the *TNW* to reprimand its followers for not following orders and to model better practices.[59] The *TNW* published models of successful letters in an attempt to both inspire and administer the Townsendites' written output. The letters reprinted in the *TNW* suggest that the movement encouraged the Townsendites to think of themselves as grassroots advocates with the power to shape the minds of those in power, while also attempting to rein in the Townsendites' exercise of that power by requesting more "considerate" and tempered exchanges with their political representatives. For example, the April 24, 1938, issue of the *TNW* provides real-time evidence of the impact proper Townsendite letters can have by describing how an Iowa club has written more than a thousand letters in support of H.R. 2. Their congressional representative ultimately submits one of their letters, "which gives in a *concise* form the reasons for the passage of this legislation," to the official *Congressional Record*.[60] The Iowa club and other carefully chosen examples provide further evidence for the power of the letter as a vehicle of protest, while also supporting the Townsend leadership's larger argument regarding the importance of upholding the standards and conventions of letter writing. When Townsendites work within the conventions of conciseness and politeness established by headquarters, the *TNW* argues, they can bend the ear of those in power. To reinforce this message, the *TNW* often provided specific messages to include in Townsendites' letters, following up these articles in subsequent issues with examples of Townsendite letter writers successfully relaying the official party line. This often took the form of reporting on Townsendite letters circulating at the highest levels of government, whether in Congress or among the club leadership.[61] So as not to appear completely authoritarian (a common critique, as mentioned earlier), the *TNW* would frequently use "The Open Forum," "The Townsend Forum," and similarly club-focused news columns to publish club members' suggestions for best practices; in this way, Townsendites could see themselves as agents with the power to direct the movement and its policies.[62]

The models included in the *TNW* were meant to highlight members' acceptance and repetition of the letter-writing standards established by headquarters (and so discourage members from going too far astray). However, even in the *TNW*-approved examples, we can see how the Townsendites recontextualized the language and genre conventions of the letter to engage in repetition-in-similarity to foreground their particular point of view. In one such example, the January 16, 1939, issue of the *TNW* reprints a letter from a Meadville, Pennsylvania, club. In the letter, the club members ask their congressional representative to address the needs of the seven and a half million elderly and youth "vitally interested in the Townsend Plan bill," describing the unique situation of those who may fall through the cracks, including those who are needy but own their own home and so don't qualify for assistance. The club decries current Social Security measures as a help to some classes, but not to "those most in need at present," such as the people who "own their own home, which they neither can eat, wear, sell at a sacrifice or borrow on, and because of this ownership, are debarred from relief assistance."[63] In its takedown of current Social Security measures, the letter adopts the clear and courteous tone encouraged by previous columns in the *TNW*. However, the letter writers also recontextualize within and across the conventions of propriety by inserting a rather stark image: the starving homeowner whose shelter becomes a liability, disqualifying him from benefits, and therefore, relegating him to penury, without food or clothes because he literally cannot eat or wear his house. The club's letter concludes with a polite reminder to the representative to follow through on his campaign promises that verges upon, but does not resort to, a threat: "We are mindful of your remarks prior to the election, when you said you would investigate the merits of the Plan and use your influence to have it brought on the floor of the House for discussion." The Townsendites' representative may have forgotten what he promised, but they have not, since they are the ones who cannot eat or wear the four walls that are supposed to protect them from indigence. In this example, we see how the letter writers worked within the bounds of conventions to call attention to the elderly who fall through the cracks: a class of people who may superficially appear to be surviving the storm because they are homeowners. The *TNW* article approves of their approach, calling for all clubs to adopt a similar method when relaying the Townsend message. In this way, the movement repeatedly reinforced the message that one letter, one interaction, can count. However, in the descriptions of such interactions, we can also see how creatively the Townsendites recontextualized the resources at their disposal to collectively raise their voices.

In another example of the Townsendites' creative recontextualization of the (un)conventional means available, a September 5, 1938, front-page article describes the meeting and correspondence between Townsendite Hannah B. Haaland of Bismarck, North Dakota, and Sen. Gerald P. Nye.[64] Haaland visited Senator Nye, providing him with a list of yes-or-no questions to answer about his views on the movement. In creating the list, Haaland works within and across the boundaries established by headquarters. She most likely composed the list based on her interpretation of official Townsend literature, so her composition works within the conventional boundaries of content and style encouraged by the movement, while also forcing her senator's hand by asking him for a straightforward yes-or-no answer to complicated questions—a move that would establish her as an expert in their interaction, which went against the instructions from headquarters. Haaland's bold move got results. After her visit, Senator Nye decided "that something more than 'yes' or 'no' answers were deserved, though your questions were so stated as to require such answers. You have been so considerate that I feel I owe you a letter which will most definitely reveal to you my views upon the Townsend Recovery Plan as incorporated in HR 4199."[65] In his letter, Nye goes on to publicly pledge his support, as "the Townsend Plan is as sound as the earth," just one of what the newspaper calls "the unusual sentences in [Nye's] letter," which it reproduces in part. Nye encourages Haaland to publish his letter and share it with others, and says that he will distribute it among the Townsendites who "have been inviting my cooperation."[66] The cynical view of such an article might point to how its message serves the Townsend leadership: Haaland's example underscores the movement's message that Townsendite letters can change minds and encourages other Townsendites to continue their grassroots advocacy efforts by meeting and corresponding with their elected officials. However, this example also points to the cleverness of Haaland and other Townsendites who recontextualized the resources available—in this case, a simple list—to gain a hearing and force those in power to take a position, which Haaland did by setting up the senator to appear more sympathetic to the people's wishes.

Leadership encouraged Townsendites to develop relationships with their local newspapers and editors, whether to advertise club meetings or to cultivate positive coverage of the movement through regular features.[67] In their work with the local press, the Townsendites developed a variety of activist literacies by occupying a number of roles: budding authors and journalists touting the plan, intermediaries between the clubs and the newspapers, educators of their local communities, surrogate marketers and distributors boosting coverage for the local newspapers, and leading voices of their communities. The *TNW* frequently reprinted evidence of their local newspaper activism. In "The Townsend Forum," for example, we hear from multiple readers about how they contacted the editors of their local papers and persuaded them to provide weekly space in the paper for a pro–Townsend Plan column. "The Honor Roll"—a column in which Townsendites' club membership drives, fundraising efforts, and social activities were regularly praised—referenced the "thousands of loyal Townsend workers and friends of the Movement [who] constantly write letters and articles for newspapers supporting the Plan."[68] One club member touts his or her success at turning a formerly "antagonistic" newspaper editor by "approaching the editors tactfully," with the result that the writer has been invited to contribute a weekly column and so encourages "all clubs to ask for space in their local papers. In this way hundreds of non-Townsendites will be taught something about the Plan."[69] To encourage advertising, one club bulletin goes so far as to provide a sample announcement to send to local papers, as some have had difficulty getting local editors to give space to advertise local meetings. The sample announcement stresses the Townsend Plan as of "national interest" to both non-Townsendites and citizens of the community.[70] The reports of the Townsendites' exchanges with local newspapers were carefully vetted and curated by the *TNW*. However, Burkhalter's archives provide evidence that the Townsendites' writing for local and regional newspapers, like their letters to politicians, reflect the calculated nature of their genre performances, in which they successfully recontextualized the style, content, and tone of the complaint letter in relation to their particular community contexts.[71]

Through their letter writing to Congress and local newspapers, the Townsendites developed their civic and political literacies, taking up the pen in ways they might not have done previously to speak out in support of a cause that would do nothing less than, as one Townsendite wrote, end poverty in the world.[72] Even as the Townsend leadership attempted to standardize how its members—who were essentially political novices—spoke for and about the movement, often registering surprise and dismay at the vehemence of their voices, the movement underwrote their everyday rhetorics of resistance in important ways. The volume (in both senses) of the Townsendites' letter-writing efforts proved the movement's power and reach, and at the same time disrupted its leadership's attempts to have a singular, coherent message, thus adding to the plan's already muddled political and ideological framework. In the next section, I delve into the records of organizer Pearl S. Burkhalter, to look behind the curtain at a more comprehensive example of the kinds of activist work engaged in by members outside of the more officially sanctioned messaging included in the *TNW*. The Burkhalter archive uncovers the diversity of the activist work engaged in by club members in their local communities, beyond the reach of the movement leadership. It also illustrates how movement members recontextualized the conventions of letter writing and other genres to more accurately and powerfully represent the material conditions of their lives and fight for the movement they believed would change the world for the better.

"I Cannot Stand Idly By . . .": The Case of Townsendite Pearl Burkhalter

As the president of Oregon City, Oregon, Townsend Club No. 1, Pearl S. Burkhalter did not hesitate to make her voice heard at all levels of government, regularly penning letters to her local, regional, and national representatives and her local newspaper editors. As a card-carrying Townsend speaker, she inspired others to join the movement. As a social coordinator, she organized rummage sales and potluck dinners. As a secretary, she recorded copious minutes of the many meetings she organized and attended. As a club president, in addition to her numerous other duties, she kept detailed receipts and budgets. As a delegate, she traveled to national conventions and wrote enthusiastically about her experiences. As an activist, she was a fighter just as willing to burn bridges as build them—a woman who did not give up. Calling attention to Burkhalter's work, which has been lost in the scholarly narratives of the Townsend Movement writ large, reminds us of the various ways the movement affected the economic, social, and political lives of its members; the untold time, money, and labor contributed by the Townsendites; and the diverse activist literacies they developed through their work. While not all of the movement's members were as loyal, hardworking, or passionate as Burkhalter, her archive helps us to better understand how and why the Townsendites were inspired by the movement to take up the pen and write, in some cases, for their very lives. Eventually, due to the collaborative efforts of thousands of individuals like Burkhalter, state and local governments developed a more compassionate approach to pensions, a fight that continues to this day, as we discuss the rise and fall of Social Security and other so-called entitlement programs.

Burkhalter's archive supplements the sanctioned narratives of letter writing provided by the *TNW* by illustrating the particular strategic choices she made when speaking back to power—recontextualizing within and across language, genre, mode, and media depending on the time, place, and space in which she was composing. Burkhalter provides a fuller representation of the (extra)ordinary everyday rhetorical resistance undertaken by Townsend Club presidents, officers, and members, who served as the chief information officers, chief financial officers, secretaries, event planners and organizers, fundraisers, diplomats, politicians, lobbyists, caregivers, and philanthropists of their activist Townsend communities. Burkhalter's archive enables us to uncover much of the unseen, unsung work of the Townsendites (including its social circulation in less formal spaces and contexts): the drafts and copies of letters sent and received (to and from all organizational and political levels); the original and copied poems composed and shared; the Townsend songbooks copied and sung; the convention programs attended and signed; the receipts paid and filed; the journals kept; the budgets developed; the meeting minutes recorded; the pins and certificates earned; the club manuals, bulletins, and pamphlets bought and distributed; the membership cards earned; and the letters to the editor and local newspaper clippings published. The Burkhalter archive provides a richer—though, of course, still incomplete—resource for studying the role that everyday rhetorics of resistance have played in shaping social movements. Through their recontextualization of the means available, Burkhalter and other Townsendites put intense pressure on those in power and so raised the stakes of the Social Security debate.

Pearl Burkhalter began her work for the Townsend Movement as founding secretary of the Oregon City club. In a February 19, 1936, letter addressed to Secretary Pearl Burkhalter, the Townsend organization (Old Age Revolving Pensions, Ltd.) officially charters the club, congratulating its "entry into this most humanitarian work" in support of a plan that is "the most unselfish and humanitarian proposal that ever originated with the people of the U.S."[73] The letter quickly gets down to the kind of bureaucratic club business that took up so much of Burkhalter's and other club members' time: their organization fee has been received, their official charter is enclosed, and all correspondence from the club should be sent to the "state area manager" with policy matters sent to national headquarters. The club was immediately put to work: fifty petition forms were included to be "circulate[d] among neighbors and friends" and would need to be sent to the state and regional offices once completed. The letter closes with a brief thank you, and a reminder to send national headquarters a monthly report of club activities; it is signed by R. E. Clements (the plan's co-founder, who eventually left the organization under embattled circumstances).[74] The letter establishing Burkhalter's club provides a glimpse into the multiple layers of bureaucratic oversight for the Townsend Clubs, which were managed at the regional, state, and national levels, as well as the intermingled roles of such clubs, as grassroots organizations gathering signatures and members on the ground, and as fundraisers for the national organization contributing dues, fees, and contributions (not to mention their role in the social lives of their members).

The Oregon City club was up and running quickly, thanks in large part to Burkhalter's efforts as secretary. According to a letter from a club in neighboring Harrisburg, Oregon, Burkhalter gathered some 171 members for her club in just three weeks.[75] The Harrisburg secretary—who met Burkhalter at a Eugene, Oregon, convention—congratulates the club for its amazing record and praises Burkhalter's efforts: "You are quite fortunate indeed in being able to secure the services of Miss Burkhalter in representing your Club at the above-mentioned convention. This lady represented you quite efficiently and stood firm in her determination."[76] Burkhalter's "determination" must have led her to rise through the ranks of her club quickly. Less than a year later, in 1937, a club permit lists her as club president and Mrs. Laura Priesler as secretary.[77]

Burkhalter was an active writer. The archives include her handwritten drafts and typed and mimeographed copies of the letters she wrote to and received from politicians at all levels—local, state, regional, and national. Her tone in the letters ranges from aggressive and threatening to diplomatic and sympathetic. In her letters, Burkhalter foregrounds her dissent rather than erasing it or framing it in polite language. Burkhalter adopts the *ethē* of interruption-interrupting, characterized by "breaks, divides, hitches, disruptions, disturbances, ruptures, or breaches—counters to traditional ways of behaving or conversing—to change the status quo of dominant values and practices."[78] As Ryan and colleagues argue, the rhetorical maneuver of interruption-interrupting enables nonmainstream composers, particularly women, to "break in to conversations" and also serves as "a means to uncover and disrupt habits that hinder communication across differences."[79] Burkhalter interrupts by refusing to play by the rules established by headquarters, instead choosing to recontextualize within and across the affordances of the genre of the letter to voice her dissatisfaction, which allows her to disrupt the conventions of politeness and correctness that so often silence the underrepresented, such as the Townsendite elderly, for whom she writes and speaks.

During the spring of 1936, when the movement's official bulletins were encouraging local club members to participate in national letter-writing campaigns, Burkhalter responded willingly to the call.[80] Immediately after establishing the club, Burkhalter wrote to the US Treasury Department, to US senator Charles McNary (a member of the Appropriations Committee), and to Louis Resnick (director of the Bureau of Information Service at the national Social Security Board) to express her support of the Townsend Plan and her unhappiness with President Roosevelt's version of pension reform, the Social Security Act.[81] In her letter to Senator McNary, dated April 12, 1936, Burkhalter, who was then club secretary, asks for fifty copies of the McGroarty Bill, H.R. 7154 (a pro-Townsend bill), and demands "that you Congressmen get behind the bill and enact it into law, and stop spending our money foolishly, remember, we are the ones that send you to Wash. to do our bidding and we are tired of being the Goat."[82] Her frustration with "being the goat" was voiced repeatedly, but the responses Burkhalter received were often perfunctory and frustratingly similar: acknowledgment and thanks for the receipt of her letter and, if she was lucky, a brief statement addressing the issues she raised. In one such measured response, Senator McNary's office writes that he is supportive of the Social Security Act but acknowledges that the policy does not do enough. He can send her a few copies of the proposed bill, but not the fifty she requested.[83] Though short, McNary's response was voluble compared to some of those received by Burkhalter, including the following curt message sent by the information office of the secretary of the US Treasury Department: "Acknowledgment is made of your letter of March 24th, [1936] addressed to this Division for attention and reply, and we wish to thank you for this expression of your views. Sincerely, James William Bryan, Chief, Information Section."[84] The response from director Resnick's office simply restates the president's awareness of the situation of the aged and his belief in the value of the Social Security Act.[85]

Perhaps frustrated with the "non-responses" she was receiving, Burkhalter writes a draft letter to Resnick directly on the front and back of his reply, stating in no uncertain terms her support for the Townsend Plan and her feelings about the failures of the Social Security Act and President Roosevelt to address the situation of people in her particular position. The letter points to her particular frustrations, including her inability to find a job, even as her father is forced to work as a janitor at the age of seventy-three, and the poor treatment the elderly continue to receive under the Social Security Act. If Roosevelt understands the plight of the unemployed aged, Burkhalter asks, "why does he not get behind the TP and work for it—for it is our only salvation whereby we will be able to make a decent and honest living."[86] In her letter, Burkhalter highlights the material conditions she faces as one of the "younger folks who can not secure employment" (she had been looking for a job for six months):

> and because I am not on relief, nor can I get relief, for I am trying to keep the house together by keeping house for my father who is 73 yrs. old and has a janitors job, and God knows he needs to be retired and in a Dis[abled] care. I tell you these things drive us mad here the President can go on a nice fishing trip and live in luxury and the majority of us have barely enough to eat. . . . how much will go to the needy aged people who really ~~need~~ deserve it and besides if they own a little then . . . become paupers. No we will not adhere to such treatment any longer. We want the T. Plan enacted into law and believe me a lot of you fellows will find out what the ax means to your necks this fall. Pres. Roosevelt said in one of his speeches a group of people well organized for a fixed purpose was irre[si]stable and we T. followers are those groups, also he said Capitol, they shall have it, well we do not want the dome of the last election, but here are 3 votes among many he will not get this fall unless he gets behind the T. Plan. and I would thank you kindly if you will see that Pres. R. gets to read this letter. Yours Truly, Mr. and Mrs. Geo. Burkhalter and Mr. Saul Koellermeier, Sr.[87]

The time for courtesy has passed, given the dire circumstances faced by Burkhalter, her family, and others in similarly difficult situations. In her draft, Burkhalter clearly ignores the admonition by headquarters for members to "be plain but positive" and to avoid threatening those to whom they write. Like so many Townsendites, Burkhalter feels left behind by the current Social Security system: she and her family must live off her father's meager salary (which disqualifies them from relief), when he should be a in a "Dis. care." This sentiment is in line with the Meadville, Pennsylvania, club members who wrote to their representative bemoaning the state of those whose homes disqualify them from relief.

In this and other letters, Burkhalter positions herself as an expert—a move headquarters cautioned against—but she does so by claiming expertise on the effects of current Social Security policy on her life and the lives of those in her community, rather than the details of the Townsend policy itself. Here, she rebukes Roosevelt for living in "luxury" and going on fishing trips, arguing that nothing is left for the elderly: "the majority of us have barely enough to eat," and because they "own a little," they are made paupers. She highlights her first-person perspective throughout ("I tell you . . .") while also speaking for the collective, both her family and "we T. followers," "the majority" who "will not adhere to such treatment any longer." Drawing on one of the only forms of agency she wields, her vote, she threatens the "ax" for Roosevelt and his cronies in the fall election, noting that her own house counts three votes: her, her husband, and her ailing father. In signing the letter with her own and her husband's name, as well as that of her father, she reiterates that she is empowered to speak for all three of them (and their votes).

Instead of drawing on the more *logos*-driven, fact-based, "clear and courteous" arguments encouraged by headquarters, in her letters Burkhalter adopts more impassioned, *pathos*-driven appeals.[88] As Victor Villanueva and Aja Martinez have argued, composers outside the mainstream often use *pathos* (sometimes seen as a less respectable appeal) to tell their stories or, as Martinez argues, "counterstories."[89] Burkhalter's *ethē* of interruption-interrupting enables her to directly counter the dominant narratives being circulated by the FDR administration that the Social Security Act would help all Americans. Burkhalter's counterstory makes the argument that it is not just the oldsters who need help and stand to benefit from the Townsend Plan, but their daughters and sons as well. She personalizes the case that Townsend officials often made: if we take care of the elderly and get them out of the work force (allow her father to retire and get disability), then we can make way for the younger people to make their own living and restore the elderly to a place of honor in their families and to a much-deserved retirement from work. Burkhalter's status as "in between," not old enough or poor enough to apply for assistance (just above the poverty line, as it were), inspired her to speak for others like herself who felt overlooked by their representatives in Washington.

According to the translingual approach, what appear to be errors or mistakes in this draft should be viewed not as deviations to overcome or overlook, but as evidence of the choices she made as a composer writing in a particular time, place, and space. Though this admittedly rough draft may have been changed later, many of the moves in this letter are typical of her finalized letters (including misspellings, run-on sentences, an informal tone); as we will see in the quilts discussed in chapter 3, she and other composers subjugate form to meaning, privileging the content of their compositions over their formality or correctness. The length and pacing of her sentences can be seen as offering a visual representation of the dilemma she finds herself in—the feeling of being pulled in several directions at once—rather than revealing an inability to write according to a particular standard. Her (in)formal tone ("I tell you . . .") conveys her spirit and also underscores her (low) opinion of the politician in question, whom she refuses to defer to in the ways typical of someone on the lower end of an asymmetrical power relationship. In addition to the more obvious forms of difference she employs throughout this particular letter, Burkhalter also cleverly uses repetition-in-similarity by recontextualizing Roosevelt's own words to make the case for the power of the Townsendites' grassroots efforts, including the "irresistible" nature of "a group of people well organized for a fixed purpose," arguing that the president should watch out for the Townsendites, who seek to use their votes to make their lives better. Burkhalter essentially draws on Roosevelt's own Democratic, civic-oriented rhetoric to make the case for the Townsendites as a group collaboratively imagining a better future for themselves.

The frustration Burkhalter voices in this letter builds, and she continues to advocate passionately for the Townsend Plan over the next several years. Some four years after the letter just discussed, in a missive of September 23, 1940, she criticizes "my dear Mr. Roosevelt" for not helping the "oldsters" during his two terms in office.[90] She has worked for seven years "for a better pension, at least a pension that our poor oldsters might have proper food and a decent place to lay their heads at night." She clarifies that though she herself remains too young to qualify for a pension, she still has sympathy for "these poor old pioneers," these taxpayers who are mistreated by "these young snobs called case workers" who do not understand the plight of the elderly:

> I cannot see why they should be so mistreated, why we treat dumb animals better than we do them, and I must say I voted for you twice but this time I will have to do otherwise, and from the information I gather from all oldsters I talk with, they all feel the same way, you have waited to long to promise the elderly people security, they have lost confidence in you, do not think I am looking for a pension my self, no, it will be a good many years yet before I am eligiable for one, but I have a heart, and when I see how badly mistreated our oldsters are, I cannot stand idly by, and not try to get some thing better for them, what we want is a National Pension, so as not to have to depend on the State for any thing, and I ask you, are they not intitled to it, if not,

> then I want to know why, there seems to be plenty money for here at home. I am a registered Democrat, but I shall have to Vote for our friend, Chas. McNary, who has always been for a decent pension, and who introduced in the Senate a Pension bill many times, in fact the first old age pension bill, therefor will have to Vote for Willkie also. Sorry you passed up the biggest issue of the day, had you take some of the money you wasted on the W.P.A. where a select few like the set up we have here in Portland get the Cream off the milk as the saying goes, instead of the ones that rightfully deserve it, you should have investigated this set up long ago,
>
> Yours truly, Pearl S. Burkhalter[91]

The use of *pathos* to shame Roosevelt, Burkhalter's strong language, and the fast pace of her sentences reflect the depth of Burkhalter's feelings about the plight of the elderly and her willingness to be disagreeable in order to get things done.[92] She strongly believes the oldsters are being treated worse than "dumb animals," and once again threatens to wield the power of her vote against Roosevelt and his party, even though she identifies herself as a Democrat in this letter and has voted for him twice (she did not fulfill the threat from her earlier letter). She again laments the inability of the administration to address the problems on the ground for the majority of those who are hurting. We hear in this letter why she does what she does: she cannot "stand idly by," and she has a heart for the elderly—unlike some others, as she not so subtly implies. She criticizes the president's allocation of money to the Works Progress Administration (WPA), which she argues has perpetuated, rather than corrected, the problem of privileging "a select few" rather than "the ones that rightfully deserve it." Throughout her letters, Burkhalter represents herself once again as speaking for those who deserve a better life, and she directly blames President Roosevelt for their continued suffering. The *ethē* she develops seeks to interrupt and wake up her audience by telling stories of the realities on the ground, as experienced at the local level. We cannot know whether President Roosevelt ever received Burkhalter's letter, which was an unsigned copy of the final version she sent, or whether he responded.

Why does Burkhalter write, when she gets so little back in response? What did letter writing do for Burkhalter, and how did it advance the cause of Townsendism? We can infer that the letters were important to Burkhalter because she chose to preserve them. And thanks to her decision, through the documents we can critically imagine and strategically contemplate within and across the gaps in the archive to develop an understanding of Burkhalter as a local pension advocate who was strong and determined, and who persevered in spite of many obstacles and challenges: a woman who used all the means available to speak back to power and organize in her local community. The relative success or failure of Burkhalter's attempts to gain a hearing with those in power remains difficult to measure and, if anything, appears to point to the failure of such letters to obtain their desired result. And yet, Burkhalter persisted in writing letters for years and years, so she must have gotten something out of the act of writing. Through the writing of these letters, she voiced her frustrations at the lack of governmental support available to her and her family. She brought attention to the particulars of her circumstances, including her frustration at keeping house for an elderly father who had a job, when she couldn't find one. Even if her letters did not lead to communicative success in the ways we might normally define it, the letters were a way for her to compose her arguments about the movement and establish her identity as an advocate for it. Through them, she recontextualized the "Youth for Work, Age for Leisure" motto of the Townsend Movement within the context of her own and her family's material conditions and made those conditions visible to those in power. What mattered for Burkhalter was the act of writing itself. Simply put, if she had not gotten something out of writing the letters, she would probably not have continued to write. Thus, the continued failure of the Townsend Plan fueled interesting rhetorical work by Burkhalter and other Townsend Movement members, and their activist literate work contributed in important ways to their communities, well after the plan had been all but forgotten on the national stage.

The letters also demonstrate how effectively and efficiently Burkhalter put her writing to work. As a Townsend secretary and then club president, Burkhalter was extremely active and was commended by her peers (as noted earlier) for her activities and her organizational prowess. Burkhalter's active letter writing served as a model for other members, whom Burkhalter encouraged to copy her letters and send them under their own names. For example, the archives include one letter written by Burkhalter to an unnamed representative asking in no uncertain terms for his support of H.R. 2, and threatening to march on Washington like the veterans (who had recently staged their own Washington, DC, protest). At the bottom of the letter she wrote in pencil, "letter I formed for our members to copy."[93] In that same letter, dated April 19, 1939, Burkhalter again engages in the kind of accusatory, threatening language the Townsend headquarters warned its followers against using: "Why is it you people back there do not get buisy and do some thing for our elderly people instead of felling your time away on so much foolishness, here we have so many oldsters that are actually going hungry, so many need a doctors care, and so many need some one to look after them and no money to do with; these Mothers and Fathers that pioneered this Country for us, instead of providing for Fish, game and dumb animals and what not, do some thing worth while once and take care of human beings for a change."[94] Burkhalter directly contradicts the maxim by Townsend leaders *not* to get involved in the nitty-gritty of policymaking by suggesting compromises and additions to the Townsend proposals, including lowering the retirement age to fifty to fifty-five years (which might have benefited her as a younger Townsendite) and giving at least $50 or $60 a month "as people . . . 50 years old can not get a job even on W.P.A. any more; before talking about tangling up with foreign countries better take care of the duties at home first."[95] In asking her fellow members to imitate her, she is also asking them to get angry, modeling how they might describe their own situations to those in power. One wonders to what extent the other club members imitated Burkhalter's fiery rhetoric, and whether and how they recontextualized *her* conventions in their own messages. In such modeling, we can see how the Townsendites circulated translingual and transmodal artifacts and so contributed to the ongoing sedimentation of the complaint letter genre.

When the Townsend Movement's efforts to establish a national version of their pension plan became less likely to succeed (and the Social Security Act more firmly established), Burkhalter and her Townsend co-workers pivoted slightly and established a new group focused on state-level reforms, the Aged Retirement Youth Employment, Inc. (ARYE), of which Burkhalter was named president. Her work at the state level reflected a larger trend within the movement: though Townsend himself had actively discouraged Townsend Clubs from engaging in or lobbying for state-level pension legislation, in the 1940s he was forced to cede some control and to acknowledge the potential value of more locally focused organizational efforts.[96] Based on the documents available in the archives, the ARYE organization represented more a grafting of the national Townsend ideology onto the state level than a complete split with the Townsend cause. Burkhalter and her colleagues still sought national reforms, but believed reforms on the state level had the most possibility of success. This ideological grafting is represented quite literally on some of the archival objects, as on the cover of a "Constitution and By-Laws and Plan of Organization" pamphlet, where Burkhalter crossed out *The Townsend National Recovery Plan, Inc., of Oregon: An Oregon Corporation Serving Oregon and the Nation* and handwrote "Aged Retirement and Youth Employment" over top. In the pamphlet itself, any mention of the "Townsend Plan" was again crossed out by Burkhalter and replaced with ARYE—a practical, frugal, and literal recontextualization of the available media. This example of Burkhalter's recontextualization of the available materials thus provides one possible example of how composers deploy language and modality in light of their particular "material social conditions of composing possibility."[97]

In addition to the ARYE, Burkhalter, district organizer Arthur Moore, and activists from other pension organizations also worked together on the Better Pensions Steering Committee, which lobbied Oregon legislators for improvements to the state's Old-Age Assistance (OAA). In a letter Burkhalter sent to US senator Charles McNary dated March 16, 1939 (her letters of 1936 were just the beginning of their relationship), she documents her frustration at the Better Pensions Steering Committee's failure to successfully lobby for local pensions using a gross income tax model similar to one that had been passed in Indiana: "I was chosen as a member of the Better Pensions Steering Committie for the State of Oregon and spent a great deal of time at the Legislature the past 60 days, and all we ask of them was to pass a bill for the State to pay $15.00 a month to match the $15.00 from the Government which would have given the old folks $30.00 . . . and they turned us down cold: had we asked for something outrages it would have been different, now a great many oldsters that have already applied as well as these that will apply for aid, will go hungry and cold unless you members of Congress come to our aid and help us to get some thing for them."[98] The letter highlights her credibility—she was chosen as a member of the committee, and she has done the work of lobbying the legislature—but her small, practical proposal has been "turned down . . . cold," and so the elderly will go "hungry and cold" without an intervention on McNary's part. Her use of repetition here, as well as her tendency to use direct address to hammer home her point, echoes the style and content of her earlier letters. She ends the letter with a stark appeal to *pathos*, citing "a pitiful case that was brought to me at our Club last Friday night, a middle aged blind man told me he had applied for aid and that they had told him his Mother could take care of him, now Senator McNary his Mother is 82 years old and they expect her to care for this blind son, why its a disgrace, that poor old soul needs some one to wait on and look after her." She concludes the letter with one last plea: "Please Senator McNary try to get them to do some thing down there."[99] Burkhalter was not above begging, and in her appeal, we see how she intelligently positions McNary as on the right side of the debate, working with her against those "down there" who were on the wrong side of things. (A Republican senator who voted against national Townsend legislation, McNary may have been more amenable to state-level reforms.)[100] Smart enough to both challenge and attempt to ally herself with McNary, she was also savvy enough to explore multiple avenues for pension reform at once, on the state and national levels. This letter and her work with ARYE suggest that she developed useful activist literacies throughout her work with the club, and as a result was even better situated to help the people like the "poor old soul" she cites in her letter.

Even as Burkhalter and her collaborators continued to be frustrated by their efforts to enact real change in Washington and on the state level, the letters between Burkhalter and her fellow organizers suggest that the club members themselves had more immediate success improving the lives of others in their Townsendite communities. For example, the archives include correspondence between Burkhalter and Arthur Moore, a long-time district organizer for the Townsend Movement and later regional director for the ARYE. Moore's wife suffered from an unnamed illness for six months, after which she died, and the letters between Moore and Burkhalter document Moore's experiences, which echo the sad stories of many of the Townsendite elderly: he was his wife's main medical caregiver and so "gave up all activity in a money making way" while caring for her. The archives suggest that Burkhalter and the others in the Oregon City Club offered the material (and emotional) support the government failed to provide, as in a letter in which Moore thanks the club for their $10 "love gift."[101] Moore also depended on his correspondence with Burkhalter to voice his own frustration with activist work. He writes that he was at a low point in his last letter, and voices his irritation that the potential recipients of the benefits they are working for are not grateful enough for his ongoing labor on their behalf. "The trouble with me was, that I wrote to you, when my spirit was at a low ebb, because of the apparent indifference of many, who would be recipients of the benefit, of all the hard work and worry that we were spending for them. If they could only realize what we are trying to do for them, and would, at least make a gesture of appreciation, it would help some."[102] Moore's letter suggests he felt comfortable expressing a sentiment to Burkhalter that could only be addressed leader to leader: the fear that all their hard work was for naught, and would (always) go underappreciated. Based on Moore's letter and her references to other club members' circumstances in her own letters, Burkhalter did what she could to channel some of the club's resources to help those in immediate need, repurposing the Townsend Club network for a nonpolitical, but no less important purpose, the charity of needy members of the community. As evidenced by her own letters and by her decision to switch directions to work more on the state level, Burkhalter did not falter in her beliefs, in spite of the negative messaging from both within and outside the movement (Moore later writes of the "hand writing on the wall" for the national movement).[103]

Following the Townsend leadership's directives, Burkhalter was also an active advocate for pension reform in her local newspapers, where she had a fairly regular presence writing as president of the ARYE club, a member of the Better Pensions Steering Committee, and a private citizen, responding to local issues and framing them within the larger arguments about how to successfully legislate the pension issue at the local level. As in her letters to politicians, Burkhalter's genre performances in these contexts suggest she exploited the limits and possibilities of the form in this particular context. The OHS includes clippings of some twenty-six letters to the editor Burkhalter published in a local newspaper, *The Enterprise*, dated between August 8, 1937, and April 4, 1941.[104] During this time Burkhalter's title changes from president of the Townsend Club No. 1 to president of the ARYE Club, No. 124. In August 1937 she published a call to arms: "It is up to the old and the young to join some club and put our shoulders to the wheel and get this plan enacted into law. For if we do not get this movement or something similar enacted into law what has the future in store for us?"[105] As early as January 29, 1939, she and other members of the Better Pensions Steering Committee published an open letter to the Oregon governor and members of the fortieth legislative assembly regarding the need for pension reform.[106] As the president of the ARYE Club 124, Burkhalter sounded a populist message: "we cannot depend on our legislature to do anything for the common people, let alone the oldsters, as they cater to special groups who already are paid a fair salary from the public trough themselves."[107] She cited her work for the Better Pensions Steering Committee lobbying the legislature as a way to enhance her credibility: "I speak from the knowledge I received as a member of the Better Pension Steering committee, and spent 33 days out of 66 at the last session of the legislature trying to get something better for our elderly people. The attitude they took was shameful, and had it not been for dog and horse racing or what not there would have been some interest shown."[108] The letter establishes her willingness to speak out, to engage an *ethē* of interruption-interrupting by lobbying for more than a month (this letter also continues her claim of oldsters being treated worse than animals by politicians).

Burkhalter's writing for the *Enterprise* demonstrates an "America First" attitude, emphasizing the importance of helping out the needy at home rather than focusing on "the sufferers in foreign countries."[109] In a piece titled "Charity Begins at Home," Burkhalter advertises the time and meeting place of the ARYE Club, which functions as both a political and social hub: the club "meets in the city hall every Friday night, with a no host supper the first Friday night in the month at 6:30, or if you wish you can buy your supper at 25 cents a plate."[110] The newspaper thus provides a venue for advertising the club and its efforts, and promoting its community engagement, as in one column when Burkhalter offers to pay for plants to beautify a highway—depending, of course, on whether the state sees fit to clear the tract in question.[111]

In her columns and letters, Burkhalter defends her honor and that of the movement against a disparaging attack by E. A. Koen of the *Banner-Courier*. In the exchange, we see Burkhalter's commitment to the movement and her view of herself as a strong defender of the elderly and the needy, who may be too weak to defend themselves: "You do not have to go through Doctor Townsend, or anyone else to take a crack at me, for my shoulders are broad and I can defend myself. In the first place I must inform you, that when you take a slam at our elderly people or the unfortunate people on relief, you can rest assured you will hear from me."[112] Koen must have sought to undermine Burkhalter's credibility by suggesting that she benefited financially and politically from her work with the movement, because Burkhalter clarifies in her letter that she has never made money from her work and is "not seeking any political office or job, but I am interested in helping to send people to our legislature that will at least fulfill some of their promises." She goes on to defend herself and other local readers from Koen's claim that they are ignorant of life and economics, correcting his use of the $200 a month version of the Townsend Plan and the age limit (sixty).[113] She is not chasing "the limelight," as he claims, and in an apparent dig at the newspaper in which Koen was published, she writes that at least her articles are published in a subscription newspaper, rather than "one thrown on my porch or in my yard if I want it or not."[114]

In these articles, republished in *The Enterprise*, and the pieces she published elsewhere, Burkhalter cultivated an identity as a defender of the downtrodden who worked tirelessly (and without earthly reward) to fight a corrupt legislature, enact legislation that works, and hold the legislature and state accountable to the promises made. As she wrote, "passiveness will not win the war and we need a change," including, as she went on to argue in this particular column, a better wartime governor.[115] She used the community forum of *The Enterprise* not only to circulate her ideas, but also to respond publicly to politicians, as when she wrote: "The only way for me to answer the letter sent me by 'Keep Governor Sprague' on the job committee, is through the press, so if you will kindly print this I will appreciate it very much."[116] Throughout her newspaper writing, instead of adopting more private means to voice her dissent, she disrupted convention by publicly listing the names of the committee members critiquing Governor Sprague on several counts, ending with, "No, we want a governor that will run that office himself."[117] Her rejection of typical public-private distinctions allowed Burkhalter to keep the pressure on politicians, exposing leaders whom she felt were not doing their jobs, or who were privileging powerful interests rather than the interests of the "common" folk.

For as radical as she may come across in her discussions of pension politics, Burkhalter's feelings about family and the workplace remained conservative (much like the Townsend Movement she supports), as evidenced by a column titled "Censures Working Mothers." In the piece, she responded to a reader's response to one of her previous letters, in which they cited the plight of one working woman seeking childcare (a family had asked an elderly woman to care for the younger woman's child while she worked). Rather than defending the working mother, Burkhalter pivoted to a discussion of working mothers and the need for them to stay home rather than work: "I say, mothers should care for their own children. We have altogether too many women who would rather work away from home than to care for their husbands. Most of these elderly people have raised a family of not one or two spoiled youngsters, but all the way from six to a dozen or more, and they did not ask someone else to care for them while they worked away from home, either; also, they did not have electric washing machines, sweepers, ironers, etc., to make their work lighter, as mothers of today have."[118] Burkhalter identified with the older generation's plight, adopting a socially conservative view of the role of women in the household, rather than attempting to sympathize with the plight of the younger generation, from whom she separated herself by identifying her peers as whiny and entitled. However, Burkhalter avoided getting sucked into an ideological battle over the nature of the American family and women in the workplace and pivoted to a more familiar message: we need to pay attention to the plight of the working elderly, "who should be at home sitting in rocking chairs" and the plight of the "broken-down, white-haired men searching in garbage cans for something to eat."[119] Rather than trying to save money, the "members of the welfare commission . . . should see that these oldsters are properly cared for."[120] Given that she herself was an aspiring working woman who never found gainful employment (at least according to the archive), or perhaps instead chose a life of community service, Burkhalter's censure of the working mother is slightly incongruous. Though we have no date for when this column was published, Burkhalter's feelings about women in the workplace could reflect a larger cultural discomfort with the increased role of women in the workplace as men fought in World War II. Her critique of the working mother focused on the younger generation's inability to understand or sympathize with the plight of their elders, who had given so much to the country. Community members could and should take small steps to help one another during difficult times, she argued, but politicians should also demonstrate their support of the well-deserving men who should be retired rather than working.

Burkhalter's columns provided her a regular forum for addressing and critiquing responses to pension reform circulating in the local community, as well as other issues. Her writing reflected the sometimes contradictory beliefs of an imperfect messenger who struggled with her desire—and often her failure—to disrupt the larger system in which she and others lived and worked, and with the lack of appreciation for her efforts shown by her peers. Burkhalter's columns repeatedly remind us of what she held most important: respecting the generations who came before. She continued to appeal to *pathos* to underline her values, as in her call for better care for the "parents or grandparents of all humanity now alive," for "they have carried civilization on their backs for several decades with joy and gladness."[121] We have learned what it means to be American from the elderly: how "to be reverent, sober and industrious, to respect the American democracy and obey its law."[122] She penned a kind of pension parable, exploiting the apparent freedom she was given in these columns to admonish those who "boastfully claim that America is a Christian society" and yet turn out the poor and elderly: "A wicked man turned a poor worn out horse out upon the commons to grub for himself. The humane society put the horse in a barn to a good feed of oats and put the man in jail; while yonder stand our grandparents trembling upon the brink as they call to us for help."[123] As she did in her letters to national politicians, she drew on an image of the elderly being treated less humanely than the animals that, in this case, sustain the local economy. She framed her opening tale as a "call" and then outlined how State House Bill 509 answered her call by providing for a $30 per month minimum pension for the elderly, who "drift across the commens from whence the horse was gathered, and while we argue, our worthy old drift out of sight and mind."[124] But to provide a pension was not enough. Burkhalter also called for her readers to "take away all stigma of pauperism" and to allow the elderly to take the pension without mortgaging their lives away.[125] In her writing for local papers, we see Burkhalter's vision more fully unleashed than in her complaint letters to politicians. In her columns, articles, and letters for the local media, she was able to purposefully reinvent her calls for pension reform so as to respond to and inspire (positive and negative) responses from her local community and contexts. In this context, she received more feedback from her audience, and she used that feedback to inspire and revise her approach to communicating her convictions.

Beyond Burkhalter's very active advocacy efforts as president of the Townsend Club and the ARYE organization, she adopted several other roles, formally and informally, during her years working for the movement, including secretary, social organizer, and treasurer. Whatever the role, Burkhalter's focus was on spreading the word about and raising money for the Townsend Plan and also having a little bit of fun, when possible. All that remains of the efforts put forth by Burkhalter and the other Townsend Club members is the detailed record kept in the archives, which include numerous "cash receipts" and "cash disbursement" sheets detailing items bought for the card parties, basket socials, dances, picnics, and other fundraisers held at the Townsend Club; handwritten journal entries about their social and political activities; business cards; meeting minutes; budgets; pamphlets; manuals; and books. Among the receipts can be found payroll records and letters requesting compensation from organizers, including one by Arthur Moore, who complained to Burkhalter when he had to pay out of pocket for gas. In his letter, Moore includes a postscript emphasizing the reasonable nature of his request: "Wouldn't have mentioned the gas expense, but *not much income*."[126] Just one of the many headaches Burkhalter must have dealt with (quite diplomatically, based on her records) on a daily basis.

Burkhalter, Moore, and the other Townsendites in the Oregon community also had an active role funding, organizing, and attending local, regional, and national meetings and conferences. On July 1, 1939, Moore ordered 300 "voter" badges, 1,000 ballots, and 250 postcards for a "Conference of Pension Minded People."[127] As secretary and president of the Townsend Club, and then president and treasurer of ARYE, Burkhalter communicated with her collaborators, maintained the clubs' finances and budgets, reserved and paid for numerous meeting halls, and arranged for and reimbursed speakers.[128] She also served as an official Townsend speaker herself, as evidenced by a letter complimenting her on her "good work for the Plan on the lecture platform."[129] In addition to certifying particular Townsendites as speakers, headquarters attempted to regulate speakers in much the same way as letter writers. An article in the July 25, 1938, issue of the *TNW* asked speakers to reference the "explanation of the real meaning of the terms, 'transactions tax,' 'sales tax' and 'gross income tax.' . . . As there has been so much confusion in the minds of many regarding the correct use of these terms, it is suggested that national representatives and all Townsend speakers clip out this article and keep it for reference."[130] Numerous references throughout the *TNW* ask readers—both leaders and normal club members—to reference the newspaper in order to clarify and better understand the movement (and its constantly shifting political strategies and ideology) so as to proselytize in an informed manner. One assumes Burkhalter stuck to the conventional script for speakers about as well as she stuck to the script in her letters.

Though her bureaucratic role could be tedious, she was also afforded opportunities to travel. In a journal describing her trip to the Second National Townsend Conference, she depicted in great detail the individuals she met along the way; the singing, supportive crowds they met in the train depots and at the conference (and also the not-so-supportive crowds); and the inspirational speeches she heard and events she attended. In her description of the conference speeches, Burkhalter re-created a chart favorably com-

Figure 1.1. Townsend convention, July 18–19, 1936, Cleveland. Oregon Historical Society, Portland, Neg. No. 76934.

Figure 1.2. Oregon delegation, Townsend convention, July 18–19, 1936, Cleveland. As part of the delegation, Pearl Burkhalter was most likely part of this group photo taken at the convention. Oregon Historical Society, Portland, Neg. No. C.N. #015-807.

paring Townsend, Washington, and Lincoln: "Picture THREE Emancipators: 1700 Washington, 1800 Lincoln, 1900 Dr. Townsend." Perhaps this is one she will re-create at home in Oregon.[131] She also described a speech by Mrs. Rittenhouse of Florida, who "opened her speech by telling Townsendites and Townsendettes, there is nothing worth getting that the women don't do a large part of—the men have to have womens help"—an argument for making women's work more visible that we are, unfortunately, still forced to make today. Burkhalter also noted the presence of many young, inspiring speakers, including a young woman who spoke about "decency."[132] Burkhalter's notes suggest that the conference was a place where she and other Townsendites came together to celebrate their leader, gain inspiration, learn strategies, and educate themselves on the plan and its politics.

Burkhalter's records, and the records of other Townsendites included in the OHS files, reveal the diverse everyday rhetorics of resistance engaged in by Townsend members at all levels—most of which have been lost because they have not been preserved. This includes evidence of the countless hours poured into funding and maintaining the organization, mostly by members such as Burkhalter, who were not themselves particularly well off or privileged by virtue of their job, position, or home life. The efforts by Burkhalter and her fellow Townsendites suggest that the movement was about more than the politics of promoting a pension for the elderly—the movement was also about believing in something bigger than oneself and having hope, part of which came from the more immediate connections established between club members as they organized and raised funds for the movement. Burkhalter's archives also present evidence of the ways the movement inspired its members' activist literacies and also their creativity, including composing poetry, plays, songs, and (as I discuss further in chapter 3) quilts and other transmodal materials.[133]

As club members, the Townsendites were inspired by the movement, but mostly by one another, to recontextualize within and across multiple genres and modes for multiple purposes, including writing, performing, and circulating poems—some inspired by local circumstances and the people in the movement with whom the writers came into contact, and some probably copied down from popular literature at the time (though it is often difficult to tell which is which from the available records).[134] In one such exchange, Mrs. D. Juttner writes a note to Burkhalter with a poem attached. In Juttner's note, she describes as her inspiration the story told her by Arthur Moore, who fell violently ill and claimed he was poisoned after visiting a neighboring (rival) club. The poem reads as a kind of paean to the heroic figure of Moore. Juttner provides the story of his poisoning as context in her note to Burkhalter: "So when you read that—"He's got just what it takes," you may know of what I was thinking."[135] The poem playfully explores the potentially fatal poisoning with a bit of a wink and a nod between the women regarding Moore, who despite Juttner's protestations to the contrary (and based on his correspondence with Burkhalter), had a flair for the dramatic. Where would Moore be without women like Juttner and Burkhalter supporting him, the poem implies.

According to the archives, Pearl Burkhalter wrote a few poems of her own, including a handwritten poem titled "How Does Our ARYE Club Grow," meant to be read aloud at the club meeting:

Listen here, club members—
How does our club grow?
By all the members staying—
Home and never attending?
No (oh, its raining to night
And in our home its so warm

The members will not expect
Me—out in this awful storm.
Please try not, to feel that way
But keep right the job . . .
Until you've shown the ARYE
That you can get a mob . . .
For we are made up of Lifters
From work we never shirk . . .
Lets attend each meeting night
Then our club will be
A club of might.[136]

Burkhalter celebrates those who sacrifice their comfort for the club and help the club recruit members; she favors the "Lifters" who "from work . . . never shirk," which will help the club gain power. Burkhalter's records include a number of similar handwritten and typewritten poems, parodies, and songs, as well as handwritten copies of "The Townsend Creed" and "The Pledge of Allegiance" (recited at the start of every Townsend Club meeting). Another handwritten poem by Burkhalter, "Many Roads Lead Home," asks readers to trust one another and God's design in spite of an uncertain future. Another, "God Bless Our Soldier Men," asks for the victorious and safe return of the men and boys "fighting for liberty."[137]

Such pieces were composed and then shared either aloud or in writing. As with "How Does Our ARYE Club Grow," the poems functioned as gentle, clever reminders of issues facing the clubs, such as continued attendance, or as encouragement for members to work hard to gain visibility for the club. Burkhalter's files include mimeographed and typed poems and short vignettes, including one, "Cock*Eyed World," a lament about the state of the political leadership during the Depression, which contrasts critiques of Herbert Hoover and FDR with a celebration of Dr. Townsend:

A very fine gentleman, by the name of Mr. Hoover,
promised two chickens for every pot.

Another very fine gentleman, by the name of Mr. Roosevelt, gave us
two bonus pots for every imaginary
chicken, but with no place in the cockeyed world to
put the pot.

There are those who promise, and those who perform
and so, now comes a country gentleman, Dr. Townsend,
with millions of followers who offers a plan to

redeem the pledges made, and give us a chicken, a pot
and a place to put it.[138]

This poem accompanies another, "How to Cook a Husband," a humorous take on how to raise a husband right that has nothing directly to do with the Townsend Plan, but must have tickled Burkhalter and some of the other (female) club members with whom she shared it.

The potentially subversive nature of Townsend-inspired poetry can be seen in a typed poem, "To Our Townsend Secretaries," which includes interesting handwritten line edits by someone (assumed to be Burkhalter, based on the handwriting). The poem, written by F. K. Maskell, laments the plight of the secretary whose work is always criticized. In the poem, the gender of the secretary is marked as male, but Burkhalter has added "s" where necessary to change the pronoun to female, so that the poem reads as follows:

If they dun a member for his dues
he's moaning.
If [s]he doesn't [s]hes's slipping
If [s]he asks for help [s]he's incompetent
If [s]he does not, she's bull-headed
If [s]he writes her ~~his~~ reports, they're too long
If [s]he condenses them, they are incomplete
If [s]he talks on a subject, [s]he is troublesome
If [s]he remains quiet, [s]he has lost interest
Ashes to Ashes, and
Dust to Dust
If others won't do it
The Townsend Secretary Must.[139]

Burkhalter knew well the plight of the secretary from experience, and perhaps recognized the truth of the poem's representation of the double bind of the secretary, in particular, and women in general: the admonition to talk, but not too much or you will be called troublesome, or to avoid silence in case you appear to have lost interest. Burkhalter's regendering of the poem as feminine, given the power dynamics at work in the right (or not) to speak, recontextualizes the poetic narrator's voice so as to speak more closely to her own experience. As with her line-by-line edits of the Townsend/ARYE pamphlet, Burkhalter rewrites (literally) the document to be corrected, revising it to fit more practically and literally the material conditions in which she lives, works, learns, and advocates.

The archive does not provide any real sense of closure to Burkhalter's life, her work, or the movement itself. However, the records of her work, and her letters in particular, make the case for developing a more flexible and fluid definition of what constitutes success when considering the everyday rhetorics of resistance employed by composers across history. As Andrea Lunsford and Lisa Ede argue, the Western rhetorical tradition's privileging of "successful communicative negotiation inevitably, albeit silently, casts misunderstanding, miscommunication, disagreement, resistance, and dissent as failure and, as such, as that which is to be avoided or 'cured.'"[140] Such a narrow definition of success can result in the exclusion and disenfranchisement of rhetors such as Burkhalter—women, minorities, and others who have been labeled as different and "troublesome" by virtue of their positionality or their discursive choices, and whose activist work may not, at first glance, seem particularly successful in attaining the stated larger goal (for example, the passage of nation-wide pension reform).[141]

In the letter-writing campaign literature circulated by Townsend national headquarters, success was defined according to the standards of politeness characteristic of the genre of the letter; Townsendites could and should dissent, but in ways that acceded to the norms of professional communication practices and so avoided upsetting their political representatives. In such a standard framework, Burkhalter could easily be dismissed from the historical record: after all, her letters suggest she was often impolite and threatening. And yet, I argue for the value of the "miscommunication, disagreement, resistance, and dissent" her work represents. Burkhalter's letters and other archival materials demonstrate how she strategically and creatively employed the everyday means and materials available to her, adopting admittedly imperfect, perhaps inconsistent, often rebellious, and often innovative approaches to the problems she encountered. By engaging in rhetorical practices that worked with and against officially sanctioned discourses and by being a troublesome woman who spoke too much, too loudly, and too often, Burkhalter paved the way for others in her community to add their voices to the conversation and "find agentive ways to transform power," leading by example and, at times, providing a literal model for other Townsendites to copy (as in the form letter discussed earlier).[142]

Burkhalter's archive therefore emphasizes the importance of recognizing the sometimes small, but never insignificant, everyday rhetorics of resistance contributed by ordinary individuals working together to improve the material conditions of their lives. The everyday rhetorics of resistance Burkhalter employed to advocate for the movement enabled her to represent her local context to those in power, who for a moment were forced to sit down and listen to what she had to say (or hear a report of what she had to say). In spite of the movement's relative failure to produce meaningful legislation at the local and national levels, Burkhalter continued to speak back to power in the ways she deemed necessary, and she continued to fight to improve the material conditions of her own life and the lives of the "oldsters" for whom she fought for years, well after the national movement had faded from the national imagination. Her persistence and commitment to advocating and interrupting for those without power points to her loyalty, passion, and commitment to the cause of pension reform. As Burkhalter writes in one letter, she's tired of watching the club members die around her and will not sit around, waiting for change: "Our Club has lost 10 members through death since the first of the year, and I tell you that makes me want to get out and put every spare moment I have to getting this Bill over so at least a few of the faithful and hopeful will reap a little benefit."[143] Her story underlines the value of taking action and fighting for a cause, even when the challenge of collaboratively imagining a better future seems insurmountable.

CHAPTER TWO

With Pen and Prayer

The Life and Ministry of Eliza P. Gurney

When Eliza Paul (Kirkbride) Gurney petitioned for a meeting with President Abraham Lincoln in October 1862, the president and the war-torn country were still reeling from two pivotal events: the bloody battle of Antietam in which the Union claimed a nominal victory, on September 17, and the Emancipation Proclamation, announced on September 22.[1] Gurney's delegation, which included several of her fellow Quakers, met with Lincoln on a dreary Sunday morning (after waiting for two days for the opportunity).[2] What could have been merely a ceremonial visit became a deeply meaningful and encouraging religious exchange between the Quaker minister and the president. As I noted in the introduction, the written correspondence between Abraham Lincoln and E. P. Gurney has been documented by contemporary scholars, who single out their exchange as noteworthy, even among the thousands of epistles Lincoln received and sent during his presidency, for what the letters reveal about the president's state of mind and religious beliefs.[3] According to Gurney's obituary and memoir, after Lincoln's assassination, she "had the mournful satisfaction of learning that her letter to the President, written nearly two years previously, had been carefully treasured up by him, and was in his breast-pocket when the fatal shot reached him."[4] This legend has circulated for years, in spite of a lack of material evidence.[5]

Gurney's letter in Lincoln's pocket would provide the perfect ending to the touching story of an unlikely correspondence between a wartime president and a Quaker woman minister. However, I argue that the myth of the letter serves a potentially darker narrative purpose—a reminder of how a powerful, feminist rhetorical figure can be pigeonholed and, as a result, remain hidden in plain sight, because her rhetorical practice is evaluated solely in relation to the men with whom she came into contact, rather than on its own merit. The existing archival records and documentation provide more than enough evidence to demonstrate the power of Gurney's rhetorical work in her exchanges with Lincoln during the last few years of his presidency, and also during the years before and after their meeting, when she traveled in the United States and Europe as a Quaker minister. In this chapter, I recover Gurney as a figure who should be studied not just for what she reveals about Lincoln, but for her achievements as an accomplished rhetorician and activist who worked to spread the Quaker message of equality, peace, and social justice. Even when Gurney gains recognition through Lincoln, her work is belittled, as when one Quaker scholar describes her as a "pious, lovable old Quaker woman."[6] The so-called simplicity and humility of her approach belies the power of her rhetoric and her ability to overcome challenges throughout her life. I look to Gurney not as a model of rhetorical or religious perfection, but as a representative example of a feminist rhetorician who recontextualized the (un)conventional means available to follow her religious calling to improve the world around her.

In this chapter, I examine Gurney's ministry before and after her meeting with Lincoln to demonstrate how she patiently, creatively, and carefully recontextualized everyday rhetorics of resistance—including silence, prayer, simplicity, *kairos*, consolation, and praise (the epideictic)—within and across the languages, modes, genres, and media available in order to speak out in both public and private contexts. As the wife of prominent British activist Joseph John Gurney and as a valued friend and mentor to other Quaker women ministers and activists at the time, Gurney held a uniquely privileged position to positively influence those inside and outside the Quaker community. From the 1840s to the 1860s, she traveled extensively throughout the United States and Europe, ministering to individuals and preaching to small gatherings and large crowds in churches, schools, hotels, palaces, prisons, and hospitals. During her travels, Gurney gained invaluable experience as a public speaker who learned to follow her inner leading to address mixed audiences of men and women, from the most powerful elites in Europe to Quakers in local meetings across the United States.

I examine the power of Gurney's rhetorical choices by considering two interconnected interpretative lenses. On the one hand, I situate her life and work in the context of the larger Quaker tradition of reform and rhetorical practice. Gurney, like many other Quaker writers and speakers, particularly women, recontextualized the nondirective, nonconfrontational, conversational rhetorical approach typical of Quaker communication to connect with her audience and redefine the terms of what constitutes successful or effective rhetorical practice. In her face-to-face encounters, Gurney strategically employed the silence for which Quaker meetings were so well known, and in her exchanges and letters she drew upon and adapted the tradition of spontaneous, spiritually inspired speech, and brought a keen awareness of the rhetorical situation, including an understanding of *kairos*—the appropriate time, place, and space for delivering her message—as well as of the effect of the body on speaker, audience, and environment.

At the same time, we can further appreciate Gurney's recontextualization of Quaker rhetorical conventions by considering her choices in relation to recent attempts to re-vision the activist possibility of classical rhetorical concepts so as to recover the depth and breadth of feminist rhetorical practice. In chapter 1, we saw how Pearl Burkhalter employed an *ethē* of interruption-interrupting to gain a hearing. Gurney's faculty for establishing credibility, authority, and communion in relation to the diverse spatial and relational contexts in which she wrote and spoke demonstrates a powerful *ethē* of relation-relating. Her ability to recontextualize the Quaker tradition of silence to calm her own nerves and to control and communicate with her audiences can be understood through the lens of Cheryl Glenn's scholarship on the rhetorical power of silence.[7] Her patience and humility—two valued Quaker qualities—demonstrate a particularly adept ability to seize upon the appropriate *kairotic* moment, which enabled her to successfully address controversial issues with powerful individuals when others had failed. And as I will discuss later in this chapter, Gurney skillfully deploys what classical rhetoric identifies as epideictic rhetoric—an underappreciated genus typically relegated to praise and blame, and often viewed as superficial or shallow. She recontextualizes prayer and praise in her writing and speech to promote more activist, potentially radical purposes. By considering how Gurney engaged both difference and difference-in-similarity—the (un)conventional and (un)familiar—we can further appreciate her ability to overcome the constraints placed on her as a woman seeking to minister to others in conditions of highly asymmetrical relations of power.

In *Man Cannot Speak for Her*, Karlyn Kohrs Campbell highlights the numerous obstacles faced by early women rhetors and the feminist historiographers attempting to recover their work. Unfortunately, early women's "words were often not preserved," with the result that many rhetorical acts by women have been lost forever.[8] In this chapter, I draw largely on what *was* preserved, relying most heavily on Gurney's memoir, posthumously published and edited by her friend and protégé, Richard Mott, in 1884. The memoir includes excerpts from Gurney's correspondence with friends and family members, and from her journals—part of the remaining evidence of the everyday rhetorics of resistance she engaged in throughout her life. On the one hand, I recognize that Gurney's memoir has been heavily edited: the letters, interviews, journals, and other documents in the memoir have been treated like so many women's words in the nineteenth century, "as historical artifacts from which excerpts can be drawn rather than as artistic works that must be seen whole in order to be understood and appreciated."[9] On the other hand, I also want to make the most of what remains. As historian Sheila Wright argues, in spite of being edited almost exclusively by men, Quaker women's journals served an educational function and organized Quaker women as a group working against patriarchal forces.[10] Just as nineteenth-century women learned about effective feminist rhetorical practice from her memoir, so can we. I begin with a brief discussion of Gurney's development as a Quaker minister struggling with and against her calling to speak publicly. I then look to the ways she recontextualized language, genre, mode, and Quaker religious and rhetorical conventions (including *ethos*, *kairos*, and silence) during her traveling ministry in Europe. Finally, I turn to her interview and correspondence with Lincoln, considering the (un)conventional recontextualization of language, genre, mode, and media she employed as a minister of consolation and encouragement.

Gurney's case provides another representative example of how, throughout history, women have engaged the rhetorical tools available to them. In the process of employing these tools, women have reshaped them for new contexts, purposes, and audiences, redefining what counts as effective rhetorical practice. Like Burkhalter, Gurney seemed to feel she had no choice but to speak out, and she claimed the right to speak by citing her religious calling and by making the most of the precedent of equality established in the Society of Friends. Though Gurney's message of social justice is couched in Quaker religious rhetoric and appears to draw on more conventional, perhaps less caustic approaches than those of Burkhalter, the tools Gurney uses and what she demands of her audiences are no less radical, and her beliefs no less passionate: in her traveling ministry, she embodies and enacts the revolutionary Quaker message of peace and equality, and in her meeting and correspondence with Lincoln, she demands a change to the status quo, an end to war, and a solution to the challenges faced by the Quakers.

Developing a Voice to Speak Publicly

During the seventeenth, eighteenth, and nineteenth centuries, the tradition of sexual equality in Quakerism empowered Quaker women to become public speakers, activists, and ministers. They provide some of the earliest and most influential examples of female participation in the public sphere—particularly notable as the Society of Friends was such a small group, operating outside the mainstream.[11] As Quaker historian Margaret Bacon notes, as early as the seventeenth century, Quaker women received "traveling minutes" from their meetings to become ministers (a minute provided official recognition of the woman as a minister, and a pledge of financial support by her meeting).[12] Quaker women's unique position in the Society of Friends therefore enabled them to transcend societal strictures—at least to a certain extent. Karlyn Kohrs Campbell argues that in the nineteenth century, as the "cult of true womanhood" sought to relegate women to the private, domestic sphere, Quaker women, "in both a spiritual and a secular sense, operated in a culture that insulated them from many of the strictures of True Womanhood." This, she says, "explains their unusually prominent roles in reform movements," and she cites the example of one of the most celebrated nineteenth-century Quaker activists, Lucretia Coffin Mott.[13] And yet, Quaker women still faced opposition from inside and outside the Society of Friends when struggling to adopt more public roles or speaking to mixed audiences.[14]

As documented in her *Memoir and Correspondence*, the calling to speak and to minister—what Gurney and Quakerism framed as a "requirement"—took a physical and emotional toll on Gurney. In spite or perhaps because of this internal struggle and reflection, Gurney found a way to channel her fear, anxiety, nerves, and dread into powerful rhetorical performances. Her ability came in part from the material, educational, and social support she received from within the Society of Friends. Born in Philadelphia in 1801, Gurney was afforded a quality Quaker education.[15] During her early years, she was mentored by a supportive network of powerful women (and men) who continually encouraged her to follow her calling. Indeed, throughout her life, much of Gurney's education came from the friendships she developed with other Quaker women activists and ministers, some of whom were prominent in the transatlantic Quaker community, who supported Gurney's own development as a minister, teacher, and mentor.[16] Later, she benefited from the wealth, status, and power associated with marrying into the Gurney family, a British Quaker banking "dynasty."[17] Her marriage in October 1841 to J. J. Gurney, a well-known and controversial Quaker minister and activist at the center of a split among Quaker sects, also put her under intense pressure and scrutiny.[18] In addition to the daily duties she faced as "mistress of Gurney's house," E. P. Gurney ministered to prisoners and the sick. Starting in 1841, she undertook a traveling ministry throughout Europe with her husband and sister-in-law, the prison reformer Elizabeth Gurney Fry, a ministry she continued after her sister-in-law's death in 1845 and her husband's death in 1847.[19]

In her letters, Gurney describes the agony and fear she experienced as she began to listen to what Mott describes as "the deepening work of Divine grace in her soul, and her earnest desire to submit herself wholly to its purifying and renewing power."[20] In an August 1838 letter to her friend and mentor, Hannah Backhouse, Gurney describes being almost, but not quite, ready to follow her heart and speak out in public:

> I told thee some years ago I had such an insurmountable and fearful dread of having to appear in public as a minister. I often prayed my life might be accepted in the place of this to me far costlier sacrifice. I cannot say what suffering the thought of this requiring has often caused me. After a time, however, it abated, and I became almost indifferent upon the subject; but for a few months past, may I confess to thee, my foster-mother, I have almost longed to tell of the redeeming love and mercy of my heavenly Father to my own poor soul. The language of my heart has often been, "Lord, open thou my lips, and my mouth shall show forth thy praise." Do tell me what thou thinks of such a change. I am sometimes almost ready to conclude the will has been accepted for the deed, and that no more will be required of me. I dreamed the other night that, in great weakness and simplicity, I uttered a few sentences in meeting, and, oh! The full sweet tide of holy joy that flowed into my bosom afterward![21]

Notably, Gurney admits she has sometimes wished she could sacrifice her life rather than speak in public. However, she feels she has made some progress, and she solicits Backhouse's counsel on her change of heart, as she now feels more open to her calling. She positions herself here as God's willing, if still fearful, instrument—almost but not quite ready to accept the call to speak publicly, which she dreams of fulfilling with ease and simplicity.

In Gurney's letters to her mentors and friends, she describes the desire to speak as beyond her control, a constraint she dare not ignore or else, she writes, "I would suffer for unfaithfulness."[22] Other Quaker women's journals describe similar compulsions and the accompanying feelings of self-doubt, inadequacy, and unfitness.[23] Such misgivings were attributed to "the voice of evil" the women called "The Reasoner," and many suffered depression and even illness as a result of their internal turmoil over the calling to speak.[24] As Wright notes in her study of Quaker women's journaling in the eighteenth and nineteenth centuries, the style and commonplaces of such writing included conversion, a discussion of the writer's struggle with the challenging realities of obeying her calling to follow the leading of the inner light, and an eventual rejection of the world in accordance with the call.[25] By representing themselves as instruments, not responsible for controversial messages, Quaker women were able to gain a voice. Gurney would most likely have been familiar with other Quaker women's experiences through her reading of their published journals and memoirs, which, as Wright notes, were meant to be circulated among Quaker audiences and in particular to strengthen and encourage Quaker women.[26]

Gurney's own experience follows the narrative arc described by Wright, Bacon, and other scholars, as we can hear in Gurney's letter to Backhouse two months after the above letter, in which she fulfills her dream of speaking with "weakness and simplicity":

> Well, my dear friend, in our large morning meeting yesterday thy unworthy child was constrained (as she believes, by the love of Christ) to supplicate the throne of grace, and was enabled, not surely by any might of her own, but by the power of the Highest, to do it calmly and distinctly. . . . I went to meeting without any apprehension of such a requiring at that time, but in a little while the impression on my mind was very strong that if I left the meeting without making a surrender I should suffer for unfaithfulness, and I besought my heavenly Father to give me some unequivocal intimation that it was indeed His own requisition, and that this was the period for yielding to it, which, in gracious condescension to my weakness I believe, He was pleased to do.[27]

Gurney speaks of an initial uncertainty that the "requiring" she was feeling was "His own requisition," but she decides that the calling is true and it is her duty to be faithful. Her letter describes what happened next, "*I felt that I must give up*, and truly I may say that from that moment to this my heart has overflowed with love and peace and gratitude to Him who wonderfully condescends to make hard things easy and bitter things sweet."[28] As Bacon notes, many Quaker women describe the experience of "giving up" as "a surrender not only of their will and pride, but also of their right to plan their own lives."[29] Given the power of the patriarchal forces at work in nineteenth-century society, even in more egalitarian, Quaker-led worship spaces the act of "giving up" was necessarily one of great bravery, a submission that was also a form of resistance and acceptance of further hardship. Gurney describes herself as a "poor" and "unworthy" instrument of God's message. As a Quaker, Gurney felt she must "surrender" and "yield" to God's will and speak to other members in the Friends' community so as to clear her conscience and relieve herself of any "inward spiritual discomfort."[30]

In Gurney's correspondence with other women, we can see her friends and family reassuring her that she was on the right path and also acknowledging the particular difficulties of speaking publicly as a woman: her memoirs include letters from Hannah Backhouse, Katherine Backhouse, and Elizabeth Fry reassuring Gurney of the importance of remaining faithful.[31]

In a letter from Fry to Gurney composed almost two years after Gurney's first public speaking experience, Fry writes, "As it respects thy gift in the ministry, I truly desire that thou mayst be faithful to thy Lord, not warped by any man; that the truths of the gospel may be upheld by thee in their purity, simplicity, and power; and may grace be given thee to keep very watchful, humble, and circumspect in all thy steppings."[32] "Not warped by any man" could be a more general reference to the Quaker desire to remain in the world, but not of it, and the need to follow the leading of the pure inner light rather than the leading of the world; however, Fry might also be (subtly) acknowledging the continued power of the patriarchy to elicit silence and fear among women, such as Gurney, who had been called to ministry.[33] In spite of her own sometimes ambivalent feelings about her role as a minister and her burden to speak publicly, the descriptions of Gurney's ministry consistently demonstrate her ability to find the right words, respond appropriately to the particular rhetorical occasion, and channel her nerves, anxiety, and apprehension into a calmness during her delivery that had a significant impact on her diverse audiences. A few months after Fry's letter, E. P. Gurney went to stay with the Backhouses in England, where she traveled with Backhouse to minister in Scotland. Mott reports that Gurney became a minister on July 20, 1841.[34] Soon after, she married J. J. Gurney and began an active transnational ministry.

Silence, *Kairos*, and an *Ethē* of Relation-Relating: Gurney's Traveling Ministry

In addition to describing the anxieties attendant on her calling, Gurney's memoir reveals her ability to creatively and constructively recontextualize the Quaker rhetorical tradition's conventions of silence, good timing (*kairos*), and good character and relation (*ethē*) in her ministry. Gurney spoke to large and small crowds made up of Quaker and non-Quaker, royal and common people in public, semi-public, and private spaces, including churches, hotels, meeting halls, and palaces. These audiences reacted to the sight of a woman minister in different ways—with surprise, confusion, curiosity, and sometimes overt prejudice. Gurney countered these reactions with a quiet but persistent presence through her recontextualization of Quaker conventions as everyday rhetorics of resistance. Gurney had a great effect on audiences—large and small, powerful and less powerful—in part because of her ability to establish an *ethē* of relation-relating, to strategically employ the power of silence, and to use her *kairotic* awareness of the appropriate time to speak.

Gurney's connection with her audiences depended greatly on her ability to determine the appropriate time to speak, gain her audience's attention, maintain decorum, and accommodate to local customs and conventions, including in some places to differences in language, religion, and beliefs about women public speakers and ministers. Both privileged and disadvantaged by her status as a Quaker, a woman, and an American who only spoke English, Gurney continually sought out situations where she could counter her audiences' surprise and skepticism at the thought of women in ministry, which she did with a calm and compassionate presence. Gurney describes times when she felt those gathered were there out of curiosity rather than Christian communion, and yet she refuses to let the obstacles she faces dissuade her from her calling to spread the Truth. Gurney's sermons, prayers, and speeches have been largely overlooked as part of the history of women's rhetorical practice; however, the everyday rhetorics of resistance in which she engaged moved the bar forward, enabling her to claim her own and other women's right to speak "in the character of a gospel minister."[35]

Quaker rhetorical conventions acknowledge the importance of the speaker's ability to read a situation and decide when and with whom to speak, and when to remain silent. This ability relates closely to *kairos*, a Greek concept that can be understood broadly as "'timing,' or the 'right time.'"[36] James Kinneavy defines *kairos* as "the right or opportune time to do something, or right measure in doing something."[37] In the *Phaedrus*, Socrates claims students must learn to "grasp the concept of propriety of time *[kairos]*—when to speak and when to hold his tongue *[aukairos* and *akairos]*." This points to *kairos* as tied not only to proper timing of speech, but to the interconnected relationship between speech and silence, and the value of maintaining one's silence—Quaker values, through and through.[38] Carolyn Miller foregrounds the "complexity and untranslatability" of *kairos*,[39] suggesting scholars consider two apparently contradictory views of *kairos*: on the one hand, "propriety or decorum . . . a principle of adaptation and accommodation to convention, expectation, predictability," and on the other hand, "the uniquely timely, the spontaneous, the radically particular."[40] In this definition, we see *kairos* as providing an opportunity for composers like Gurney to recontextualize the means available by accommodating convention and also pushing the boundaries by engaging in more "radically particular" work.

Quaker practice emphasizes both aspects of *kairos*—propriety and timeliness/spontaneity—while also enacting a more ecological approach to *kairos* in line with current rhetorical conceptualizations of *kairos* as "gather[ing] and giv[ing] possibility to the subjects, bodies, and circumstances it renders available."[41] When preparing to worship (and possibly speak), Quakers are encouraged to engage in rigorous self-reflection—"a general preparation for life and character."[42] They should prepare to adapt to any context, circumstance, or occasion, but should not engage in "explicit preparation for a special occasion," instead focusing on "general fitness" and allowing the seeds of a message to grow slowly, a process that could take "days or months." Quaker practice also rejects explicit attempts at persuasion: "The speaker does not argue."[43] The cult of true womanhood defined the public sphere as "competitive, driven by ambition," and public speaking as similarly "competitive, energized by the desire to win a case or persuade others to one's point of view"—all traits that were seen in nineteenth-century society as masculine.[44] Quaker conventions against explicitly persuasive speech may thus have worked to Quaker women's advantage by providing a way for women to engage in a less masculinist, but no less effective, rhetorical practice. For Quakers, both women and men should avoid such competitive forms of public speaking in favor of more mindful, simple, and communally oriented practices. Quaker convention also suggests approaching one's audience in simplicity: "The simplicity of the gospel may be obscured by learned discourse and elaborate discussion. . . . All unusual words and oratorical flourishes should be discouraged."[45] Quakers sought equal opportunity for both speaker and audience, so that all could potentially understand the message, regardless of education or class status. Gurney's ministry illustrates an ability to spontaneously respond to diverse contexts and determine the appropriate time for speech and silence (and the relationship between the two), which she would attribute to an ability to listen to the leading of the inner light, but which she also developed through attentive, disciplined rhetorical practice. Though Gurney continually doubts her leadings, and at times despairs that she has led her delegation down the wrong path, she returns time and again to a belief that she is "doing the right thing at the right time *and for the right reasons*."[46]

Kairos is "intimately related" to two aspects of the ethical appeal: good character and good sense.[47] However, as Joy Ritchie and Kate Ronald point out, the ethical appeal, or appeal to character, "by definition, has been historically denied to women."[48] In response to this denial, Ritchie and Ronald argue, women rhetors have "developed alternative means of persuasion," as when women draw on "appeals to experience, to irony, and the constant assertion of their own *ethos*."[49] And though Ritchie and Ronald suggest that women's efforts to establish their *ethos* were sometimes contradictory or unsuccessful, women continued to fight to establish themselves as credible speakers.[50] Fortunately, recent feminist scholarship moves us away from the more homogeneous, static, and individualistic construction of *ethos* as limited to the establishment of one's credibility or character by virtue of reputation, intelligence, and good will, or the accompanying definition of *ethos* as idea of custom, abode, or habit.[51] A more imaginative, flexible understanding of *ethos* as *ethē* "open[s] up new ways of envisioning *ethos* to acknowledge the multiple, nonlinear relations operating among rhetors, audiences, things, and contexts (i.e., ideological, metaphorical, geographical)."[52] For Gurney, as for Burkhalter and other women rhetors, "*Ethos* is neither solitary nor fixed. Rather, *ethos* is negotiated and renegotiated, embodied and communal, co-constructed and thoroughly implicated in shifting power dynamics."[53] Gurney's *ethē* of relation-relating enables her to constantly (re)negotiate with her Quaker collaborators and her non-Quaker audiences, communally adapting and co-constructing her words and work in relation to the particular time, place, and space of her practice.

In Gurney's letters and journals, we get a sense of the physical and emotional labor required in order to remain open to the inner light, follow its *kairotic* leading, and develop an *ethē* of relation-relating that enabled her to speak out in places and spaces where she was often uncomfortable. Gurney describes many instances where she felt the need to speak out but struggled with the calling, times when she "felt true peace in giving up my own stubborn will, which always, I think I may say, rises against it."[54] In one of her first encounters while traveling in Europe, she admits to the kind of dread and apprehension she reported as a younger woman anxious to speak at meetings, though in this instance she was speaking more publicly, to a potentially less receptive, non-Quaker audience: "my heart was like lead all day, under the apprehension that I should have to declare some plain truths to a company of Protestants and Catholics, which it seemed to me it would be impossible to utter."[55] Here, we experience not only her attunement to the calling to speak, but also her dread at the thought of fulfilling that calling: *kairos* for Gurney meant waiting for the appropriate time, when her audience was ready for her, and she was ready for them. Gurney managed to speak, however, and delivered a message of charity and simplicity to the wealthy and powerful. She moved cleverly from blessing those assembled to cautioning against "praising the gods of silver and gold"—a message that reflects her unease with the lack of "seriousness" and "self-denial" she had noticed during her visit with the French Christians.[56] In her letter reporting on the experience, Gurney writes that her audience received her message with "great satisfaction," and reiterates the difficulty and labor of such work on her physical and mental being, "I cannot say the weight that was taken off my soul by being faithful, but it was no small effort, as thou mayst suppose," particularly to such large assemblies of, in this case, over seventy distinguished guests.[57]

Gurney's letters and accounts of her travels in her memoir also repeatedly demonstrate her strategic and effective recontextualization of the Quaker tradition of silence. The creativity and potentially disruptive nature of her use of silence could easily be overlooked, if not for an understanding of such a move as a strategic example of a composer working within and against the constraints of her particular temporal, spatial, and material location. Silence is, of course, foundational to the Quaker religious practice, and traveling Quaker delegations often asked for silence, no matter the purpose, context, or audience—Quaker or non-Quaker, religious or political. Gurney, who often spoke after her better known husband and sister-in-law, was particularly adept at using silence as a way of sharing Quaker religious practice. During such meetings and opportunities, "silence . . . is not seen as an end in itself, but as a means of quieting the inward person to hear the voice of Christ."[58] And though her approach does not depart significantly from silence as Quaker religious practice, she recontextualized silence for particularly rhetorical purposes.

Gurney recontextualized silence as a way to gather herself and calm her nerves and anxiety at the start of meetings; as a way to explain and demonstrate Quaker beliefs and experience to non-Quaker audiences; as a way to establish her right to speak in front of crowds that were less than friendly to women speakers; and as a way to make public spaces more private and intimate (and, therefore, amenable to a quieter, more conversational delivery). She also used silence rhetorically to refocus the room's attention on herself and her message, and to establish a sense of communion so her audience could listen to and receive her message. For Gurney, silence was a form of empowerment, an active, expressive act. As Cheryl Glenn notes in her research on the rhetorical power of silence, "silence is too often read as simple passivity in situations where it has actually taken on an expressive power. Employed as a tactical strategy or inhabited in deference to authority, silence resonates loudly along the corridors of purposeful language use. Whether choice or im/position, silence can reveal positive or negative abilities, fulfilling or withholding traits, harmony or disharmony, success or failure. Silence can deploy power; it can defer to power. It all depends."[59] Though there were times when Gurney was part of a larger delegation and may have been silent or silenced due to the strictures against women speaking or preaching, her own memoir suggests that she often reconstructed silence to her advantage, using it as a "tactical strategy" that "resonated loudly" with her audience. Silence was a fundamental aspect of her ministry, sharing prayer, blessings, and scripture with audiences in formal and informal settings, while also subtly challenging the beliefs of those whom she met, including people in powerful positions. Gurney's recontextualization of silence as a powerful rhetorical tool built upon Quakerism's understanding of the generative power of silence. As Howard Brinton writes in his discussion of the Quaker spoken word during meetings, silence is a living thing, and speech and silence are intimately connected: "It is no light matter to break the *living silence.* This should be done only with a sense of humility. Spoken words should not come as an interruption of the silence but rather as a component part of it. The tone of voice and manner of the speaker must harmonize with the character of the meeting. As the worshiper sits in silences one message may arise out of the depth of his soul which he recognizes by its nature to be intended not simply for himself but for the gathering as a whole. If he does not express it, he finds himself burdened with a sense of omission, but if he faithfully utters it there follows a sense of clearness and relief."[60] Throughout her ministry, Gurney struggled with whether and how to break (or not break) the living silence by delivering the messages welling up inside her, but often chose to unburden herself, a process that also required a great understanding of *kairos.*

One particular trip highlights Gurney's recontextualization of *kairos,* an *ethē* of relation-relating, and Quaker conventions of silence. In May 1843, Gurney, her husband, and Fry had the opportunity to meet with the French king Louis Philippe I, his sister, the queen, and other members of the royal court. Gurney wrote to Backhouse about the visit, describing her anxiety before the meeting, caused in part by the thought of the power and prestige of their interlocutors. She writes that she regrets being included in the invitation in spite of feeling some special "attraction" to the royal family.[61] However, she trusts the leading of the inner light, preparing herself for what is to come, while remaining open to the spontaneous speech she may be required to deliver: "it seemed to be sealed on my spirit that if I went in simplicity, and was faithful to what was made manifest, I should feel a greater flow of peace and joy than I had yet experienced since I came to Paris."[62] After Fry spoke to those assembled about the prison issue and J. J. Gurney spoke on his recent travels to the West Indies, E. P. Gurney engaged further in conversation with the group, but finally made a *kairotic* choice to speak: "I found I dare not leave it here, and actually had courage to request permission to express what was resting on my mind toward them . . . and *after a short pause* I was strengthened to address them for several minutes in an unexcited manner, and with more quietness of spirit than I have often known when speaking to the humblest individual. I think in mercy I was raised above all fear for the moment . . . and they were all profoundly attentive."[63] In this passage, we hear Gurney's struggle with whether she should assert herself after her companions have already spoken, for to assert herself means she has something unique to add or her fellow delegates have left something important unsaid. Throughout her journals, we see Gurney engage in explicit discussions of the timing of her testimony, even as she gains more and more experience as a speaker. Of course, Gurney's memoir mostly includes examples where her timing was good, a probable result of the friendly editing of Richard Mott.

However, Gurney's letters and journals highlight the kind of reflective self-knowledge Amelie Frost Benedikt views as fundamental to an effective use of *kairos*, for "*kairos* begins to achieve morally good results only as a result of reflection upon the 'goodness' or 'badness' of one's 'timing.'"[64] In her letters and journals, Gurney constantly questions her attunement to the particular temporal-spatial context, which prepares her to better judge the right time and proper measure in future encounters.

As the previous account suggests, Gurney would often take a short, silent pause to gather herself and those assembled, a silence that served multiple purposes: the pause would draw the gathering's attention to her and away from those who had just spoken, and it would enable her to gather her own nerves. In that moment, she was able to appear calm and quiet in spirit, rather than nervous, and so was able to relate to a gathering of people who would ostensibly be quite opposed to the simplicity and humility practiced and preached by the Quakers. During this and other visits with "the great ones of the earth," Gurney chose to address her audience "in simplicity," and with a calmness that affected her audience deeply: as she notes at the end of the passage quoted above, "the ladies, including the queen, directly dropped their worsted work in which they were busily engaged, and they were all profoundly attentive" and "the king in the kindest manner exclaimed, 'Allow me to return you our heartfelt thanks for your good wishes and prayers for our family.'"[65] Her message was delivered in a spirit of compassion, but was nonetheless radical in its Quaker bluntness and directness: she spoke of the importance of humility and of how "even kings and princes are not exempt from the common lot of humanity," a reference specifically to the death of the queen's son, which brought tears to the queen's eyes.[66] As they left, not only the Princess Adelaide but the king himself repeated their thanks to Gurney, the king even taking her by the hand and offering "my warmest and most grateful thanks."[67] For this, Gurney felt "abundantly rewarded . . . for my first act of dedication before the great ones of the earth," and her husband "said he had been so reminded of [Backhouse's] prophecy that 'I would one day see more of royalty than ever my sister Fry had done.'"[68] Here and elsewhere in his own journals and in his letters to others, J. J. Gurney—who had during their travels at times excluded E. P. Gurney from his antislavery work—notes with pride his wife's ability to influence the most powerful.[69] Gurney's professed simplicity of manner, which she often speaks of in a derogatory way in her letters, even calling her approach in one meeting with Prussian royalty "stupid," was nonetheless highly effective.[70]

Later that same year, Gurney recounts another *kairotic* encounter in which we see the challenges she met with when trying to patiently follow her inner leading in the face of numerous practical obstacles and doubts, even from within her own delegation. In August 1843, J. J. Gurney felt led to seek a meeting with the king of Württemberg, but gave up after making some inquiries and finding out that the visit would take them seven days out of their way and the king would be unlikely to be in town when they arrived. However, E. P. Gurney patiently persisted, because, as she wrote in a letter to Backhouse, she felt "it was clearly impressed on my mind that we should go to Stuttgart, and that we should see the King."[71] Even though the probability of meeting the king was not good, the party traveled out of their way to Stuttgart. Sometimes finding the appropriate time requires putting yourself in the appropriate place, and waiting for longer than most potential speakers would be willing to wait. While waiting, the delegation faced continued setbacks to arranging the meeting, but Gurney was once again encouraged in her decision when "the words of our Saviour very unexpectedly revived in my mind: 'Your times are always ready, but my time is not always,' accompanied with a strong belief that we ought to wait His time."[72]

The words Gurney hears in this instance reinforce her ongoing struggle between *kairos*-time and *chronos*-time. As Benedikt writes, "kairic time, therefore, marks opportunities that might not recur, moments of decision. Whereas *chronos*-time is absolute, universal, and objective, *kairos* is interpretative, situational and, therefore, 'subjective.'"[73] The delegation was subject to the tight schedules of those with whom they wanted to meet, many of whom they would only have a brief, one-time chance to encounter; Gurney's inner leading reinforced her belief in the *kairic* opportunities before her in spite of these constraints. After Gurney repeated her inner leading to her companions, the delegation followed her lead and waited a day longer for the opportunity to meet with the king. Finally, however, the other delegates felt they had to leave. Gurney was shaken by what she saw as a repudiation of her inner leading, her subjective *kairotic* assessment of what she saw as the best opportunity to meet with the king, and she wrote of how deeply disturbed she was in that moment: "If this [deep impression to meet with the king] proved a delusion, how could I believe that any of my former experience was true? I threw myself on the bed and wept in agony of soul which was known only to the All-seeing Eye."[74] While she was in the depths of despair, a request came in for another meeting that evening, which extended the delegation's stay. That same afternoon the king came to town, a fortuitous event which meant the delegation could again try to see him, but after hearing this seemingly good news, Gurney wrote that she felt a bit of regret, since "it [was] such a solemn undertaking."[75] The following morning, in spite of being told the queen was unavailable and "the King did not receive ladies alone," the Quaker delegation patiently waited until they found themselves, finally, in front of the king and queen that evening.

That evening, the delegation faced what E. P. Gurney described as a "formidable" group, including members of the royal family and thirty to forty ladies and gentlemen. In the events that followed, Gurney demonstrated an ability to recontextualize the affordances of the modes available to her in this particularly opulent, potentially unreceptive setting—including speech, silence, and speaker-as-body-and-voice. As we can see in her own description, Gurney made the most of the limits and possibilities of her material environs by making the public space more private. She writes that "in such a party, standing in the open balcony, I felt it was impossible, and in a strength that truly was given me, *I asked the King and Queen if they would kindly allow us to sit down together in silence*; to which they assented at once and, followed by the crown prince and the two princesses, walked into the drawing-room, the Queen herself placing our chairs just opposite to them."[76] Gurney's audacious request enabled her and her husband to gain the audience's full attention and so speak to and sit in contemplative silence with the royal family in a quieter space. Aristotle's *Rhetoric* includes a discussion tying the concept of *kairos* to gaining and reawakening an audience's attention: "Wherefore, when the right moment [*kairos*] comes, one must say, 'And give me your attention, for it concerns you as much as myself'; and, 'I will tell you such a thing as you have never yet' heard of, so strange and wonderful."[77] Gurney's use of silence sends that same message—though with fewer words—finding the appropriate time to speak and engage silence to transcend the asymmetrical power relations at work and establish an *ethē* of relation-relating. As Glenn argues, the power of silence should not be underestimated: "silence—the unspoken—is a rhetorical art that can be as powerful as the spoken or written word. Like speech, the meaning of silence depends on a power differential that exists in every rhetorical situation: who can speak, who must remain silent, who listens, and what those listeners do."[78] Whether speaking with royalty or ordinary people, Gurney employed silence to level the playing field, speaking across power, gender, and religious differences and so gain a hearing that enabled her listeners to experience the silence in a new way and, ultimately, listen to the power of the words of Gurney and her companions. On this occasion, Gurney also demonstrated an ability to navigate and even disrupt the social hierarchies at work, rearranging the space and the seating so that she could meet those in power as (near) equals. And when the Gurneys and the royal family left the balcony, they found out the royal court had been listening in to their private meeting from the next room, "so that we had in fact been holding a meeting with them all."[79] Gurney's move to physically separate her group from the larger gathering so that she and her immediate interlocutors could be more comfortable made it possible to have a more intimate setting for both the royal family and, to a lesser extent, their court, listening at the door—and so break down the distinction between public and private (an already blurry line in the royal court, as the image of the eavesdroppers suggests).

In spite of her adroitness at navigating such socially and politically tricky situations, in her private letters and journals, Gurney reveals how she suffered from the pressure of scheduling meetings and waiting for the right *kairotic* moment. Gurney would have had to demonstrate remarkable rhetorical dexterity to navigate the conflicts between her practical need to schedule and plan meetings, and her religious requirement to not prepare, but instead be spontaneously inspired.[80] She often made preparations for meetings even though she did not feel an inner leading to speak and so worried she would not have anything to say; she speaks in one letter of the stress of having to schedule multiple meetings with "my mind a perfect blank," relating how she had to trust that the inner light would come to her when she needed it.[81] Moreover, Gurney was deeply affected by the prejudice, surprise, and negativity she encountered from audiences. In 1843, Gurney reports on a stressful encounter in Geneva, where the delegation spoke to "devoted pastors" who nonetheless held "a strong prejudice . . . against women's ministry."[82] The pastors' prejudice added to her anxiety and their curiosity objectified her, making her feel like a kind of sideshow: "and, with the burden which was certainly laid upon me towards the people I was placed in the most painful and apparently indissoluble bonds. I scarcely know which was the most annoying, the objection in the minds of some, or the strong curiosity and inclination in others, inducing them to beg that I would speak." Toward the end of that same visit, the delegation held a breakfast with twenty-one people, including said pastors and "several other serious gentlemen."[83] Gurney felt constrained to speak, and reports of the difficulty she felt in front of the intimidating and hostile crowd: "It was no small trial to me to be faithful on this occasion, especially as the two ministers who were said to be so entirely opposed to women's ministry were sitting near me; but instead of being offended by what I said, they were as cordial as possible afterward, hoping the Lord might bless our labors of love, and expressing with many others the comfort and satisfaction they had had in the opportunity." Though she does not recount her exact words in this moment, reading between the lines, we can suppose that Gurney was able to develop an *ethē* of relation-relating with even this intimidating crowd, who moved from a position of skepticism to a listening disposition in which they blessed her continued ministry and thanked *her* for "the opportunity." But the reality of the historical-material conditions in which Gurney spoke still caught up with her. Gurney follows her discussion of this relatively successful encounter with a difficult audience by noting that she was unable to take part in several other meetings, in part because of the spaces where they were held, as when J. J. Gurney spoke in the local church's oratory and "I could have no part in them, as women are not allowed to speak in their churches."[84] Although J. J. Gurney was able to intercede on his wife's behalf, sometimes divining that the reported prejudice did not in fact exist, there were many such times where E. P. Gurney was prevented from speaking.[85] She reacted with annoyance at the prejudice and obstacles to speaking she encountered, but also, on occasion, with relief. For example, in Nîmes, when prevented from speaking in church by the "law of the Sanhedrim," which forbids women from doing so, Gurney reports that "my naughty heart was ready to jump for joy." But the delegation found a workaround, holding a gathering in a more neutral space at the hotel. Gurney's "soul was in greater heaviness all the evening than I can describe," and in front of a crowd of 170 people she finally gave in to the burden to speak: "my spirit was enfranchised from its bonds . . . to deliver a very close communication to a mixed company, and felt true peace afterward."[86] As in her early ministry, speaking was a pleasurable relief of a (required) burden.

After her husband's death in 1847, Gurney took a leadership position, traveling with fellow delegates who provided strength during her moments of anxiety and enabled her to spread the gospel message, even in the most remote communities. Sometimes, the isolated villages to which she traveled had never before seen a woman minister, though this did not mean they were unaccepting. In 1856, Gurney undertook a treacherous trip through the mountains of northern Italy to minister to small communities.[87] In a letter from Perosa, Italy, Gurney described how "[n]o woman Friend has ever visited this place before in the character of a gospel minister; but, as the moderator observed, 'the people expressed no surprise, but appeared quite prepared to receive our gospel messages as coming from the Lord.'"[88] Gurney described herself, humbly, as "the weakest of the flock," but she still felt blessed by God, admitting that she was happy to have her companions' help, since she had "felt the weight of the meetings, as well as the preparatory baptisms,—which, I assure thee, have not been small,—rather heavy upon me."[89]

Gurney and her companions did not allow themselves to feel too discouraged when they encountered "a little scruple in their minds against women's ministry," as oftentimes the local ministers encouraged them to understand any initial resistance or shock as a result of the newness of women in ministry, rather than an intransigent set of beliefs.[90] Even when introduced in a "cold" way by a pastor during a meeting in Turin with some three to four hundred people in attendance, Gurney persevered, recontextualizing silence to gain the audience's rapt attention: "However, after a short but solemn silence, I was enabled thoroughly to relieve my mind to a most serious and attentive audience on the faith and the words of Abraham, 'God will provide Himself a lamb.'"[91] After Gurney's talk, the delegation received a warmer welcome, and the pastor himself kneeled and prayed they would listen to her message. During that same visit, they visited two schools, and Gurney wrote that during her time with "the mountaineers," "[w]e have found large openings for books and money everywhere we have gone, and I have felt so much interest in many of their objects that I have been ready to wish my purse had no end."[92] In this way, Gurney continued to win over her audiences (large and small) by reinventing silence and prayer rhetorically and by engaging in other, more practical forms of missionary work, such as distributing money, books, pamphlets, and tracts.

Gurney also encountered ignorance from more cosmopolitan, upper-class people, as during her visit with the dowager empress of Russia that same fall. Gurney wrote that the empress was open to but confused by her and Elizabeth Fry's work as women preachers, "which she could not exactly understand," a reaction that Gurney said made it more difficult to complete her duty: "it was no easy matter to address her as a minister just after she had expressed her astonishment that women should ever be called upon to preach."[93] However, Gurney wrote that she felt "empowered" by her faith.[94] The empress was moved to tears by Gurney's words, and the two women "sat together in solemn silence for a little while," after which the empress commended Gurney, saying that "she understood every word I said, because I spoke so 'simply and so distinctly.'"[95] Silence became a way to extend and affirm Gurney's message to her audience, and in spite of the empress's professed skepticism and hesitancy to view Gurney (or any woman speaker, for that matter) as credible, Gurney was able to establish an *ethē* of relation-relating that enabled her to reach her audience with simplicity and directness.

Gurney fundamentally believed in the power of silence both to enable and to encourage communion, and also to serve as a testimony to the presence of God (and the power of her own words). Gurney faced the added pressure of having to educate the ministers and pastors they met about the Quakers' seemingly odd practice, particularly when faced with large crowds. For example, she relates how a pastor in Anduze was anxious about the Quaker delegation's insistence on using silence to open a meeting of some three to four hundred people. The minister was confused, arguing that he could not guarantee how his people would react, since some were there just out of curiosity. She writes that he told her, "Would it not be better to begin with a hymn? Etc. I told him I did not think that was necessary, that we had generally found there was a Power over us which could silence them without the intervention of man, and I believed we might trust it on the present occasion."[96] Gurney responded to the minister's doubt and his inability to grant her authority or understand her approach, by doubling down on the divine power of silence to quiet even potentially raucous or unpredictable crowds. She felt it was the right time and the right place, for the right purposes, and in this instance, she was right: the silence was "profound," and Gurney writes, "I never witnessed a more serious or attentive assembly."[97] In a different gathering at Nîmes, the attendees remained after Gurney and her companions left; the gathering continued to sit in silence, until an Evangelical pastor "recapitulated all I had said, commending it to their serious consideration, and expressed an earnest desire that they might never forget the gospel truths that had been proclaimed amongst them."[98] Gurney's words and her ministry of silence circulated even after she and her companions had left. Mott includes several other instances when Gurney faced down dissenters, and writes of how the incidents often led to a deeper communion, or to more people being persuaded of the power of women in ministry, rather than to the disruption and doubt that the dissenters desired.[99]

During her life Gurney actively worked to spread Quaker truth and values. Although Gurney's memoir holds her life up as a model for other Quaker ministers, contemporary scholars could easily view her rhetorical practice as more religious and less explicitly "activist" when compared to the work of her outspoken husband J. J. Gurney and her sister-in-law Elizabeth Fry, well-known Quaker social reformers at the time. However, I argue against such distinctions. Gurney was a participant in Quaker conversations about slavery, prison, and education reform due to her affiliation with the Gurneys and the network of other orthodox Quaker activists, her membership in multiple Quaker meetings in Britain and the United States, and her attendance at the Quaker yearly meetings in London and New England.[100] During her ministry, Gurney often participated in activist efforts by preparing the way or providing closure for her better known activist colleagues, a sometimes thankless, but necessary role. She also dedicated her public and private ministry to the promotion of the Quaker values of equality (across lines of race, class, and gender), a dedication to the pursuit of Truth, and the importance of serving one's fellow man in humility and kindness. Gurney's religious ministry functioned as a form of activism, one that the historical record may be less inclined to appreciate given contemporary biases toward more secular forms of activism, but which is no less powerful. The everyday rhetorics of resistance in which she engaged throughout her ministry touched the hearts and lives of people in the United States and Europe.

"A Most Interesting Interview"

In his introduction to Gurney's notorious political meeting with Lincoln, her memoirist Richard Mott identifies the exigency of her visit as Gurney's concern for America's wartime leaders: "E. P. Gurney, in common with her peaceful sect, naturally felt her sympathies called into their fullest exercise for those at the head of affairs, that they might be rightly guided in this momentous crisis."[101] Notably, Mott fails to mention the depth and breadth of the challenges faced by Gurney and the Society of Friends, for whom the Civil War represented one of the biggest tests of the Quaker peace testimony since the seventeenth-century.[102] In his prefatory remarks, Mott may have assumed a Quaker readership who would already be familiar with the persecutions and challenges Quakers faced from without, or he may have wanted to gloss over the internal disagreements over how Quakers should respond to war and slavery. As advocates for peace and against slavery, the Society of Friends found itself in a difficult position with regard to the Civil War. Many Friends upheld the Quaker peace testimony and refused to be drafted, to fight, pay war taxes or bonds, or make supplies for war.[103] As Bacon notes, Lincoln and his secretary of war, Edwin Stanton (the son of a Quaker), were considered "lenient toward Quaker conscientious objectors, and their enemies described them as belonging to 'The Quaker War Cabinet.'"[104] However, many Quakers still struggled with the implications of nonviolence, and balked at the choice between paying a bounty for a substitute or joining the army without cooperating. Southern Quakers in particular suffered greatly for their opposition to slavery and the war: many Quakers in the South were imprisoned (as were some Friends in the Northeast), and some young southerners even lived for years in the woods as "bushwhackers" rather than take part in the war.[105] Two Draft Acts were passed in 1863, and as a result of the second, Quakers could theoretically choose between medical work, work with the freedmen, or paying $300 to a freedmen's or hospital fund.[106] Although many Quakers took advantage of the policy, Quaker meetings in the Northeast remained opposed to paying a fine or paying for a substitute.[107] In the case of those Quakers who declared themselves "absolute objectors," Lincoln continued to parole them home, as he had done in the past for other Quakers who had suffered violence and even torture in the army.[108] Other Friends did join the war to support the Union, and according to records of the Western and Midwestern Friends' meetings, those who fought for the Union were spared from disownment by their home meetings after the war.[109]

Unfortunately, Gurney's memoir does not provide documentation of her writing or thinking about the ongoing political turbulence before her meeting with Lincoln. Instead, Mott simply states that in October 1862, Gurney "felt constrained to pay a religious visit to Abraham Lincoln . . . in which she was accompanied by John M. Whitall, Hannah B. Mott, and James Carey," whom we know from her journals and letters to have been among her closest friends and confidantes.[110] Several accounts of the meeting between Lincoln and Gurney exist: the Abraham Lincoln Papers at the Library of Congress contains an original copy of the interview; Gurney's obituary, written by J. B. Braithwaite and published in *The Annual Monitor*, contains an eyewitness account; and Gurney's memoir combines an eyewitness account with excerpts from the account in her obituary.[111] The various renderings differ in their representation of Gurney and Lincoln's exact words during their meeting; however, Gurney's underlying message of encouragement to and praise for Lincoln remains consistent.[112]

Gurney's obituary writer, Joseph Bevan Braithwaite, establishes the exigence for the meeting: Gurney's *ethē* as a purveyor of God's word in her prior ministry, and her timing, what I would point to as her highly attuned sense of *kairos* developed in part during her experiences as a traveling minister. Braithwaite writes of Gurney's "solemn interest" as she watched the course of the war, and notes he is unsurprised by her sympathy for and desire to speak with Lincoln, given her experience "pleading the cause of her Divine Master before those in authority in the old world."[113] Braithwaite points, specifically, to the timing of Gurney's visit: "[b]ut she knew that for every right step there is the appointed time; and for that she was willing to wait."[114] If we can trust the reports that the meeting occurred in mid to late October, Gurney would also have known of Lincoln's Emancipation Proclamation, announced on September 22, 1862. A column in the *National Republican* on September 30, 1862, describes the proclamation as evidence of the administration's determination to end the war, praises its timing on the heels of the Confederate army's failed attempt to invade the North, and identifies the need to finally end slavery, "the admitted cause of the war," which "the country and the President feel that it is time to strike a blow" to remove.[115] At the time of the Lincoln-Gurney interview, then, the country and President Lincoln had entered a period of some small hope, even as men continued to die in horrifying numbers.[116] In addition to the weight of responsibilities Lincoln faced as commander-in-chief, he continued to suffer from what some contemporary scholars have identified as a prolonged struggle with clinical depression, due in part to the loss of his eleven-year-old son Willie to typhoid earlier that same year.[117] As Gurney had done when seeking a meeting with the king and queen of Württemberg, she waited for the appropriate *kairotic* moment, listening to her inner leading and refusing to leave Washington, DC, without meeting Lincoln. Braithwaite's only quote from

Gurney about the visit notes the relief she felt when, finally, "the great iron door seemed to open of itself, and a most interesting interview we had."[118]

As she did in her previous encounters with royalty in Europe, Gurney recontextualizes several modes—speech, silence, and speaker-as-body-and-voice—in the opening moments of the meeting to establish her presence, an *ethē* of relation-relating and sympathy, and her right to speak to Lincoln; she also opens by citing the spiritual requirement for her visit. Gurney and the delegation begin with conversation and then, according to the eyewitness accounts, Gurney seeks to further connect with the president by moving physically closer to him and to relate to him intimately on an emotional and spiritual level, communicating what Braithwaite calls a "sympathy not easy to be described" that she felt for the beleaguered president.[119] After some brief conversation, Gurney gets down to business, taking off her bonnet, and moving her chair closer to Lincoln.[120]

Once she had the attention of the room, Gurney established the exigence for her visit, reassuring Lincoln that she came not out of self-interest, but as a messenger of sympathy and consolation. Throughout her life, Gurney served as a "messenger of consolation," a required form of social testimony in the Society of Friends that was both difficult and potentially burdensome, but could lead to social and political reform and, consequently, the relief of spiritual distress.[121] Gurney's obituary singles out her ministry of consolation to those who had suffered and lost loved ones, suggesting that her abundant experience with suffering and loss (including the deaths of her fiancé, her husband, and other close family members and friends) allowed Gurney to sympathize with others who were suffering and mourning (and to develop an *ethē* of relation-relating). Framing consolation as a duty provided yet another avenue for Gurney and other nineteenth-century Quaker women to address the double burden they faced as women ministers, and so helped them establish their right to speak out in more public spaces and to cross some of the established boundaries of acceptable roles for women in nineteenth-century domestic ideology (which carried over to the Society of Friends, in spite of protestations to the contrary).[122] In the interview with Lincoln, Gurney stepped into the familiar role of "messenger of consolation," explaining that she had been led to call on him out of a sense of religious duty and obedience to follow God's leading.[123]

> I can truly say it is not from any motive of idle curiosity that I have requested this interview. I come in the love of the gospel of our Lord and Saviour Jesus Christ,—that blessed gospel which breathes glory to God in the highest, peace on earth, and good will to men. In common with the members of my own Society,—may I not say in com-

> mon with every true-hearted citizen of the United States?—my spirit has been introduced into *near sympathy* with our Chief Magistrate in the heavy weight of responsibility that rests upon him; believing, as I do, that in the faithful discharge of his various and important duties he does endeavor to preserve a conscience void of offence toward God and man. And earnestly have I desired that when weighted with cares and anxieties he may commit his way unto the Lord, that he may be careful for nothing, but in everything, by prayer and supplication with thanksgiving, he may let his requests be made known unto God; and then, whatever the trials and perplexities he may have to pass through, the peace of God, which passeth all understanding, will keep his heart and mind, through Jesus Christ our Lord.[124]

Gurney positions herself as a representative of "the members of my own Society" and a messenger for a higher sovereign power. In expressing her sympathy for Lincoln's responsibilities, Gurney (tentatively) claims to speak for a larger, national constituency, "—may I not say in common with every true-hearted citizen of the United States." Establishing one's *ethē* of relation-relating is necessary for the epideictic rhetor to reinforce shared values, and as Gurney does here, epideictic rhetors often speak as an acknowledged member of and spokesperson for community members and supporters.[125]

In her opening, Gurney acknowledges both the difference in their positions and the (im)possibility of their fully understanding one another. And yet, when Gurney speaks of her sympathy with Lincoln, there is a discrepancy between the transcription of her words in her memoir and in the Lincoln Papers, and though the difference is small, I believe it provides some insight into how Gurney may have chosen to approach Lincoln and navigate the asymmetrical power relations in the room that day. According to the Lincoln Papers, Gurney told Lincoln, "[M]y heart is in *full* sympathy," but in her memoir, she is quoted as saying, "[M]y spirit has been introduced into *near* sympathy."[126] The full quotation from the memoir, given just above, can be compared with the same excerpt from the Lincoln Papers, which reads: "In unison with the feeling of the people of my persuasion, my heart is in *full sympathy* with our Chief Magistrate. I believe him weighed down by cares and responsibilities of no ordinary magnitude, and desirous as he is to preserve a conscience void of offence, both before God and his fellow men, I would encourage him not to be careful for things over which he has no control, but to place his trust on Him, who is Mighty, and able to save."[127] The difference between *near* and *full* sympathy speaks volumes about Gurney's motivation. To be in full sympathy would suggest, following the Oxford English Dictionary definition of sympathy, two parties in complete agreement:

sympathy speaks to affinity, similarity, and harmony, "conformity of feelings . . . community of feeling; harmony of disposition."[128] Perhaps the White House stenographer changed Gurney's "near sympathy" to "full sympathy" so as to erase any potential ambivalence or challenge on the part of Gurney about Lincoln's leadership or her ability to align herself with his policies. But I believe the nuance of "near sympathy" better reflects Gurney's difficult position: encouraging the leader in charge of the war she cannot rightly support, even if she agrees with its goals. Religious studies scholar Michael Birkel identifies the concept of "near sympathy" with the teachings of eighteenth-century Quaker abolitionist John Woolman, defining it as "a way to engage in love those whom we would otherwise be tempted to regard as different and threatening."[129] Lincoln held great power over the Quakers, some of whom were suffering persecution for their refusal to join the war. In this sense, Lincoln was both different from and threatening to Gurney and the Quakers, and speaking across the boundaries between them required engaging in near sympathy, a nineteenth-century version of rhetorically listening across cultural, linguistic, and other forms of difference.

Throughout her speech, Gurney works to establish an *ethē* of relation-relating, part of which depends on conveying her near sympathy for Lincoln and developing "the fact or capacity of entering into or sharing the feelings of another or others," or what the *Oxford English Dictionary* identifies as "fellow-feeling."[130] However, Gurney knows that she cannot truly understand or share Lincoln's feelings or experience, because of the difference between their positions (and his immediate power and her relative lack of power to shape the war) and their belief systems (for instance, his record on slavery). Gurney's use of near sympathy suggests an ability to recontextualize more formal, constrained modes of speech so as to transcend the limits and possibilities of the rhetorical occasion. In her interview, she also engages in a strategic use of praise that falls short of blame but highlights subtly and carefully the distinctions between her and Lincoln. To the abolitionists, Lincoln did not do enough, quickly enough, to end slavery, and Lincoln was fairly clear in the early years of his presidency that he was not fighting the war to end slavery.[131] Gurney would have been well aware of Lincoln's sometimes contradictory position on the Union and slavery, both during and after the war. However, on that day, in her words to Lincoln, she chose not to criticize Lincoln or focus on the difference between the Quaker values of justice and equality, and Lincoln's own values; instead, she chose to encourage him toward a continued path of peace and thanksgiving. She praised Lincoln for "he does endeavor to preserve a conscience void of offence toward God and man," and she prayed that he would continue to use "prayer and supplication with thanksgiving, [that] he may let his requests be known unto God" and then experience the peace that God can provide.

In this interview and in her subsequent exchanges with Lincoln, Gurney demonstrates an ability to strategically employ epideictic rhetoric—the genus of rhetoric devoted to ceremonial speeches of praise and blame, including *epitaphios logos* or eulogies/funeral orations for fallen fighters, *panegyric* festival orations, and *encomia* praising the acts of accomplished individuals—recontextualizing prayer and praise to challenge the status quo.[132] The epideictic has long held an ambivalent place in the rhetorical canon, with scholars describing it as a "difficult and puzzling" genre, "the most problematic" of the three species of rhetoric, and "self-indulgent and artificial."[133] However, rhetorical theory has come to recognize the epideictic as a complex, valuable, and potentially disruptive genre, with applications beyond Aristotle's original, more limited classification of it, which focuses on the present; constructs the epideictic audience as mere observers, not judges meant to take action; and outlines the goals of the epideictic orator as relegated to praise or blame of the subject.[134] Rather than an empty affirmation of commonly held beliefs, or a stylistic showcase for the skills of the speaker, epideictic rhetoric has come to be seen as having a key role "in the instilling, preservation, or enhancement of cultural values"—a means by which rhetor and audience reaffirm shared values and also investigate points of conflict and contestation, a way to have a social and political impact.[135] Moreover, as Cynthia Miecznikowski Sheard has argued, the epideictic can be a powerful and disruptive force to "address private and public 'dis-ease,' discomfort with the status quo" and "invoke shared values as a basis for promoting a vision of what could be."[136] Thus, scholars have made a strong case for understanding the epideictic as more complex, fluid, and important than previously acknowledged.[137]

Even before her meeting and correspondence with Lincoln, Gurney employed the epideictic in (un)conventional ways. Two reports from her memoir describe examples of Gurney using epideictic rhetoric in an expected space and place: upon the death of her brother-in-law (husband of Elizabeth Fry), Samuel Gurney, and on the "burial day" of her close friend William Forster (though we know she spoke at other burial days and occasions throughout her life). In both accounts, Gurney engages difference-in-similarity, appropriately praising the dead and calling upon those around her to uphold Quaker values, while also using the epideictic occasion to go one step further and ask her audience to join her to take action and evangelize the values they hold in common, which she claims are at risk of being lost as the current generation dies off, and future generations take over.[138]

In her meeting with Lincoln, Gurney takes the opportunity afforded by the circumstances and context, a more formal though small meeting, to speak words of encouragement to Lincoln in order to achieve a common epideictic objective, establishing a sense of communion with one's audience. However, her reassuring words of prayer and praise also engage in a more radical form of the epideictic by challenging the status quo and visualizing a peaceful, utopian future in line with the Quaker peace testimony, which rejects war "for any end or under any pretense whatsoever."[139] In this way, the epideictic rhetoric that Gurney utilizes throughout their interview recontextualizes what is essentially an activist Quaker call for peace in a non-offensive manner suitable to the ceremony of the occasion.

Much has been written on Lincoln's religious beliefs, and although he never openly attended or aligned himself with a certain denomination, he was known to be an independently religious man who spoke about God in his speeches and claimed to have some Quaker ancestry.[140] The biblical passages Gurney quotes and paraphrases would most likely have been familiar to Lincoln, but they were also fundamental to the Quaker peace testimony and, therefore, the Quakers' refusal to fight in the Civil War or engage in any conflict. In the second section of her speech (as defined by the paragraph breaks provided in her memoir), Gurney references a well-known passage from Isaiah 58, in which the prophet criticizes God's servants who hypocritically engage in the spiritual practice of fasting without attending to the economic and social injustice experienced by those around them, including slavery. As she has done before, Gurney highlights the values shared between her and Lincoln's multitude of supporters. "In common with the thousands and tens of thousands on both sides of the Atlantic, my heart has rejoiced in the noble effort which our honored President has made to keep the true fast,—the fast which the Lord hath chosen,—to loose the bands of wickedness, to undo the heavy burthens, to let the oppressed go free; and I assuredly believe that for this magnanimous deed the children yet unborn will rise up and call him blessed in the name of the Lord."[141] According to Michael Barram's exegesis of the passage from Isaiah that Gurney references, the true fast aims to "foster well-being and justice," and so is not just about helping others, but also helping oneself.[142] Gurney's words suggest Lincoln is acting in accordance with God's will, and that he will no doubt be praised by future generations for keeping the true fast, though she goes on to say that he will endure "trials and persecutions," which are "the lot of all who endeavor to maintain a just weight and a just balance, and who desire to be found walking in the path of uprightness." Gurney continues with a message of the power of faith and belief from Psalm 46, aligning Lincoln and herself with other Christian believers, who are reassured by the idea "that God is [the believer's] refuge and strength, a very present help in trouble. Therefore will not we fear, though the earth be removed, and though the mountains be carried into the midst of the sea, though the waters thereof roar and be troubled, though the mountains shake with the swelling thereof." Interestingly, Gurney does not reference verse 7 in the same Psalm, which would seem to be most pertinent to a time of civil war: "Though nations rage and kingdoms totter, God's voice thunders and the earth trembles." Instead, she chooses to focus on the more peaceful, strengthening, and refreshing image of a "river of God," to which she has "earnestly desired . . . the President might repair day by day . . . that thus his spirit may be strengthened and refreshed, and be fitted for the right performance of his various and arduous duties."

Gurney then shifts from a message of encouragement and consolation to an imaginative reconstruction of a more utopian future in direct contrast with the trials and tribulations the nation and Lincoln currently face. She prays that "by the grace of God [Lincoln] may be made an instrument in hastening" the time when earthly kingdoms become God's kingdoms, and foretells a time "when swords shall be beaten into pruning-hooks, when nation shall no longer lift up sword against nation, nor the people learn war anymore." This last passage comes directly from Micah 4:3, a verse also quoted in the Quaker peace testimony. The peace testimony was a foundational document written by George Fox and others in January 1661, "a declaration . . . against taking up arms, either on behalf of an earthly kingdom or to inaugurate the kingdom of Christ."[143] Gurney continues, "What a glorious transition would be witnessed here, from a scene of desolation and sorrow and suffering to one of peace and joy and love! The wilderness would become as Eden, the desert as the garden of the Lord; joy and gladness would be found therein, thanksgiving and the voice of melody." Gurney's Edenic description of the future Lincoln might bring if he continues in his effort to loosen the bands of wickedness engages in idealization, one of the potentially revolutionary functions of the epideictic identified by Sheard and, I argue, a form of recontextualizing the means available to Gurney in the particular time, place, and space of her meeting. Sheard writes, "By bringing together images of both the real—what is or at least appears to be—and the fictive or imaginary—what might be—epideictic discourse allows speaker and audience to envision possible, new, or at least different worlds."[144] As scholar Peter Brock points out, the early Quakers viewed the state as potentially a force for positive change: "the Godly ruler was no contradiction in terms. Rulers also could be ruled by the Spirit."[145] Gurney's vision for a better future aligns with Lincoln's, but requires constant vigilance to seek the will of God. Brock labels Gurney's approach in her meeting and correspondence with Lincoln as "nonpolitical lobbying in favor of peace"—what I would identify as an attempt to recontextualize the peace testimony in a way that might be more acceptable to her audience, the commander-in-chief of the US armed forces.[146] In quoting the testimony—which adamantly rejects war as an option in any situation, for "[h]e that takes the sword, shall perish with the sword,"—Gurney lobbies both in favor of peace and, very subtly, on behalf of the Quakers who have refused to go to war, though she does not name them explicitly.

Just as the purpose of the Quaker peace testimony was meant to absolve its signers "from that aspersion cast upon us, that we are plotters," so Gurney asks Lincoln to understand the Quakers' position on peace and war: Quakers could be both against war and supportive of Lincoln, but they could not engage in war themselves. To outsiders, this might seem contradictory, but to Gurney and other Quakers, the contradictions made sense, and they could live with the paradox. Gurney concludes the second section by addressing Lincoln as a friend, "if so I may be permitted to call thee," and paraphrasing the priestly blessing from Numbers 6: 24–26, "may the Lord bless thee and keep thee, lift up the light of his glorious countenance upon thee, and give thee peace." She goes on to suggest that God will protect and cover Lincoln and offer him security and refuge (a passage from Psalm 91). Although Gurney's words during their ceremonial encounter appear to participate in more conventional epideictic praise of Lincoln, her strategic recontextualization of scriptural passages aligned with the Quaker peace testimony produces difference-in-similarity, calling on Lincoln to heed the spirit and serve as a human instrument for fulfilling God's utopian promise of peace.

In the third section of her speech, Gurney concludes by praying that God may continue to guide Lincoln and provide him with the "unerring counsel" he needs to survive "the remaining difficulties of thy wilderness journey." She seeks to reassure Lincoln through praise and encouragement by foretelling a time when he will have come through the trials and tribulations he now faces, to victory. She reiterates her faith in his attempts to follow the will of God, while also making the case for persisting in his pursuit to divine the will of God. She also suggests that the Union's victory is foretold, and in her speech she recontextualizes apocalyptic imagery from the Book of Revelation—after "the Beast" had been conquered by God's people—to make a more political argument: "and, finally, when thou shalt have served thy generation according to the will of God, through the fullness of His atoning, pardoning love and mercy in Jesus Christ our Lord, [may our Father] receive thy ransomed spirit into that rest which remaineth for the people of God, unite it to the *glorious company of victors* whom the apostle saw standing on the sea of glass mingled with fire, having the harps of God in their hands! And they sang the song of Moses and the song of the Lamb, saying, 'Great and marvelous are Thy works, Lord God Almighty, just and true are all Thy ways, thou King of saints. Who shall not fear before Thee and glorify Thy name, for Thou only art holy.'" Gurney prophesies a future, after the trials and tribulations of war are complete, when Lincoln will be positioned among the "glorious company of victors" over evil, who sing the praises of the "Lord God Almighty," but are also themselves blessed. Apocalyptic imagery was not without precedent in Quakerism; early Quakers had "an apocalyptic belief in the imminence of a new age of history, which would commence with their own victory in the 'Lamb's War' (a phrase early Quaker writers liked to use to denote the struggle against sin and the 'world'). . . . They believed in the transforming power of the Holy Spirit, a power that would enable them to convert and remold the peoples of the whole earth. Theirs was to be a *total victory*."[147] We see Gurney recontextualizing the prophecy from Revelation 15 to foretell a "total victory" against sin, a future that might have seemed impossible to imagine at that point in the Civil War, but which she believes will be achieved if Lincoln continues to seek a righteous path.

According to her memoir, Gurney then "knelt in fervent prayer for her country and for the President, who appeared bowed under a sense of his deep responsibilities."[148] Here, as she has done so many times before, Gurney recontextualizes the Quaker tradition of silence and prayer to establish an *ethē* of relation-relating with her audience. One of the delegation members remarks on "the deep solemnity, the almost awful silence that reigned within that room," and says the president was moved to tears while Gurney spoke to him.[149] Though the Lincoln Papers transcription does not mention the president's emotional response, it does comment on the prayer Gurney offered as "short but most beautiful, eloquent, and comprehensive."[150] The president responded to Gurney's words with deep gratefulness and humility, as reflected in his remarks to her, which acknowledge the heavy burden of his responsibility and the consolation provided by her words. In the description of the visit included in Gurney's obituary, the speaker-as-body-and-voice is highlighted: the president is reported to have taken Gurney's hand before leaving, "holding it for a few moments in silence," evidence of the intimate connection they had made, even in the rather public space of the White House.[151] Both the Lincoln Papers and Gurney's memoir report Lincoln's response. According to her memoir, he paused and then "very deliberately, nearly in the following words," said, "I am glad of this interview. In the very responsible situation in which I am placed, as a humble instrument in the hands of my Heavenly Father, I have desired that all my words and actions may be in accordance with His will; but if, after endeavoring to do my best with the light which He affords me, I find my efforts fail, then I must believe that, for some purpose unknown to me, He wills it otherwise. If I had my way the war would have ended before this, but nevertheless it still continues. We must conclude that He permits it for some wise purpose though we may not be able to comprehend it; for we cannot believe that He who made the world still governs it. I repeat that I am glad of this interview."[152] Lincoln responds positively to Gurney's earlier plea that Lincoln "be made an instrument" of God's peace, calling himself a "humble instrument in the hands of my Heavenly Father." Though he is a willing instrument, Lincoln suggests that even when he seeks out God's will, he cannot understand it, nor can he comprehend why God would allow war to continue, rather than bringing about the peace both he and Gurney desire. He makes this point by referencing "the light which He affords me," a nod to the Quakers' belief in the inner light, which also puts a human spin on it (there is only so much light given, and only so much Lincoln can see). If Lincoln fails to succeed with that light, he must believe that was also God's will. Lincoln does not purport to know God's will, only to seek it out, even if it does not align with what he thought was best for the country. In the Lincoln Papers, he even more clearly states his desire for peace, using repetition to underline the difference between what he desired and reality: "If I had had my way, this war would never have been; but nevertheless it came. If I had had my way, the war would have ended before this; but, nevertheless, it still continues." God is in control, even if we cannot understand why he would permit such an awful war to continue.

Gurney could not have known it at the time, but her discussion of the will of God fell on particularly fertile ground, as it was a topic heavy on the heart of Lincoln, who in September 1862 (the month before Gurney's visit) wrote the "Meditation on the Divine Will," a personal memo later found by Lincoln's secretary John Hay.[153] In it, Lincoln tries to reconcile the concept of God's will for the divided North and South: "The will of God prevails. In great contests each party claims to act in accordance with the will of God. Both *may* be, and one *must* be, wrong. God cannot be *for* and *against* the same thing at the same time. In the present civil war it is quite possible that God's purpose is something different from the purpose of either party—and yet the human instrumentalities, working just as they do, are of the best adaptation to effect his purpose. I am almost ready to say that this is probably true—that God wills this contest, and wills that it shall not end yet . . . Yet the contest proceeds." Lincoln rationalizes his responsibility to both God and the American people, and struggles over how both sides can claim to be following God's purpose, a purpose unknown to him and others, but which includes the continuation of a horrible war.

Lincoln's "Meditation on the Divine Will" suggests that Gurney's words came at the perfect *kairotic* moment to assuage Lincoln's deep sadness over his inability to control, or even make sense of, the Civil War. Gurney appeals to Lincoln's values, reinforcing his desire to act in God's will, even if they as humans are imperfect instruments of that will.[154] Gurney approached Lincoln as a sympathetic Christian open to and in need of hearing words of Christian encouragement and fellowship, and unlike some other Christian ministers Lincoln received, she did not try to impose upon Lincoln her own beliefs or her own interpretation of God's will. Lincoln must have appreciated this, as he expressed frustration with another Christian delegation who approached him during the same fall of 1862 on the issue of national emancipation: "I am approached with the most opposite opinions and advice, and that by religious men, who are equally certain that they represent the Divine Will. I am sure that either the one or the other is mistaken in that belief, and perhaps in some respects both . . . I hope it will not be irreverent for me to say that if it is probable that God would reveal his will to others, on a point so connected with my duty, it might be supposed he would reveal it directly to me; for, unless I am more deceived in myself than I often am, it is my earnest desire to know the will of Providence in this matter. And if I can learn what it is I will do it! And I can assure that the subject is on my mind, by day and night, more than any other. Whatever shall appear to be God's will I will do."[155] The frustration that Lincoln voices about that encounter has been avoided in his meeting with Gurney, in part because she was led to echo Lincoln's own sentiments on God's will, and also because she expressed an earnest desire for Lincoln to be led by God down the right path. Part of the power of Gurney's rhetoric, then, was that she asked nothing of Lincoln and offered him the opportunity to be the observer, to simply take in her words of epideictic encouragement, ostensibly asking nothing in return, though in reality pushing for nothing less than peace.[156]

"My ~~Dear~~ Esteemed Friend": Gurney and Lincoln's Written Correspondence

Gurney's visit touched the president deeply enough to lead him to ask, almost a year later, for her to write to him (the request was relayed through an intermediary, US agriculture secretary and Quaker Isaac Newton, who "offers to be the bearer of a paper messenger").[157] Her letter of August 1863 prompted a written response from Lincoln in 1864, during one of the darkest periods of his presidency as he faced almost certain defeat in the presidential election. Throughout this exchange, Gurney demonstrates remarkable patience and an ability to wait for the *kairotic* moment to make her case to Lincoln, which she does by continuing to recontextualize a rhetoric of consolation, prayer, and praise, and by further developing an *ethē* of relation-relating. I examine each letter in turn and point out how Gurney employs these strategies to move from more subtle appeals for peace to a more apparent discussion of the cause of Quaker conscientious objectors in her final letter to Lincoln.

In Gurney's letter dated August 18, 1863, she reconstructs the rhetoric of consolation and encouragement of their meeting, and also praises Lincoln specifically for proclaiming a day of thanksgiving, which she commends as an act inspired by the Holy Spirit.[158] Here, Gurney appears more comfortable in the role of spiritual advisor to Lincoln. She recognizes Lincoln's request to write to him as a request for continued encouragement, and in this letter, she offers up even more specific praise and gratitude. However, she also continues to respect the fine line between praise and flattery that is so important for the epideictic rhetor, who must never appear insincere or trite.[159] Gurney encourages Lincoln by envisioning a different reality and providing figurative evidence for the realization of that ideal. Gurney's choices, then, align with Sheard's view of the power of epideictic rhetoric to engage in and challenge the status quo through civic discourse. Sheard writes that "epideictic discourse alters the reality in which it participates by making its vision a reality for its audience and instilling a belief that the power for realizing the vision lies with them."[160] Throughout the letter, Gurney recontextualizes the same vision of a peaceful world she conveyed to Lincoln during their interview (albeit in a different mode, writing) and attempts to convince him, using the figurative language of the Bible, that he has the power to enact God's vision by serving as His instrument.

In the first paragraph of the letter, Gurney tells Lincoln that she has thought of him often since their meeting—"my mind has turned towards thee with feelings of sincere and christian interest"—and reassures him of her "continued hearty sympathy in all thy heavy burthens and responsibilities." The "near" sympathy of their meeting becomes "hearty sympathy" in her letter, perhaps a recognition by Gurney that Lincoln's request that she write him represents a personal appeal for the praise and comfort she provided in their meeting a year earlier. Gurney recognized this appeal for what it was, and refrained from taking the opportunity either to criticize Lincoln's policies on conscientious objectors or to explicitly call for peace, which she saves for her next letter. In the opening paragraph she does not identify herself as a spokesperson for the Quakers, but speaks more generally of her belief in "the prayer of many thousands whose hearts thou hast gladdened by thy praiseworthy and successful effort 'to burst the bands of wickedness, and let the oppressed go free.'" Gurney repeats many of the

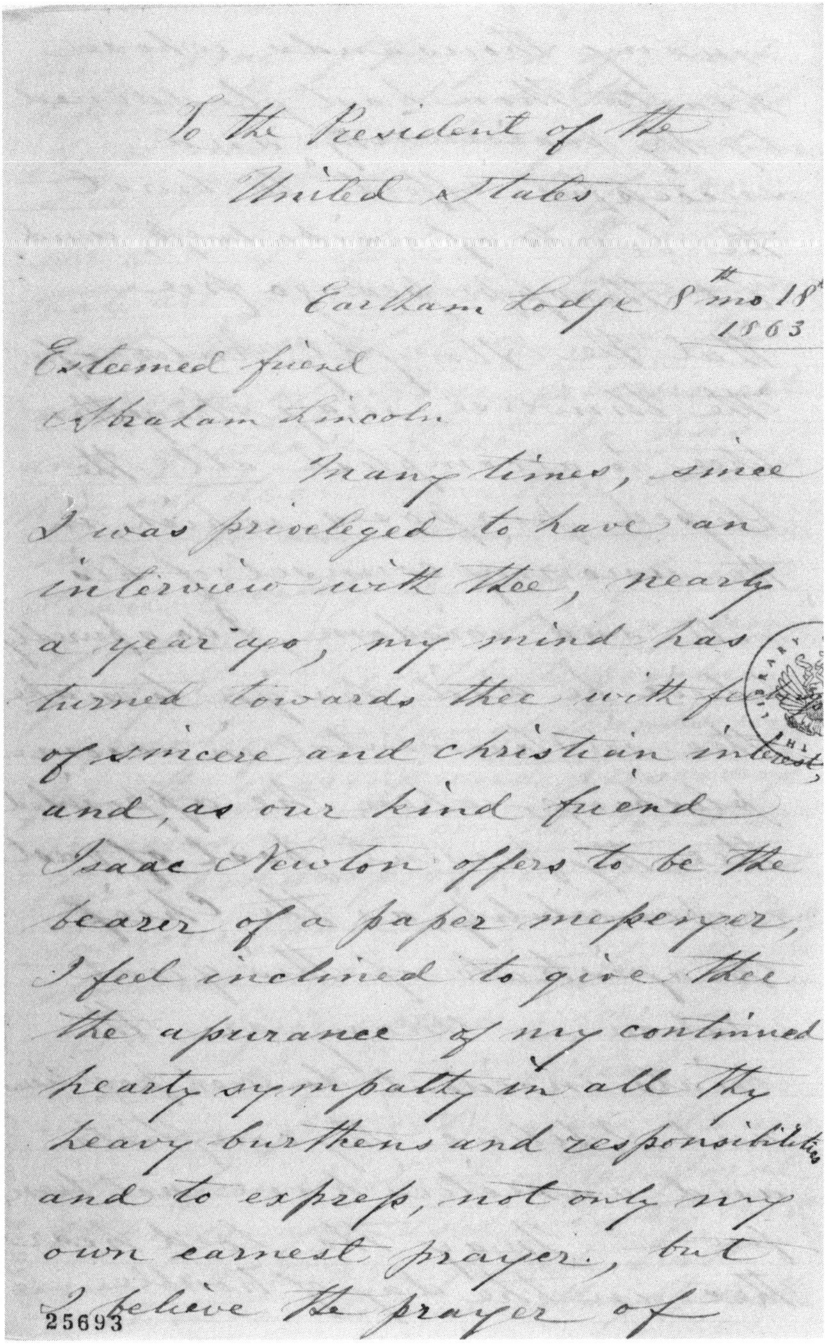

To the President of the
United States

Earlham Lodge 8th mo 18th
1863

Esteemed friend
Abraham Lincoln

Many times, since I was privileged to have an interview with thee, nearly a year ago, my mind has turned towards thee with feelings of sincere and christian interest, and, as our kind friend Isaac Newton offers to be the bearer of a paper messenger, I feel inclined to give thee the assurance of my continued hearty sympathy in all thy heavy burthens and responsibilities and to express, not only my own earnest prayer, but I believe the prayer of

Figure 2.1. The first page of a letter from E. P. Gurney to President Abraham Lincoln, August 18, 1863. Abraham Lincoln Papers, Series 1, General Correspondence, 1833–1916, Library of Congress, Manuscript Division, http://hdl.loc.gov/loc.mss/ms000001.mss30189a.2569300.

affirmations and scriptural references she made in their meeting a year earlier, suggesting that by keeping the true fast Lincoln serves as a liberator, someone whom God has placed in power as "Chief Magistrate" (the same identifier she used in their meeting) and as an instrument of His will: "—that the Almighty Ruler of the Universe may strengthen thee to accomplish *all* the blessed purposes, which, in the unerring counsel of his will and wisdom, I do assuredly believe he did design to make thee *instrumental* in accomplishing when he appointed thee thy present post of vast responsibility, as the Chief Magistrate of this great Nation." Gurney recognizes the difficulties of Lincoln's position: "Many are the trials incident to such positions and I believe thy conflicts and anxieties have not been few." She prays that the Lord may hear, defend, and strengthen Lincoln, as well as answer his prayers. As in their meeting, Gurney finds herself in the awkward position of reassuring and encouraging the Chief Magistrate responsible for the current war—a war the Quakers stand against though they are on the side of the Union—and she navigates this tricky position by using the modal form "may," a form the Cambridge dictionary notes that speakers use "to ask for, give and refuse permission" in a formal situation.[161] Here, she calls on and asks for God's permission on behalf of Lincoln, recontextualizing a blessing from the Psalms with an exhortation from Isaiah: "'May the Lord hear thee, in the day of trouble—the name of the God of Jacob defend thee—send thee help from his sanctuary, and strengthen thee out of Zion.—The Lord fulfil all thy petitions that are put up in the name of the Prince of Peace, of the increase of whose Government and of whose Peace, he has himself declared there shall *never* be an end." In this same passage, she enacts a vision of a peaceful future by referring to the Old Testament prophecy of the "Prince of Peace," a prophecy Christians believe was fulfilled with the coming of Christ, and which reminds Christians of God's power as the chief arbiter of peace over all governments and people: "For unto us a child is born, unto us a son is given: and the government shall be upon his shoulder: and his name shall be called Wonderful, Counsellor, The mighty God, The everlasting Father, The Prince of Peace."[162] Gurney's reference to the prophecy from Isaiah enables her to recontextualize the language of scripture and prayer in her writing so as to provide support for Lincoln in the difficult position in which he finds himself as commander-in-chief, while also continuing to forward a more radical message aligned with Quaker peace testimony. All she asks is that he pray to the Prince of Peace for guidance, and in this she can give him her full support.

Gurney goes on to commend Lincoln for his proclamation of a day of thanksgiving, which he had called for in July and which was observed in August following the Union victories at Gettysburg and Vicksburg: "I can hardly refrain from expressing my cordial approval of thy late excellent proclamation appointing a day of thanksgiving for the sparing and preserving mercies, which in the tender loving kindness of our God and Saviour, have been so bountifully showered upon us."[163] In addition to the rhetoric of consolation and sympathy Gurney had expressed in her previous encounter with Lincoln, here Gurney describes her gratitude that Lincoln is so obviously continuing to act under "the immediate influence and guidance of the Holy Spirit." Cleverly, she praises the proclamation itself rather than the impetus for the proclamation, the victories in the war—after all, she cannot explicitly offer thanks to Lincoln (or to God) for the death of soldiers in war. Gurney also clarifies that she will not observe the day of thanksgiving herself, since the Quakers do not celebrate in that way. However, she is thankful for the document's "recognition of an all-wise and superintending Providence . . . as well as the immediate influence and guidance of the Holy Spirit, which perhaps never, in any previous State-paper, has been so fully recognized before."[164] In particular, Gurney praises the proclamation's message of care and consolation for the American people, a way to encourage Lincoln's own role as a messenger of consolation, even as she consoles him. She ends with a final sentence pronouncing a blessing upon Lincoln and his family, "in a feeling of true Christian sympathy and gospel love," that God may take care of them, invoking the metaphor of God as the shepherd willing to give his life for his sheep, for whom he has secured "an everlasting inheritance." Gurney signs the letter as she opened it, with friendship, "thy assured friend, Gurney."

Although he took almost a year to respond, Lincoln eventually sent a personal reply to Gurney on September 4, 1864. Lincoln's letter has been the most cited aspect of their correspondence among scholars today and in the newspapers of the nineteenth century, when Lincoln's response was published under headlines such as "Interesting Letter from President Lincoln" and "Remarkable Letter from Abraham Lincoln." Lincoln opens by acknowledging their memorable encounter and explaining to Gurney (and to more contemporary readers) why her rhetoric has been so powerful to him. The Library of Congress archives include the original draft with Lincoln's edits. He chooses to address her in the same way she addressed him, with esteem:

> My ~~dear~~ esteemed friend.
>
> I have not forgotten—probably never shall forget—the very impressive occasion ~~of the visit of~~ when yourself and friends ~~to~~ visited me on a Sabbath forenoon two years ago. Nor has your kind letter, written nearly a year later, ever been forgotten. In all, it has been your purpose

> to strengthen my reliance on God. I am much indebted to the good Christian people of the country for their constant prayers and consolations; and to no one of them more than to yourself—The purposes of ~~God~~ the Almighty are perfect, and must prevail, though we erring mortals may fail to acutely perceive them in advance. We hoped for a happy termination of this terrible war ~~ere~~ long before this; but God knows best, and has ruled otherwise. We shall yet ~~perceive his~~ acknowledge His wisdom, and our own error therein—Meanwhile we must work earnestly ~~by~~ in the best light He gives, us, trusting that so working still conduces to the great ends He ordains—Surely He intends some great good to follow this mighty convulsion, which no mortal could make, and no mortal could ~~hinder~~—stay.

Lincoln's opening paragraph points to the power and effectiveness of Gurney's rhetoric, which he says has stuck with him since their meeting two years before. He notes that her purpose has been both to strengthen his reliance on God and to pray for him, and writes of how indebted he is to his supporters across the nation, who also pray for him and offer consolation; however, he does not lump her in with his many supporters (the thousands she named in her own letter), instead saying she stands out among these supporters and so he is *most* indebted to her. He repeats his message of two years earlier: God has a perfect plan, though we may not be able to perceive it, and the terrible war continues. We may understand God's plan in the future, and understand where we went wrong, but right now we must work with the light He gives us, a kind of blind trust that we are moving in the right direction. God must have a greater good in mind, beyond what we can control or even imagine.

Modern scholars cite the letter as a window into Lincoln's religious beliefs as later expressed in the second inaugural address, and they argue over the extent to which the letter portrays Lincoln's belief or skepticism in a greater power.[165] Unsurprisingly, most contemporary scholars fail to acknowledge Gurney's agency or power as a rhetor in the exchange, instead simply noting briefly the context of Lincoln's words as addressed to a Quaker woman minister. However, one scholar, John Burt, praises Gurney's ability to avoid some of the pitfalls of prior delegations (as referenced earlier). Burt describes Lincoln's response to Gurney as, at once, grateful for and skeptical of her message of God's will to end the war.[166] Burt posits that Gurney's lack of "self-righteousness" may have contributed to Lincoln's response.[167]

I expand on Burt's claim by arguing that Gurney's lack of "self-righteousness" or her humility can be better described as a powerful ability to recontextualize the language, media, and modes available to seize the *kairotic* moment and engage in epideictic rhetoric appropriate to the occasion, while also cleverly managing to avoid the pitfalls of appearing overly "preachy" about how the will of God should be carried out by Lincoln. Gurney recontextualizes her Quaker message of peace across speech and writing; as she did in her interview, in her letters Gurney demonstrates a facility for persuasively employing the Quaker practice of consolation to shape Lincoln's thinking on the issue of the war, God's will, and the possibility of a peaceful future envisioned by figurative scriptural references to God's promise for peace, both in the past (the Old Testament book of Isaiah) and in the future (the New Testament book of Revelation).

In the second paragraph of his letter, Lincoln acknowledges the difficulties the Quakers have faced during the Civil War. He repeats rhetoric similar to that which Gurney employed in her earlier correspondence to him, also adopting an epideictic approach by highlighting their common beliefs and shared values, and pointing to the action he has taken and hopes to take in response to the "great trial" faced by war-resisters:

> Your people—the Friends—have had, and are having a great trial. On principle and faith, opposed to both war *and* oppression, they can only practically oppose oppression by war. In this hard dilemma some have chosen one horn and some the other. For those appealing to me on conscientious grounds, I have done, and shall do, the best I could and can, in my own conscience, under my oath to the law. That you believe this I doubt not; and believing it, I shall still receive, for our country and myself, your earnest prayers to our Father in heaven,
>
> Your sincere friend,
> A. Lincoln.[168]

Lincoln identifies his and Gurney's belief in God as the common thread by which they can both continue to deal with this "hard dilemma." He pushes back subtly, however. He has done "the best I could and can, in my own conscience, under my oath to the law" for the conscientious objectors. As with the conscientious objectors themselves, his conscience directs his decisions, and is qualified by his "oath to the law."

Notably, in their meeting and in her letter of a year earlier, Gurney never actually referenced the difficult position of the Quakers in the Civil War. She stayed silent on the issue, but her silence was rhetorical. As Lincoln's letter demonstrates, he heard her messages of encouragement, prayer, and consolation, but he also recognizes that though she stayed silent on the issue of conscientious objectors during their initial meeting, it was part of what motivated her to visit him. Gurney chose to wait for the appropriate time to seek a meeting and speak with the president, and she also chose to recontextualize the Quaker tradition of silence, waiting patiently for the president to bring up the issue she had been seeking to address all along; in this case, her silence paid off, eventually.

Just four days after Lincoln's letter was written, Gurney responds to Lincoln, which suggests that as soon as she received Lincoln's letter opening the door to a discussion of the "Friends" question, she immediately took the opportunity to address it with him.[169] She opens by addressing him, once again, as an esteemed friend, and notes that "I like to address thee in thy own familiar way." Both Lincoln and Gurney use this form of address within the bounds of the Quaker convention of addressing one another as friend; however, by recontextualizing his form of address in her own letter, Gurney takes a greater risk, establishing that she wants them to speak to each other as equals. However, she also notes the imbalance of power at work by thanking Lincoln for "thy valued and valuable letter, which I shall keep among my treasured things, and *for* which, allow me to return thee my sincere and grateful thanks." In her first paragraph, she thanks him again for taking the time to write, given the "close and absorbing occupation of thy daily life," and writes that she could not have anticipated his response to her letter, which came out of "a motive of sincere and Christian interest" to communicate her "unfeigned regard" for him. She repeats that her meeting with him was initiated out of "a true concern," and she views herself as God's instrument in their exchange. In this letter, she recounts their meeting and earlier written exchanges with greater confidence, a result of her knowledge that their first encounter was described by Lincoln as an unforgettable, "impressive occasion." She also may have heard the echoes of her own words in Lincoln's letter, and so have gained the confidence to go on to address the question at hand.

Gurney then unleashes her most passionate plea for peace and for Lincoln's sympathy with and understanding of the position in which the Quakers find themselves. "'Friends' *have* been placed as thou has justly said, in a peculiar, and somewhat *anomalous* position—Decidedly opposed to all oppression, and believing as they do, that the holding of our fellow men, in cruel bondage, is a sin of the deepest dye, in the sight of a just and holy Judge, and earnestly desiring their enfranchisement from the galling chains imposed upon them by their hard taskmasters, nevertheless they cannot conscientiously resort to arms, even to effect this blessed, and 'devoutly to be wished for' end.—The weapons of their warfare, are *not* carnal—The Saviour has commanded them to *love* their enemies, therefore they dare not *fight* them." Gurney opens this paragraph by identifying the Quakers as Lincoln did, as "Friends," a way to underline and highlight—as she has done throughout their correspondence—the Quakers' belief in equality even with people such as Lincoln who occupy the most powerful positions. Gurney calls theirs "a peculiar, and somewhat anomalous position," suggesting that the Quakers' experience in and approach to the war deviates from the standard, normal, or expected. They, like the other rhetors in this book, are situated outside the mainstream by virtue of their position and beliefs. The "Friends" believe "the holding of our fellow men, in cruel bondage is a sin of the deepest dye," and yet "they cannot conscientiously resort to arms, even to effect this blessed, and 'devoutly to be wished for' end." She underlines that their weapons are "*not* carnal," and that they must "love their enemies," not fight them.

As she did in her interview, she recontextualizes several key biblical passages for political ends. The passage from the New Testament book of John proclaims the power of living faith to bring victory: "The only victory, which they, as followers of the Prince of Peace, can, with consistency, rejoice in, is *that* which is alone obtained, through the transforming power of the Grace of God—over the world, the flesh and the Evil one. 'This is the Victory that overcometh the world,' saith the Apostle—'even our Faith.'—and again, 'Who is he, that overcometh the world but he that believeth that Jesus is the Son of God.'" Gurney's reference to the "Prince of Peace" within a call for a peaceful resolution to conflict suggests that she may have been holding back from fully addressing the Friends' position in her earlier discussions. Here, she clearly states that the "only victory" comes through "the Grace of God." She quotes directly from 1 John 5:4, "[For whatsoever is born of God overcometh the world:] *and this is the victory that overcometh the world, even our faith*," a message echoed in verse 5, which qualifies the only possible victory as coming through the Prince of Peace.[170] Gurney once again recontextualizes conventions of language by using the modal form "may" to communicate her yearning that Lincoln might be blessed by, but also listen to and act on, her words, and she combines her plea with a verse from Hebrews 11:1, for Lincoln to believe in the power of faith.[171]

> May this vital, operative Faith, which is the substance of things hoped for the evidence of things not seen, be more abundantly bestowed upon us—then, though the surface may be tempest tossed, (being justified by Faith,) the Believer in Jesus, will have "*peace with God*"—a holy calm, a *deep* still undercurrent of soul-satisfying happiness which even the rudest storms of Time fail to disturb, and none of the vicissitudes of Life have any power over.—an heir of Heaven, with child-like confidence, he can adopt the language, "The Lord is my **light** and

> my salvation, whom shall I fear?"—"The Lord is the strength of my life, of whom shall I be afraid"?—"For in the time of trouble he shall hide me in his Pavilion—in the secret of his Tabernacle shall he hide me—He shall set me up, upon a Rock—And now shall my head be lifted up above mine enemies—*therefore* will I offer in his *Tabernacle sacrifices of Joy*."—That this may be thy blessed experience is the fervent desire of my heart.

Gurney qualifies the faith referenced in Hebrews, describing it as not just "faith," but a "vital, operative faith," a powerful faith, one that justifies those who believe and provides "*peace with God*." In describing this peace, she adopts the language of Isaiah 54:11 to describe the conflict in which Lincoln, the Quakers, and the country find themselves: "O thou afflicted, tossed with tempest, and not comforted." She uses the metaphor of the storm to describe the peace provided by God, who gives "a holy calm, a *deep* still undercurrent of soul-satisfying happiness which even the rudest storms of Time fail to disturb, and none of the vicissitudes of Life have any power over." She reiterates the victory provided to those who believe over their enemies, quoting Psalm 27:1, 5: "The Lord is my light and my salvation, whom shall I fear? The Lord is the strength of my life, of whom shall I be afraid?" She then references verses 5–6, wherein the Lord offers shelter and victory over enemies. She ends with a blessing for Lincoln: "That this may be thy blessed experience is the fervent desire of my heart." Interestingly, the passage from the Psalm ends with a call for the faithful to wait on the Lord, a quality of Quaker practice that Gurney exhibits throughout her correspondence with Lincoln.

In this letter, Gurney demonstrates an ability to develop an *ethē* of relation-relating that speaks "directly to the states of her hearers," as noted by those close to her in her memoir.[172] In Daniel Bassuk's *Abraham Lincoln and the Quakers*, he lists all the known meetings between Lincoln and the Quakers, and while Lincoln was mostly cordial and sometimes open to their encouragement, there were times when he chose to respectfully disagree, as in the case of one meeting with Progressive Friends, or in another case, when Lincoln reacted much more negatively to a Quaker woman who attempted to prophesy "like the prophetess Deborah."[173] However, because of her rhetorical adroitness, Gurney's prophecies did not put off the president, a testament to her attunement and sensitivity to each *kairotic* opportunity.

In her meeting and correspondence with Lincoln, Gurney reinforces and reconstructs the values they have in common—praising his work to let the oppressed go free—and at the same time she redefines victory as born of love and faith rather than carnal warfare or weapons. Gurney acknowledges the tempest experienced by Lincoln and the nation, and at the same time offers up an alternative vision of the means by which Lincoln might obtain victory, faith, light, and salvation through God. She prophesies a utopian vision of peace at odds with Lincoln's values as commander-in-chief, choosing instead to call him the "Chief Magistrate," with the judicial power to make the right choices. She acknowledges Lincoln's suffering but offers him comfort, blessings, and even joy (something far from Lincoln's heart, most likely, at that time). Gurney's message of faith, love, and peace was radical, but she does not hesitate to use the means available to push her agenda when given the opportunity.

Gurney ends the letter with a more practical political message by reassuring Lincoln that, in spite of the differences between the Society of Friends and Lincoln, they support his election:

> In conclusion, I would just remark, that the very kind consideration for the religious scruples of the society of Friends, which has been so invariably and generously manifested by the Government, and especially by our honoured Executive, has been fully and gratefully appreciated—I think I may venture to say, that Friends are not less loyal for the lenity with which their honest convictions have been treated, and I believe there are very few amongst us who would not lament to see any other than "Abraham Lincoln" fill the Presidential chair—at least at the next election—believing as we do, that he is conscientiously endeavouring, according to his own convictions of right, to fulfil the important trust committed to him, and to discharge the solemn duties of his high and responsible office, "not with eye service," as man-pleaser, but "in simpleness of heart, fearing God."—
>
> May our worthy Chief Magistrate yet see the day, when the Prince of Peace, the wonderful counsellor shall rule and reign over this now distracted country—The Union unbroken—the opprest set free—and instead of the sounds of lamentation and woe, which now, so often fill the heart with mourning, "Joy and gladness shall be heard therein, thanksgiving and the voice of melody."
>
> That the Lord in his infinite compassion may hasten the day, is the frequent prayer of thy sincere and
>
> obliged friend E P Gurney

Gurney ventures to speak for the Society of Friends as a whole and describes Lincoln's handling of the Quakers thus far as upstanding and kind; she strongly hints that Quakers will remain loyal to Lincoln in the election. She situates the "honest convictions" of the Society of Friends as different than, but not opposed to, Lincoln's own actions. She acknowledges Lincoln "is conscientiously endeavouring, according to his own convictions of right" and praises him for seeking to please God, not man. Here, Gurney engages in repetition-in-difference, cleverly identifying Lincoln as he identified the Quakers in his own letter, as "conscientious." In equating the "conscious" and "conscientious" approach taken by the two sides (Lincoln and the Quakers), Gurney maintains the role of the epideictic rhetor by acknowledging the points of their agreement rather than their disagreement: both the Quakers and Lincoln conscientiously cite their duty and the law as explanation for their choices, and both feel limited by their duty and the law, and the circumstances of war. They must agree to disagree, even though they have a great deal in common. Gurney closes with her belief that the war will end and joy will come, and she closes her letter by once again highlighting the equality of their position and their friendship, by signing, "obliged friend."

As she did throughout her life as a traveling Quaker minister, in her relationship with Lincoln, Gurney took on the role of speaking for those outside the mainstream who found themselves in a "somewhat anomalous position." Throughout these exchanges, Gurney gained a hearing with the most powerful man in the United States by establishing an *ethē* of relation-relating that enabled her to address him in near sympathy, as a friend and equal. She recontextualized familiar, conventional messages of praise and consolation into more radical messages of hope and peace in both implicit and—as her friendship with Lincoln developed over the years—more explicit ways. Gurney's meeting and exchanges with Lincoln thus stand as worthy of study independent of the context of the second inaugural address, which is often the prism through which Gurney is viewed by contemporary scholars. Her rhetoric represents a form of consolation and a challenge, both to sympathize with the Quakers as a community, and also to collaboratively imagine a peaceful future won through God's grace and love, an ostensibly inconceivable possibility during a time of great bloodshed. The meeting and correspondence between Gurney and Lincoln therefore provides an interesting case study of how, throughout history, women rhetors have adopted typically underappreciated forms of rhetoric, such as a rhetoric of consolation and the epideictic, in transformative new ways for their particular purposes.

CHAPTER THREE

"The Needle as the Pen"

Recontextualizing the Discourses of Quilts and Quiltmaking

We was taught there's so many different ways to build a quilt. It's like building a house. You can start with a bedroom over there, or a den over here, and just add on until you get what you want. Ought not two quilts ever be the same. You might use exactly the same material, but you would do it different. A lot of people make quilts just for your bed for to keep you warm. But a quilt is more. It represents safekeeping, it represents beauty, and you could say it represents family history.
—Quiltmaker Mensie Lee Pettway

I never did like the book patterns some people had. . . . I work it out, study the way to make it, get it to be right, kind of like working a puzzle. You find the colors and the shapes and certain fabrics that work out right. . . . I stayed with what I started with: old clothes that I could tear up. It always come out level.
—Quiltmaker Annie Mae Young

A Nation Is Known By Its Treatment of Youth and of Its Aged.
—Townsend Plan quilt

In their descriptions of the quiltmaking process, as seen in the epigraphs to this chapter, Gee's Bend quiltmakers Mensie Lee Pettway and Annie Mae Young detail a complex set of composing practices: the women recontextualize within and across modes and media, engaging both difference and difference-in-similarity in their compositions, and making decisions about when and where to start, what materials and colors to use, and how to design their quilts so they will "come out level."[1] In the quotation from the Townsend quilt—a signature quilt created by Townsendites in Mitchell, South Dakota—we see the quiltmakers recontextualizing a common refrain of the Townsend Movement (see chapter 1) within and across modes and media to express their support of and to raise funds for pension reform. In this chapter, I move from a consideration of extant examples of the ways women have imaginatively and effectively engaged pen and voice in (un)conventional ways in their letters, meetings, and speeches, to a discussion of how women across history have also engaged the needle as pen, recontextualizing the resources available to craft everyday rhetorics of resistance. This chapter thus responds to the call to explore women's material culture as a discursive practice, and I do so by studying what I identify as the transmodal literacy practices of the Gee's Bend and the Townsend Plan quiltmakers. How do the women write their lives in and through their quilts? What are the implications of considering quilts as a "*form* of discourse"? What can rhetoric and composition scholars learn from studying how women's quiltmaking practices blur the lines between the verbal and the visual?

Previous scholarship has considered quilts and quiltmaking as a form of protest rhetoric, as "a metaphor in literature, politics, and philosophy," as evidence of US commemorative practices, as "a particularly embodied form of material culture," as a nineteenth-century technology to promote memory- and meaning-making, as a form quintessential to a "Native belief system, worldview, or sense of identity," and as a way for women and men to protest US immigration policies.[2] I extend the conversation by applying a translingual and transmodal framework informed by feminist rhetorical practice, quilt studies, art history, and material culture studies to consider quilts as transmodal literacy practices—a move away from the ideology of a single language / modal norm and toward an understanding of the transmodality of all composition practices, even and especially "older" technologies, such as quiltmaking. Applying such a framework to quiltmaking makes sense, given the arguments forwarded by scholars such as Maureen Daly Goggin, who has studied women's needlework as a material rhetorical practice. Goggin's scholarship disrupts narrow understandings of what constitute meaningful semiotic practices, arguing that "the longtime scholarly privileging of the 'word' in limited material terms—primarily scripted, printed and, more recently, digital pages" has left "other kinds of semiotic material practices . . . under, if not un-theorized."[3] Like Goggin, I seek to challenge the field to push the boundaries of "What counts as rhetoric? And who counts in the creation/ transformation and circulation/performance of meaning?"[4] As Heather Pristash, Inez Schaechterle, and Sue Carter Wood have argued, needlework functions as a "vehicle through which women have constructed discourses of their own, ones offering a broader range of positions from which to engage dominant culture."[5] Needlework does not function "as an *alternative to* discourse, but as a *form of* discourse; that is, we think of the needle *as* the pen"; it is "a form of rhetoric with the potential to shape identity, build community, and prompt engagement with social action."[6] In this chapter, I argue that studying quilts as everyday rhetorics of resistance helps to recover the ways women across history have engaged quiltmaking to represent their lives, and to collaboratively imagine a better future for themselves and their communities.

Quilts represent their makers' literacies—their "ways of being in the world, forms of life"—as well as their makers' "histories (multiple, complexly interanimating trajectories and domains of activity)."[7] We can and should consider the material diversity and contexts of quilts as transmodal literate practices. A transmodal approach focuses on process over product and so uncovers the complex recontextualizations at work in quiltmaking practice. As with translingual approaches to language, transmodal approaches to material objects and artifacts consider them within the time, place, and space of their production. Therefore, a temporal, spatial, and material approach considers the discursive nature of quilting as a site for understanding how marginalized groups have employed "alternative semiotic resources and acts of meaning making."[8] In this chapter, I explore how both sets of quiltmakers "select from, (re)structure, fiddle with, and transform the material and social worlds [they] inhabit,"[9] a practice identified by Paul Prior and Jody Shipka that aligns with recontextualization.

Just as there are many ways to build a quilt, so there are many ways to tell the story of the Gee's Bend and Townsend Plan quiltmakers. When treating the quilts as a form of discourse, I heed John Dixon Hunt's argument that object analysis entails a "series of translations" in which speakers "encode their messages, with certain goals, within given linguistic and other cultural contexts, and while attending to traditions or conventions of production and . . . hearers decode . . . within different schemas, in fresh contexts that involve both pragmatic and intellectual control."[10] I also rhetorically listen to Malea Powell's invocation that "ghost stories are *both* the stories of material colonization *and* the webs and wisps of narrative that are woven around, under, beneath, behind, inside, and against the dominant narratives of 'scholarly discourse.'"[11] I cannot tell the whole story of the Gee's Bend and Townsend Plan quiltmakers, but I can critically imagine and strategically contemplate the quilts and their makers, listening respectfully and responsibly to their work and words. Quilts serve as more than a metaphor for the imbrication of subject, object, and text—they also provide insight into their creators' everyday rhetorics of resistance.

In what follows, I begin with a consideration of the Gee's Bend quilts. I look at the complex cultural politics at work in the production, reception, and consumption of the quilts, and how the quiltmakers recontextualize form and meaning in their quilts to engage with quiltmaking as an African

American female literacy practice that disrupts outsiders' categorization of their quilts and the quilts' value. I then turn to the example of the Townsend quilt, which offers a representative example of how movement members recontextualized the movement's message both transmodally and translocally, working across space and place to create a gathering place for Townsendites from across the country to passionately defend the pension plan. Both examples provide further evidence for how women have historically always already reworked and reshaped the languages, modes, and media available to them, working within and across the boundaries of language, mode, media, and culture to reshape and reposition the tools and resources on hand so as to actively seek change.

The Gee's Bend Quilts as Translingual and Transmodal Practice

In designing their quilts, the Gee's Bend quiltmakers do not follow a prescribed pattern (see figure 3.1 for an image of one quiltmaker at work). Instead, as we have seen in the epigraphs to this chapter, the women "puzzle" over how to rework flour and fertilizer sacks, old work-clothes, and factory remnants into quilts that serve the practical purpose of keeping their families warm, and a larger purpose as objects that represent, for Mensie Lee Pettway, "safekeeping," "beauty," and "family history." Gee's Bend, Alabama, has periodically gained and lost the attention of journalists, historians, ethnographers, folklorists, government workers, and art critics, who have created a narrative of the community as a "civilization unto itself" whose "geographic isolation and . . . unusual degree of cultural continuity" have made it an intriguing site to study the experience of African Americans in the rural South during slavery, Reconstruction, WPA programs of the Great Depression, and the civil rights era. Gee's Bend has also been described as a haven of creativity for its inhabitants who create brilliant, abstract work-clothes quilts in conditions of extreme poverty and "isolation."[12] The women's quilts came into and vanished from the national spotlight several times during the twentieth century, but it was not until the twenty-first century that the women and their quilts became an internationally celebrated cultural phenomenon, thanks to controversial collector and promoter of southern African American vernacular art, William Arnett, who brought the quilts to the attention of the "high art" community. The art community heralded the women for their modernist, abstract, painterly use of color and brilliant designing of leftover materials, and the women quickly saw their work move from clotheslines and beds to museum walls.

The Gee's Bend quilts defy traditional definitions of both high art and "traditional" quilting—they include patterns, materials, stitching, and colors

Figure 3.1. An unidentified Gee's Bend quiltmaker at work. Photograph by Carol M. Highsmith. Library of Congress, Prints and Photographs Division, LC-DIG-highsm -07201, http://hdl.loc.gov/loc.pnp/highsm.07201.

that result in combinations that should not work but somehow do. "Discovered" by Arnett and eventually exhibited at the Houston Museum of Fine Arts in 2002, the women's work-clothes quilts initially received a fairly ambivalent response in Houston and then New York. However, this changed when coverage moved from the antiques and style sections of the newspapers into their arts sections.[13] The transition from treating the quilts as "mere" craft to viewing them as serious artistic objects worthy of critical appraisal was cemented with *New York Times* art critic Michael Kimmelman's review of the 2002 Whitney Museum exhibition of the quilts. Kimmelman heralded the quilts as "some of the most miraculous works of modern art America has produced,"[14] and the Whitney exhibition quickly became one of the must-see art shows of the year.[15] The popularity of the Whitney exhibition would lead to a highly successful run in eleven other cities, followed by spinoff exhibitions, including one called "Gee's Bend: The Architecture of the Quilt."[16]

The quilts left art critics like Kimmelman scrambling for ways to place them—often drawing comparisons to well-known Western, modernist artists, such as Paul Klee, Barnett Newman, Mark Rothko, or Frank Stella.[17] At the same time, while some people in the quilting community embraced the abstract, work-clothes aesthetic of the quilts, others took issue with what they perceived to be the quilts' sloppy, haphazard quilting, stitching, and piecing. Critics questioned whether the quilts should be compared to Western art and aesthetics, or whether they should be seen as having antecedents in West African art. I argue that it is important to acknowledge that the quilts have been produced both outside of and within the boundaries of tradition—a consideration that challenges where, how, and in what modes creativity, meaning-making, and resistance can occur. If we hear the dissonances in critics' efforts to situate and describe the Gee's Bend quiltmaking tradition, we can see how the idea of tradition itself should be thought of "not as a fixed body of knowledge but an action."[18]

As translingual and transmodal composers, the quiltmakers tackle the dilemma that Lu and Horner argue all composers face: what kinds of difference to make, how to make that difference, and why.[19] How we read and respond to the similarity and difference represented in the quilts relates to how we read and respond to similarity and difference in writing. In looking to the processes and practices at work in the quiltmakers' compositions, we are reminded to think carefully about how we categorize and classify so-called difference, no matter what the medium or mode. A translingual and transmodal framework considers how all composers constantly translate and renegotiate meaning and so contribute to the ongoing evolution of conventions and traditions in both expected and unexpected ways.[20] Although we might see the Gee's Bend quiltmakers' recontextualizations as deviation or error—breaking the rules of quiltmaking, as it were—I argue that we should understand their choices as evidence of the fluidity of quiltmaking conventions and standards, which are a function of sedimentation and not inherent to the medium itself.[21] Standards and conventions are constantly being recontextualized as users engage in everyday rhetorics of resistance, as we see in the case of both the Gee's Bend and Townsend Plan quilts. However, as Keith Gilyard reminds us, translingual and transmodal composers are stigmatized for straying from the standard in different ways. In the critical discussions surrounding the quilts, we can see the need to rhetorically listen to the particular ways the women and their quilts have been (de)valued, by whom, and why. I would argue for the importance of supplementing a translingual and transmodal orientation to the quilts with a consideration of the quilts as what Elaine Richardson has called an *African American female literacy practice,* in order to work against the problematic equalizing (or fetishizing) that could potentially occur when considering the temporal, spatial, and material contexts of the quilts.

As a case study, the Gee's Bend quilts demonstrate the "double burden" placed on "subordinated groups" who deviate from the norm,[22] while also pointing to the importance of considering the material contexts of the production, consumption, and reception of the quilts as communicating African American female literacies, defined by Richardson as "ways of knowing and acting and the development of skills, vernacular expressive arts and crafts that help females to advance and protect themselves and their loved ones in society. African cultural forms that are constantly adapted to meet the needs of navigating life in a racist society influence these practices and ways of knowing and coping."[23] Quilting allows the women to cover, protect, and enrich the lives of their loved ones and themselves. At the same time, the long history of quilting in the Gee's Bend community must be considered within the time, place, and space of the quilts' production, for as Richardson reminds us, African American female language and literacy practices reflect the women's socialization in a racialized, genderized, sexualized, and classed world in which they employ their language and literacy practices to protect and advance themselves. Working from this rhetorical situation, the African American woman develops creative strategies to overcome her situation, to "make a way outa no way."[24] The women's quilts have been shaped by the difficult material contexts in which they lived. The social, economic, racial, and political oppression they experienced as farm laborers, factory workers, mothers, wives, grandmothers, sisters, teachers, healers, and religious and community leaders guided their artistic and design choices, requiring and inspiring them to "make a way outa no way." To this day, the women employ quiltmaking as a vehicle to construct their own discourse(s)—a way to (re)write and resist the material conditions of their lives.

While some audiences (especially critics) celebrate the differences in the quilts, others (including other quiltmakers) perceive the differences in the quilts as "evidence of deviant lack."[25] As a result, many critical reviews focus on attributing intentionality and purpose to the quiltmakers' designs. For example, in the foreword to the first exhibition catalogue, Houston Museum of Fine Arts director Peter Marzio writes: "The quilts pulsate with a disciplined beauty that is rooted in both symmetry and a conscious decision to deviate from that order."[26] To make the case for museum audiences that the quilts deserve to be seen as works of art, Marzio feels he must establish the intentionality of the quiltmakers' decision-making process. I argue, following the translingual and transmodal approach to composing, that instead of viewing the quilts' features as "errors" or attempting to codify or classify the quilts in particular ways, we should listen for the semiodiversity of the quilts as texts full of multiple, perhaps conflicting, meanings that communicate the quiltmakers' particular experience and help them to "advance and protect themselves and their loved ones in society."[27] Rather than attributing intentionality to the quiltmakers' work in order to legitimize them as artists (as Marzio does), we should recognize the possibility that difference and difference-in-similarity in texts represent acts of meaning-making that challenge the idea of a fixed norm or tradition. In the quiltmakers' own responses to whether and how their quilts can be considered "art," they point out how the quilts function as an African American female literacy practice, "created to carve out free spaces in oppressive locations."[28]

When recontextualizing the modes available in the quilt, including layout, piecing, and stitching, many of the quiltmakers choose to spend less time on elements typically foregrounded in quilts. Take, for example, curator Jane Livingston's description of a denim quilt by Lutisha Pettway: "these women subjugate stitching as an element that might define the object to a passive role. Stitching helps to demarcate areas, or to hold things together, or to separate them, in the service of the larger design. . . . Most of these quilts are simply pieced together, but are done so in ways that create groundbreaking works of art."[29] The quiltmakers' recontextualization renders the function of stitching as a means, not an end—subjugating form to meaning. In the worn condition of the materials used in Pettway's quilt—strips of faded, torn jeans whose monochromatic blue color is disrupted by less-faded dark blue pockets—Pettway communicates her material circumstances, including the limited time and means she had to spend on stitching and piecing. Work clothes represent labor not compensated, "the icons of a race-based casted system."[30]

Similarly, China Pettway's quilts use corduroy throwaways from the Freedom Quilting Bee, established in nearby Rehoboth, Alabama, in 1966 to market the women's quilts to a national audience.[31] Livingston cites the intentional variation of China Pettway's techniques: "Such 'inconsequential' techniques . . . while they may seem arbitrary or functional rather than deliberately artful, could not be more consciously deployed. It is in such details as this, as is true in most serious composition, that the difference between craft and art is forged."[32] The variation Livingston points out represents fertile mimesis at work. The seeming simplicity of the quilts' designs, the variation of their piecing, should be seen not as "arbitrary or functional," but instead as recontextualizations that disrupt standard forms of quilting by using stitching and materials that make art out of used objects in order to represent the impoverished social, material, and cultural conditions of the women's lives. The quilts help us to understand how creativity can be forged out of difference, but also out of the "inconsequential" and everyday.

If we listen to the quiltmakers' words, we can hear how they resist codifications (such as art versus craft) imposed upon them by outsiders. The women insist upon considering their form of quiltmaking as the norm, rather than as deviant or alternative to a dominant tradition. In the following quotation, Mary Lee Bendolph (one of the most recognized and celebrated quiltmakers to come out of Gee's Bend), relates how the concepts of "art" and "artistry" fit into her experience:

> I didn't know anything about art. I ain't never heard [my mother] say nothing about art. Never as I know did she ever say anything about art. If she knew anything, she didn't tell me. But she didn't tell me everything she knew. But I doubt she knew anything about art. All they would do was make quilts to keep us warm. I see other people's quilts like when the spring of the year come. The women would hang their quilts out, and we would just go from house to house looking at the people's quilts. And I would take a pattern from looking at their quilt and try to make one like it. But it don't never be just like the quilt I see hanging on the wire. When people go around looking at the quilts, we wanted them to be pretty and make them look better than the next one. We didn't have no museum in Gee's Bend, but we would go from house to house looking at quilts and getting ideas about how I would like to lay mine out. People go from museum to museum checking out other people's work. Sometimes they like it, sometimes they don't. They go home and try to make it, too. I think that was the same thing we was doing back then. They have a name for it—art—and we didn't. And ours was hanging on the outside. When people would go to your house, they want to see your quilts. And they look at the quilts on the bed. They'd tell you if it looked pretty. That would make me feel good about my quilt. I would go and make more by them looking at my quilts and saying they was pretty.[33]

Bendolph intentionally circumvents the distinction between art and craft Livingston and others forward in their arguments over intentionality. Although Bendolph's mother may not have known or taught her about art, the community has long carried out artistic practices—forming a kind of makeshift "museum," but one in which objects that would traditionally be hung on the inside are hung on the outside. The women were inspired by each other, recontextualizing each other's patterns in light of their own particular experiences. The women adopted a "communitarian" approach, "sharing visual strategies."[34] They experimented because it made them "feel good," even if the quilts were everyday objects of necessity. Bendolph resists attempts by outsiders to retroactively apply the label "art" to the community's quilts, but that does not mean what the quiltmakers were doing for all those years was not unique or original or did not share the goals of the critics who now call it art. For Bendolph, intentionality is not a question, but a given; difference is the norm—an act of resistance, in and of itself.

Recently, the circumstances of quilt creation have changed. In 2006, Bendolph participated in a workshop with her daughter-in-law, Louisiana P. Bendolph. In the workshop, the women used technology to create art prints and work with multiple mediums. Both, however, still dedicated themselves to recontextualizing designs such as the housetop pattern "of concentric squares and frames" or what Louisiana Bendolph calls a new generation of "un-housetops."[35] The means may have changed, but the impetus to recontextualize remains. Mary Lee Bendolph, her daughter-in-law, and other Gee's Bend quiltmakers are beginning to recontextualize their own tradition(s) in the context of twenty-first-century technologies.

In the critical discussions forwarded by many of the curators, reviewers, and art critics published in the exhibition catalogues, there is a recognition of the difficulties inherent to placing the quilts (literally and figuratively). Though critics acknowledge the possibility of West African antecedents and the reasoning behind comparisons to Western abstraction, the goal of those most closely associated with the exhibitions, especially William and Paul Arnett, is to forward a uniquely "Gee's Bend" quilting tradition that privileges the improvisational aesthetic so highly valued by today's artistic community. The historical narratives accompanying the exhibitions tend to romanticize the isolated circumstances of the quilts' production; outside influences by governmental, commercial, and charitable interests are most often viewed as sullying the "pure" abstract aesthetic developed by generations of Gee's Bend women. In reviews and exhibition catalogues, the quilts have been compared to the use of striped patterns in the West African aesthetic tradition; the use of improvisation in the jazz music tradition; and the use of asymmetry and abstraction in the Western aesthetic tradition.[36] Attempts to situate and categorize the quilts' artistic heritage inevitably fall short, in part because the quiltmakers' sense of originality cannot be traced to just one tradition or set of material circumstances.

However, I argue that it is also important to consider the difference represented by the Gee's Bend quilts as just one of the forms of quilting literacy employed by African American women, historically. Quilt scholars Cuesta Benberry, Shelly Zegart, and Carolyn Mazloomi emphasize the importance of recognizing *all* African American quiltmaking traditions, including the tradition of making fancy, patterned quilts.[37] In Benberry's 1992 exhibition *Always There: The African-American Presence in American Quilts*, she argues that the rising interest in African American quiltmaking has brought an attendant privileging of visual criteria such as those found in the Gee's Bend quilts over strong evidence that more mainstream quiltmaking traditions also exist among African American quiltmakers, past and present.[38] Benberry asks that we situate African American women's quilts within the lived contexts of their makers, even if those histories counter our understanding of "the" African American quilting tradition.[39] Her approach is in contrast to those who are more interested in privileging the exotic "Africanisms" they read into quilts or creating a history linked to the underground railroad that lacks substantial support or evidence.[40] Recognizing the diversity of African American quilting traditions offers a glimpse into "every facet of African American involvement in America."[41]

Fetishization of difference not only ignores, but also silences, important contributions by minority groups invested in working the familiar in unexpected ways. There is evidence that multiple trajectories existed within the Gee's Bend tradition and that the women incorporated recontextualization of convention in different contexts, for different purposes. Rather than arguing over whether the quilts do or do not fit into a singularly defined, static conception of "the" African American quilting tradition or using the quilts to establish a new tradition altogether, we should consider how the Gee's Bend quiltmakers recontextualize tradition(s)—how they employ semiodiversity within the space of one quilt and disrupt singular definitions of the Gee's Bend tradition. This allows us to see the innovative ways composers outside the mainstream have engaged in everyday rhetorics of resistance—including material means and traditions—to represent and gain agency over their lives.[42] As A. Suresh Canagarajah notes, any effort to forge a new approach to rhetoric must consider not only Jacqueline Jones Royster and Gesa E. Kirsch's "three Rs" (rescue, recovery, and [re]inscription), but also the dangers of romanticization.[43] I suggest that the seemingly mainstream aspects of the quilts are no less generative a site for difference, difference-in-similarity, meaning-making, and resistance for the quiltmakers, whose technique and imagination flourished in unlikely conditions, including poverty and isolation.

Take, for example, the debate over a quilt pictured in Arthur Rothstein's April 1937 WPA photograph (see figure 3.2).[44] In the photo, Lucy Mooney sits at a sewing machine, while her two granddaughters, Lucy P. Pettway and Bertha Pettway, stand beside her. The two girls hold a Dresden Plate–patterned quilt that was popular in the 1920s and 1930s.[45] William Arnett notes that no such traditional quilts of Mooney's survive today and cites interviews with Mooney's granddaughter, who "could not recall Mooney ever making any pattern quilts such as those in the photographs."[46] Arnett argues that the "fancy, patterned" quilt was inserted into the picture, and that Rothstein chose to ignore the women's abstract quilts because "they would not have fit his employer's populist agenda."[47] Although there is evidence that WPA photographers often staged photos of their subjects for maximum effect,[48] the "fancy, patterned" quilt remains in the picture, raising questions

Figure 3.2. Lucy Mooney in her living room with her granddaughters Lucy P. Pettway and Bertha Pettway. Photograph by Arthur Rothstein. Library of Congress, Prints and Photographs Division, FSA/OWI Collection, LC-DIG-fsa-8b35946, http://hdl.loc.gov/loc.pnp/fsa.8b35946.

about how to include more traditional quilts in the abstract artistic tradition of Gee's Bend privileged by the Arnetts and others today. The controversial picture points to the difficulty of identifying particular quilting traditions and practices as African American, because so many of the quilts made by African American women during slavery and reconstruction were created for others, and so were not identified or saved as the work of their African American creators.[49]

If we pair the words and work of the women themselves with the words of quilt scholars who argue for a broader understanding of African American quilting tradition(s), we can see the possibility that two (or more) trajectories in the community's tradition existed simultaneously, which communicated African American female literacy practices in different ways. In Nancy Callahan's research on the Freedom Quilting Bee, she conducted interviews with quiltmakers who pointed to the existence of a fairly strong tradition of elaborate, highly patterned quiltmaking in Gee's Bend, even before the FQB was established.[50] In particular, quiltmaker China Grove Myles was renowned in the Bend for her highly elaborate "Cuckle Burr" or "Pine

Figure 3.3. Quilter China Groves Myles standing next to one of the last Pine Burr quilts she made before her death in 1976. Photograph by Rhodes Johnston Jr. Courtesy of University of Alabama Press.

Burr" quilt, a "pattern involving hundreds of tedious swatches that unfold before the eye in a breathtaking three-dimensional effect" (see figure 3.3).[51]

Myles passed on this and other patterns to the women of Gee's Bend and is said to have taken pride in the small stitches it required.[52] The pattern is both traditional (in the sense that it requires minute attention to details of stitching and patterning) and innovative (her niece Lucy Mingo says Myles first created the pattern for pillows and then made quilts using the pattern at the prompting of FQB sales representative, Stanley Selengut).[53]

In the pattern, Myles recontextualizes the tendency toward specificity in quiltmaking, foregrounding the creative, critical labor required by quiltmaking in a different way than those who "subjugate stitching . . . to a passive role."[54] Loretta P. Bennett and her mother, Qunnie Pettway, later chose to re-create the Pine Burr quilt pattern—in part because it was so challenging—as part of a project funded by the Alabama State Council on the Arts.[55] In their re-creation, Bennett and her mother demonstrate a valuing of all aspects of the Gee's Bend quilting tradition. Together, they recontextualized the pattern of the quilt, in this case for the purposes of creating a living history of their community's quilting artistry. The grant subsidized the labor Bennett and her mother put into teaching and learning the pattern—a process that had not been recognized or subsidized by the government in this way before—while also allowing for the quilt to be displayed to future generations of Alabama quiltmakers. The Pine Burr pattern lies somewhere between the tradition of abstraction, asymmetry, and improvisation privileged by the Arnetts and more mainstream traditions of highly patterned, fancy quiltmaking. It includes some familiar aspects, such as extremely detailed stitching and pattern-making, and makes of them something new—creating semiodiversity via a highly patterned tradition (not uncommon in any form of quiltmaking). Although the Arnetts do not erase evidence of this tradition from their catalogues, they do not foreground it.

Interviews with the quiltmakers by the Arnetts as well as others involved with the recent exhibitions reveal the quiltmakers' own ambivalence toward outside influences, including the FQB, on Gee's Bend quiltmaking traditions.[56] The quiltmakers responded to the "standardization of patterns, materials, sizes, and techniques" with both accommodation and resistance. Nettie Young suggests that the FQB brought economic opportunity while also introducing patterning that "broke the ideas I had in my head. I should have stayed with my own ideas."[57] We see this push-pull between the patterning and standardization introduced by the FQB and the quiltmakers' desire to innovate in curator John Beardsley's description of two quilts made by Nettie Young and Candis Pettway, another quiltmaker who worked for the FQB.[58]

If we look at Beardsley's analysis of the two quilts by Young and Pettway—made for the women's own use during the FQB years—we can see how the quiltmakers recontextualized by sneaking in and combining elements that they valued with the elements of patterning and color introduced in the FQB.[59] Although both women use bee patterns and cloth, their quilts "are chromatically distinct."[60] In Beardsley's description, we can hear how the women recontextualize elements of the patterning required by the FQB with color and design combinations of their own. Young "confound[s]" the standardized bee pattern through her choice of colors, particularly her use of white strips, producing fertile mimesis so as to resist and accommodate the FQB's influence. The women were able to "transform the conditions" of their lives by making use of the economic security their jobs afforded them, while also working against outsiders' proscriptions.[61] The quiltmakers used the FQB to advance themselves economically, sustain their quilting heritage, and negotiate competing interests: public and personal, commercial and artistic.

It is only fitting that, so many years later, the women have achieved even more success than they did during the FQB years by making the quilts "their" way; however, it is important to note, as Beardsley does, that the quilts currently being celebrated came out of the "complex interactions between local tradition and market demand" seen in the FQB quilts.[62] The idea of the Freedom Quilting Bee as a "mixed blessing" speaks to the "mixing" that was necessary for the women—they have had to quilt in relation to the specific conditions of their lives, and the changes represented by the FQB mark another set of changes they dealt with through recontextualization. The "limitations" introduced during the FQB years also introduced a larger variety of quality fabrics that quiltmakers in and out of the FQB were able to put to use artistically for their own purposes.[63] The quiltmakers' recontextualization of fabrics and patterns enabled them to challenge the standard and, ultimately, provided more resources to make quilts their way.

In all the Gee's Bend styles, we see the women working with and against tradition and convention to recontextualize the affordances of the modes available to them and draw attention to the temporal-spatial framework of the quilts' creation, including conditions of poverty, lack of time, and heavy physical work. The women reworked quiltmaking as a form of rhetorical resistance. Outsiders to the community have come to appreciate the quilts by resituating or renaming them in terms of particular artistic or cultural traditions, but the Gee's Bend quiltmakers have always known the practical everyday use of the quilts and their rhetorical and aesthetic power, and do not see the multiple purposes as mutually exclusive.

Art historian Anna C. Chave criticizes the Arnetts' decision to situate the quilts in relation to a modernist, Western aesthetic, which she argues "deracinate[s] these talented women." She argues that the quilts should be categorized not as art, but instead as "something else, just as complex and complexly aesthetic," a "destabilizing" stance that points to how "craft can no longer be presumed to be 'mere,' relative to art."[64] Chave draws on feminist theorist and cultural critic bell hooks to argue that the Gee's Bend quilts should be considered within the larger context of African American aesthetic practices, which historically served a political function.[65] Although Chave problematically cites scholars who define African American quiltmaking largely according to an improvisational aesthetic (such as Eli Leon or Maude Southwell Wahlman) and fails to cite quilt scholars who emphasize the diversity of African American quilting traditions (such as Benberry), Chave's argument provides a useful starting point for thinking through the ways the Gee's Bend women's quilting practices, as a form of discourse, circulate, gain, and communicate particular values and literacies. Chave's work also reminds us of the importance of applying Krista Ratcliffe's concept of *rhetorical listening* to our study of the cross-cultural exchanges that have occurred around the "discovery" of the quilts.[66]

Building on Chave's use of the work of bell hooks to define the aesthetic value of the quilts, I would argue that bell hooks can also help us in our consideration of the quilts as an African American literacy practice. In hooks's discussion of her grandmother's quilting practices, she takes issue with the view of the African American quilter as "exception."[67] And although Chave and others describe African American quiltmakers, such as the Gee's Bend women or hooks's own grandmother, Baba, as "illiterate," we can see in hooks's description a purposeful avoidance of that particular term. Instead, hooks suggests that Baba's handiwork constituted a literacy that communicated her artistic imagination and skill: "Baba did not read or write. She worked with her hands. She never called herself an artist. It was not one of her words. Even if she had known it, there might have been nothing in the sound or meaning to interest, to claim her wild imagination. Instead she would comment, 'I know beauty when I see it.' She was a dedicated quiltmaker—gifted, skillful, playful in her art."[68] hooks goes on to suggest that African American quiltmakers fully appreciated the "aesthetic value" of their practice, citing nineteenth-century quiltmaker Harriet Powers's understanding of the value of her quilts, "not solely as regards skill, time, and labor but as the unique expression of her imaginative vision."[69] However, hooks expands the definition of African American quiltmaking's aesthetic value beyond what Chave notes, pointing out quiltmaking's role as a "meditative practice";[70] hooks also points to how quilts function as "maps charting the course of our lives . . . history as life lived,"[71] and as storytelling vehicles for remembering "the particulars."[72] Notably, hooks's grandmother made improvisational "crazy quilts" as well as more fancy, patterned quilts: while her grandmother preferred the fancy quilts, hooks preferred those made for everyday use. hooks writes, "Working through generations, [Baba's] quiltmaking reflected both changes in the economic circumstances of rural black people and changes in the textile industry."[73] hooks helps make the case that multiple traditions existed for many African American quiltmakers, often in the same house—quilting traditions changed as the material circumstances of quiltmakers changed.

In a sense, quilts have functioned as, and have enabled African American women to create, everyday rhetorics of resistance, what hooks describes as "homeplaces," sites of "resistance and liberation struggle," places "where all black people could strive to be subjects, not objects, where we could be affirmed in our minds and hearts despite poverty, hardship, and deprivation, where we could restore to ourselves the dignity denied us on the outside in the public world."[74] Loretta Pettway, Mary Lee Bendolph, and other quiltmakers describe their struggle to survive and to provide for large households in the most dire of material circumstances, where they suffered physical abuse at the hands of husbands and worked long hours in the fields.[75] In creating quilts to cover their families despite oppressive economic and social circumstances, the women created homeplaces for themselves and their families, while also learning from their mothers and passing down to their children a literacy different from, but no less important than, reading and writing, one that communicates the "particulars" of their experience. Listen, for example, to Mary Lee Bendolph's description of her experience teaching her daughter: "I was teaching her to make quilts to keep warm. Life is like making a quilt. Not just to keep warm, but to help her go through life, to understand life. Quilting ain't easy. It takes work. It takes time. It takes faith. It takes a mind to do it. It takes patience. Sometimes you have to give up pleasures of your life to make a quilt. . . . Sometimes it won't work, but you have to keep on and go on anyhow because you need to do that to help you go through life. . . . I do what I can do, not what other people could do. Sometimes she may want to make a quilt like me, but she have to do what her mind tell her. Quilting teach all of this to her."[76] In this passage, Bendolph lays out the ways quilts and quiltmaking operate as more than a means to keep warm: as a way to understand life, a way to learn about and resist the challenges that the women encounter. For Bendolph, quilting teaches the lesson that life is hard, and that it takes work, time, intelligence, faith, patience, and compromise. The quilter needs to persist in spite of the many challenges she encounters and must believe in the value and originality of her own ideas and approaches. Mihaly Csikszentmihalyi argues that "objects give concrete evidence of one's place in a social network as symbols (literally, the joining together) of valued relationships."[77] Quilts occupy this space as sentimental objects, but also, in the case of the Gee's Bend quiltmakers, as "vehicles of memory," a piecing together of a husband's old clothes done "for love" because, as Mary Lee Bendolph suggests, "old clothes carry something with them."[78]

A notorious encounter between William Arnett and Annie Mae Young points to how the Gee's Bend quiltmakers define and communicate the value of their quilts in ways that might be misunderstood or misinterpreted by outsiders. In the late 1990s, William Arnett saw a picture of a quilt by Annie Mae Young in a book by southern folk life documenter Roland Freeman. Based on the photo, Arnett tracked down Young and her quilt, eventually buying it for what he describes as "a lot of money" in spite of Young's seeming protestations.[79] Chave provides a different interpretation, pointing out some possible linguistic and cultural misunderstandings that may have occurred during the encounter between Young and Arnett that would have led him to view Young as undervaluing her own quilt (because it was kept under a mattress, for example and because she called it "ugly").[80] Citing hooks, Chave suggests that keeping the quilts under the bed could be interpreted as a form of "safeguarding," not a dismissal of the quilts' value; citing South African critic Sarah Nuttal, Chave suggests that calling the quilts "ugly" might be a holdover of "African diaspora aesthetics."[81] Here, Chave adopts "a code of cross-cultural conduct" that allows her to rhetorically listen to the cross-cultural exchange between Arnett and Young—remaining open to alternative interpretations of the values being communicated by Young.[82] In this example, we hear how the quiltmakers draw on and make use of rhetorical strategies that have not always been recognized or valued by the (often white) outsiders who have come to represent them to the larger world.

In the early 1990s and then again in the late 2000s, Tinwood Ventures—the Arnetts' organization to promote, support, and manage the intellectual property of the Gee's Bend Quilting Collective and Foundation—came under fire for its practices in dealing with the artists it represented, including yard artist Thornton Dial and, later, the Gee's Bend quiltmakers.[83] In 2007, quiltmakers Annie Mae Young, Lucinda Pettway Franklin, and Loretta Pettway sued the Arnetts, claiming that the Arnetts and Tinwood Ventures took advantage of the women and cheated them out of their intellectual property and quilt earnings; although eventually dismissed and resolved with an undisclosed agreement in 2008, the lawsuits created a rift between the three quiltmakers, on the one hand, and, on the other, those in the community who support them or who continue to support the Arnetts, including those associated with the Gee's Bend Quiltmakers Collective (including Mary Lee Bendolph).[84] Although many in the art and quilt communities stand by the Arnetts, there is no doubt that the circumstances surrounding the Gee's Bend quilting "phenomenon" reflect a complex set of race, gender, class, and cultural politics. Unfortunately, the lawsuits have led some museums to avoid acquiring the quilts for fear of controversy.[85]

Through the Gee's Bend quiltmakers' recontextualization of "traditional" quilting techniques, the women have forced audiences to see the quilting "norm" differently, shifting audiences' definition of the standard for what makes a "good" quilt. An online discussion on the topic of the Gee's Bend quilts reflects the reactions of quilting community members to the quilts: "It's wonderful to see these sweet, humble women recognized for their creative eyes and enduring spirit." "I had a very mixed reaction to these quilts. Up close, I hated them, but on[c]e I saw them from a distance, I was very struck by their graphic quality and really loved them. . . . I don't think it's completely fair to judge these quilts, as quilts, by today's standards although

I also believe that one's own individual emotional reaction, whatever it is, is completely valid."[86] One commenter even connects to the concept of a language standard: "Mostly what I can see, I can only speak for myself, is courage and a glorious celebration in whatever good came their way. Their language m[a]y be ungrammatical, according to Webster, but their sensibilities are infinitely refined."[87] In another quilting forum, one commenter writes, "Now, these quilts are not straight, or flat or anything. Most of them have big knots all over the top of quilting threads. Several quiltmakers had more 'issues' with their sewing machines than I do. But, man, those quilts are *amazing*!"[88] In these comments, we can see how these online audience members struggle with their inability to place the quilts, at least according to "today's standards" and conventions. However, in describing their own difficulties, the writers point to the ways the women manage to make the "ungrammatical" something more "refined." At the same time, other commenters still have trouble attributing intentionality to what one describes as the quiltmakers' sewing "issues."

In the "shock" that art critics such as Kimmelman have felt at their own extremely positive responses to the quilts (noted by Chave, Sally Anne Duncan, and others),[89] as well as the surprise of quilt forum participants, we hear echoes of Royster's description of the reception her work on nineteenth-century African American women non-fiction prose writers receives from audiences: the "surprise" that "rather 'naturally' emerges in a society that so obviously has the habit of expecting nothing of value, nothing of consequence, nothing of importance, nothing at all positive from its Others, so that anything is a surprise; everything is an exception; and nothing of substance can really be claimed as a result."[90] Rhetoric and composition can add to the critical discussion surrounding African American quilting practices by allowing us to rhetorically listen to the literacies and everyday rhetorics of resistance represented by the quilts—asking how we can respond to the work of "Others," while also working against dominant discourse practices. Rather than responding with shock or seeing the quiltmakers' practices as exceptional, we need to work to create "better practices so that we can exchange perspectives, negotiate meaning, and create understanding with the intent of being in a good position to cooperate, when, like now, cooperation is absolutely necessary."[91]

We can see how the quilts demand that we push against what counts as rhetoric and writing, and who counts in its production. The women not only wield the needle as pen, they create their own discourse(s), responding to the challenges they encounter in their everyday lives and finding creative ways to respond to those challenges by recontextualizing difference and difference-in-similarity in their quilts. The quilts underline the argument that we should listen to the semiodiversity of texts, rather than codifying or judging the formal elements with enumerative categories based on a static understanding of particular traditions or standards. We should look at instances that do not "look right" as challenges for writers and readers to take agency over their work, negotiate meanings, explore the particular contexts that they want to highlight, and understand the multiple options for making it "look right." The Gee's Bend quilts represent just one example of how women have (re)written the particular contexts of their lives through strategic, creative deployment of repetition and difference. The example of the Townsend Plan quilt, to which I now turn, can help us to better understand the everyday rhetorics of resistance employed by the Townsendites.

The Townsend Quilt as Translingual and Transmodal Practice

As discussed in chapter 1, many Townsendites chose to express their support for the movement through writing; however, based on the evidence of club activities presented in the *TNW* and the archives, club members were never engaged in just one form of activism. The Townsend Clubs encouraged members to participate in fundraising; canvassing for new members; getting out the vote and seeking signatures for various petitions; advertising; delivering speeches; and holding and attending rallies, conventions, and parades, among other undertakings. Movement members creatively recontextualized the modes and materials already accessible to them, including the literacies and tacit knowledge that might have less value in other contexts. The women of the clubs were able to monetize the transmodal literacies they brought to the table—such as quiltmaking and other forms of needlework—to generate funds and organize for the movement. The *TNW* and the OHS provide evidence of the many activities of the clubs and their ladies' auxiliaries (often in charge of the clubs' social activities). These included rummage sales and raffles to auction off quilts, pillowcases, tablecloths, and other homemade items; potluck dinners to raise money and also help feed hungry members of their community; Townsend-inspired entertainment, including kitchen bands, and original and official Townsend plays; and the decoration of parade floats, billboards, and other signage to promote the plan in the community. Numerous articles in the *TNW* celebrate the activities undertaken and funds provided by these community efforts, often accompanied by photos of the designers, creators, and affiliated club officers. Throughout its pages, the *TNW* reiterates over and over the importance of communicating the Townsend message anywhere and everywhere. Photos and advertisements in the *TNW* describe the buttons, medallions, calendars, hats and costumes, aprons, banners, penny banks, kitchen band instruments, hymnals, records, and other items that Townsendites bought, circulated, and created to promote the movement. Members also frequently wrote the *TNW* to share with other Townsendites the best practices for organizing social activities and turning them into fundraisers.[92] The Townsend Clubs valued the resources their often impoverished elderly members could provide in spite of their material conditions, and so paved the way for creative recontextualizations within and across a variety of media and modes for the purpose of improving their material conditions.

In my investigation of the transmodal means Townsendites employed to promote the Townsend message, I focus particularly on one of the largest and best preserved objects associated with the movement, the Townsend Plan quilt, created in 1940 in Mitchell, South Dakota.[93] An analysis of the transmodal and translingual literacy practices represented by the quilt helps us to understand the complex ways the quilt's composers recontextualized within and across the affordances of the modes available in the quilt. The layout of the quilt and the content of the signature blocks foreground the Townsend Movement's odd-to-our-eyes mixture of religious and entrepreneurial rhetorics. The blocks themselves represent Townsend Clubs from across the nation and so represent the translocal connections the Townsend Movement enabled, in spite of its supposed failure as a national policy. (The quilt was created well after the movement's heyday.)

Quilting, long associated with church picnics and bazaars, was the perfect kind of social gathering to provide the opportunity for members to heed the Townsend leadership's call to mobilize resources, raise funds, and advertise the movement—a way to pool the resources of multiple clubs and work across state borders. Articles detailing the quilts created by movement members (mostly women) often focused on the amount of money raised by the sale or auction of the quilts, which ranged from less than $20 to more than $100. The money was then used to send local Townsendites to the national Townsend conventions, raise money for club activities and resources, or contribute to Townsend national headquarters—as in the case of the auction of a quilt made by the women of Whitehall Club No. 1, which brought in $20, "[t]he entire proceeds [of which] were sent to Dr. Francis E. Townsend to be used as he sees fit."[94] Issues of the *TNW* include photos of the quilts made by members and usually picture the women quiltmakers holding up the quilt in question. One photo, titled "Quilt Sale Swells Several Funds," describes how members used the sale of a quilt to finance the club's delegate to the national convention: "How to send a delegate to the Third Townsend National Convention was somewhat of a problem until Mrs. J. S. P. Johnson of Berea, Calif., Townsend Club came forward with a beautiful quilt which she had made to donate to the cause. Sale of the quilt not only financed the delegate, but brought enough to top the needed amount by $10, and this was promptly sent as a donation to National Headquarters. Mrs. Johnson appears in the center of the picture, with Mrs. Edwin Thornburg who assisted in making the quilt standing on her right. Mrs. Leslie Thwing, the Club's delegate, appears on her left." In the photo, the three elderly women, all wearing flower-patterned dresses, hold up a beautiful, intricate quilt. Although the article does not state the specific amount earned by the sale of the quilt, the *TNW* frames the donation of the quilt as a practical, homegrown solution to a larger problem (how to finance one delegate's trip to the national Townsend convention), and praises the women's decision to "promptly" send the remaining money to national headquarters. The movement depended on the small donations of movement members like these three women, and the *TNW* wanted to encourage others to follow in their footsteps and find ways to make money from everyday materials and resources (no matter how small the donation might be).

The quilts created and circulated by Townsend Movement members served as fundraising vehicles and as a means for the women to position themselves in relation to other club members at the local, regional, and national levels. The *TNW* represents quiltmaking as a small, but not insignificant node in the larger Townsend network, as seen in an article from October 1938, which summarizes the multiple activities engaged in by Townsend Club No. 1 of Paris, Texas, during the prior year:

> Paris, Texas—Townsend Club No. 1 of this city looks back over its activities in 1938 and finds it has done much to further the Movement. It has grown in numbers and in influence, for other Clubs are appealing to it for guidance and advice. It has held many important meetings at which Dr. Carl E. Lunn, national representative in the Lone Star State; Dr. and Mrs. H. A. Chappell, Miss Roberta Schmale and Tiffin Reed have been speakers. It has won from the newspapers here space for intelligent "letters-to-the-editor" and informative, factual accounts of its meetings. In addition, it has been instrumental in increasing the circulation of the Townsend National Weekly and in getting Townsend adherents in other communities to organize Clubs. Special commendation for devoted service is given by Mrs. Francis H. Reha, secretary to Mrs. M. L. Rogers. Mrs. Rogers made a beautiful velvet crazy quilt which she gave to the Club to sell and, although she is 84, she has spent a great deal of time and energy distributing the National Weekly and other Townsend literature.[95]

The description judges the importance of the club and its activities in terms of the club's relative geographical reach and its impact on other local clubs (for example, citing the club's mentorship of other clubs), the number of meetings the club held, the speakers hosted and cultivated by the club, the national forums engaged in (the *TNW* being the most important), and the funds raised and members brought in. The club celebrates the labor of one member in particular, Mrs. M. L. Rogers, who created and donated a velvet crazy quilt for the club to sell (though we do not know for how much). Notably, other articles meant to spotlight individual club members often note the age of the members as this article does, a way to counter the narrative that the elderly are weak or indigent. The article, "Woman of 75 Finds Way to Help Plan," describes "Mrs. George Harris, 75, [who] is unable to attend club meetings because she lives twelve miles from this city and the nearest club. But Mrs. Harris has done what she could for the movement. She made a quilt and gave it to a club with the request that it be sold and the proceeds sent to the Foundation Fund."[96] Even those like Mrs. Harris, who were unable to attend meetings due to their material circumstances, were able to participate in the movement from afar by contributing material items such as quilts. Such news articles encouraged other Townsendites to dig deep and think creatively about the resources and skills—the transmodal literacy practices—they might contribute. The articles also made the argument for the continued relevance and importance of even the most isolated or forgotten elderly members of society who, the *TNW* suggests, have the potential to donate "a great deal of time and energy" to the Townsend cause. The movement enabled the Townsendites to view themselves for the first time not only as a political constituency, but also as functional members of society, vital to their local communities, who could and should be valued more by American society at large.

Based on the photographic evidence, many of the quilts auctioned off by clubs were conventional quilts meant to appeal to the aesthetic desires of potential buyers (mostly other club members in the local community). However, the Townsendites (or Townsendettes, as Pearl Burkhalter referred to the women of the movement) also designed quilts meant to uniquely represent the Townsend Movement and its message. Quiltmaking thus served a rhetorical purpose, functioning as a transmodal means by which Townsendites could proclaim their right to a pension, and the respect and honor that came with it. As we have already seen with the case of the Gee's Bend quiltmakers, the Townsendite quiltmakers cleverly recontextualized the conventions of quiltmaking so as to make the most of their meager resources, value the labor and skills they brought to the table, and represent their local context to a larger audience.

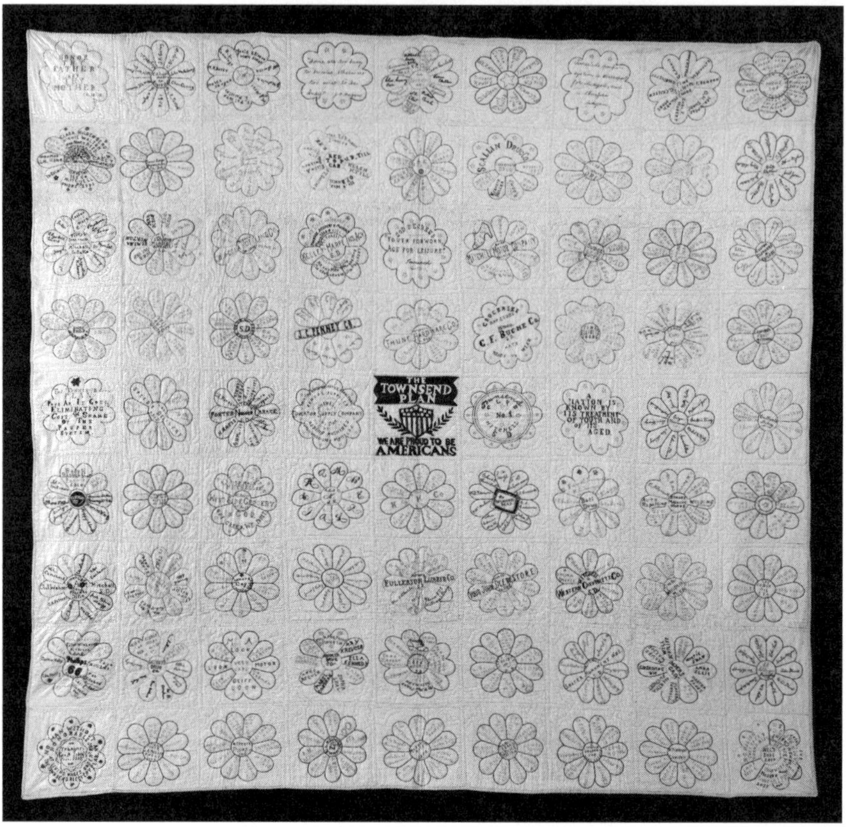

Figure 3.4. Townsend Plan quilt. 92 × 94 in. Courtesy of Wolfsonian–Florida International University Object Collection, accession no. TD1990.122.1, https://digital.wolfsonian.org/WOLF014858/00001.

Stored at the Wolfsonian-Florida International University museum in Miami, the Townsend quilt pictured in figure 4 is an album or signature quilt with eighty-one quilted flowers (nine quilt blocks on each side), surrounding a center panel boldly proclaiming, "The Townsend Plan: We Are Proud To Be Americans." The flowers are stitched in red, yellow, and gold thread, and the overall effect presents a consistently patriotic "red, white, and blue" color scheme to the quilt's viewers. Throughout the quilt, the composers recontextualize the available modes (including writing, images, layout, and color) with the affordances of the media (including choice of fabric, thread, patterning, stitching, and embroidery) to cleverly visualize their support of the Townsend Plan. Each flower includes the names of local people, businesses, and vendors; the space in each block was most likely sold for fundraising purposes, as I discuss further below. The center of each flower includes the names (and sometimes contact information) for local insurance agencies, drugstores, shoe stores, hotels, gas stations, and ice cream parlors, as well as national retailers such as J. C. Penney, and coal companies. The flower petals include the signatures—in script and block print and of varying levels of embroidering ability—of individuals and sponsoring businesses. Townsend Clubs in other cities and states are also represented, including clubs in Colorado, Nebraska, Illinois, and Massachusetts. In addition, there are quotations by the founder of the plan, Francis Everett Townsend, popular messages and maxims circulated by the movement, and Bible verses.

Though we know very little about the creation of this particular quilt, the *TNW* provides evidence for how similar quilts were created and circulated among the Townsendites. An article in the October 10, 1938, issue of *TNW* describes and pictures a similar quilt created by a California woman: "The sale of the autographed counterpane pictured above brought $61.50 into the treasury of Club No. 12, Glendale, Calif. The idea of making it is attributed to Mrs. Julia McKinnan, shown in the picture. At the left is James A. Light, president of the club. Members of the Ladies Auxiliary assisted Mrs. McKinnan in the quilting. Mrs. McKinnan sold space on the quilt at ten cents to each of 98 persons, whose names and addresses were embroidered in. There was no more room for a great many who also wanted to contribute. The balance of the $61.50 was made when the Club sold the counterpane." The article credits the quiltmaker Julia McKinnan with coming up with the idea of selling space on the quilt, and suggests that the demand exceeded the available space. Notably, the picture also includes McKinnan's (male) club president, who must have wanted to share in the glory of the $61.50 raised for the movement, even though one doubts he shared in the labor or innovation involved in the creation of the quilt itself.[97] On June 16, 1939, the *TNW* describes a Townsendite quilt that, like the Fargo quilt, portrays the national reach of the Townsend Plan: "Kelso, Wash.—The Ladies Auxiliary of Kelso Club No. 1 has completed a quilt with blocks representing each state in the United States and Alaska and Hawaii."[98] Perhaps the Mitchell, South Dakota, club members took note of these or other articles in the *TNW* about the fundraising activities of other clubs and designed their own project to gather sponsorships from within and beyond their community to create the quilt and then to auction it off for even more profit.

As an example of transmodal literacy practice, the Wolfsonian-FIU Townsend quilt can tell us something about the members who made it, the sponsors who underwrote it, and how the producers and consumers of the quilt saw themselves in relation to the movement and its politics. When we look at the quilt blocks—at the people, places, and values represented therein—

we see how the quilt might represent what Brea Barthel in her discussion of the AIDS quilt has called "a gathering place."[99] The quilt pieces were most likely created separately by members from across the United States and then stitched together by members of the Mitchell, South Dakota, Townsend Club where it originated. The final product serves as what Barthel calls a "shared 'invisible' community" for its producers.[100] The quiltmakers recontextualize difference and difference-in-similarity in the space of the quilt, framing (literally and figuratively) the continued strength of the movement's support in the local community, while also foregrounding the club members' identity as a political constituency with connections beyond their small town, fundraising power, and a voice in national politics.

Building on Barthel, I add that the community represented in the quilt could be an example of another set of invisible networks—what I call translocal networks, following sociolinguist Jan Blommaert. Blommaert uses the idea of the translocal to recognize the ways that local diasporic communities are connected to larger global communities, either through family networks or through social media. Space, for Blommaert and other translingual theorists, is active, not passive.[101] Blommaert asks us to think of the horizontal space of a neighborhood, community, or street as intersected vertically by the political, cultural, and social.[102] We can see how the space of the quilt is active, connecting disparate communities to larger national, and perhaps even global, networks (see the coal company in one of the blocks, for example). The quiltmakers recontextualize the modes available to foreground the horizontal spaces of the neighborhoods, communities, and streets in and beyond Mitchell, South Dakota. For example, single blocks select and arrange multiple individuals and businesses in the local community, and I imagine the sponsors of the quilt may have had connections both relationally and spatially in and beyond Mitchell. Numerous small businesses are represented, including local drugstores, cleaners and tailors, garages, diners, grocers, delivery services, auto repair shops, and lumber companies. A block at the top right corner of the quilt demonstrates the complex dynamics at work: Yellow Cab is arranged in the center circle of the flower with the message "Phone SOS."[103] As with the rest of the quilt, the lines between the petals represent the connections or divisions between sponsors. In the same quilt block, Milwaukee Rooms and the people who work there take up four undivided petals but are separate from smaller donors "A. J. Stebbins" (one petal), "Cities Service" (one petal), Hamm's standard service (two petals), and Hoon's café (one petal).

Nationally recognized corporate businesses and franchises also sponsored individual quilt blocks, gaining more of the viewer's attention by virtue of (perhaps) donating more to the Townsend cause; these include Coca-Cola

Bottling Co., "Your John Deere Store," a Texaco Service Station, a Phillips 66, and J. C. Penney Co. The advertisement for Penney's is embroidered in blue at the center of a block near the middle of the quilt, with the names of people in the community in each of the petals (one wonders whether sponsors had to pay more for prime positioning toward the middle of the quilt). The names in another block are connected by the relative power and prestige of some of the people represented, but the exact relationships are unclear: the names of the chief of police and the national Townsend representative for North and South Dakota, Jerome A. Owens, are listed, along with other individuals and three women associated with "Artesian North Dakota." Though we do not know their positions in the community, the individuals in this block held some recognizable form of power across local, regional, and state lines. The *TNW* includes several articles featuring Owens, even including a note about his wife's travel habits, along with a write-up of a speech and visual education program Owens delivered in front of three hundred people on May 11, 1940.[104]

In addition to visualizing the translocal relationships among individuals and business sponsors, the quilt also recontextualizes messages related to the movement within and across the modal resources of the quilt as medium. At first glance, these blocks could be understood as the rote repetition of patriotic, religious, and entrepreneurial values (and clichés). However, when considered more closely, the quilt's messaging actually represents the recontextualization of repetition-as-difference by advocating for a more disruptive political message in support of a new way of seeing the elderly: as central, not marginal, to the American dream; as heads of their households, rather than a burden on the next generation; as leaders of their community, not paupers. The Townsendites recontextualized potentially subversive arguments in a seemingly benign medium; because quiltmaking has often been devalued as "women's work," it has rarely been considered as a space or place where one needs to look for (or censor) radicalism.[105] In spite, or perhaps because of, these associations, the composers were able to transform the medium of the quilt into a transmodal means of working toward social change. As one block claims, citing both God and Townsend (or perhaps Townsend as a God-ordained prophet): "God Decrees, 'Youth For Work, Age for Leisure.' Townsend." If quilts "can be used to create and reshape *ethos*," as Barthel states, I argue that the Townsendites of Mitchell, South Dakota, took the creation and circulation of this quilt as an opportunity to establish their credibility as contributors to and sponsors of their local, regional, and national communities, and their importance to the achievement of the American dream.

See, for example, the patriotic appeal in the center block, which proclaims "The Townsend Plan We Are Proud to Be Americans." Townsend meetings proclaimed their patriotism repeatedly. Club meetings began and ended with pledges of allegiance, both to the flag *and* to the Townsend Club, and members would also sing "America the Beautiful" and other songs and hymns derived and improvised from the patriotic canon.[106] It was important for the quilt's producers and consumers to put patriotism front and center to establish an *ethē* of advocacy from which they could challenge the American system as a whole. And yet, the Townsendites chose "America the Beautiful" because it acknowledges America as a beautiful, but flawed space. ("America! America! / God mend thine every flaw, /Confirm thy soul in self-control, / Thy liberty in law!").[107] The quiltmakers (and the Townsendites in clubs throughout the United States) recontextualize familiar patriotic messages as a way to challenge the status quo.

In spite of repeatedly proclaiming their patriotism at club meetings, events, conventions, public gatherings, and objects such as this quilt, the Townsendites were attacked by the public, and even certain members of Congress, as un-American. In "An Open Letter: To Representative Martin Dies," the *TNW* defends the movement against Dies's claims that the Townsend Plan and other populist movements, such as the Ham and Eggs movement, reflect the growing power of Marxism in the United States.[108] The *TNW* responds: "You link Townsendites with all the undesirables and un-Americans—and thus damn them with a phrase. You must know that the Townsend Plan is the most American movement in this country, dedicated to the preservation of American standards and American ideals. . . . All the things you condemn are born out of desperation of the unemployed. To destroy them, destroy the cause of this discontent by bringing back employment, by restoring business, by raising living standards."[109] Nothing is more American, the article argues, than preserving and raising "American standards and American ideals" and, most important, American living standards so that the elderly, who worked so hard to make America great, can be taken care of and restored to their former glory—a populist argument that has gained strength today, in the far right reaches of American politics. The article blames the desperation of the unemployed on the government; Marxism will remain until unemployment is vanquished once and for all. Even as it slyly supports Marxism given current material conditions, the article clearly rejects the un-American label and argues that nothing could be more American than the Townsend Plan. As another quilt block proclaims in bold red capital letters: "A NATION IS KNOWN BY ITS TREATMENT OF YOUTH AND OF ITS AGED." In this *TNW* article and in the quilt, we see how the rhetoric of the Townsend Movement cleverly recontextualized conventional messages of patriotism and loyalty, using those messages to provide the foundation for more revolutionary pro-elderly, pro-pension (and anti–Social Security Act) arguments.

The Townsend Movement often drew on familiar religious messages to shame the government and those who did not fully support old-age pensions outright. The quiltmakers also engage in this strategy, recontextualizing religious rhetoric in several blocks. One such block reads: "America's pauper system is disrespect for it's aged, and is therefore pagan." The cursive script is sewn neatly in blue thread and is bedazzled with four yellow stars, surrounded by the red outline of the outer edges of the flower (the petals themselves are not outlined, which would have interfered with the block's quotation). In this way, the block recontextualizes the modes and media of the quilt itself, including writing, image, layout, and choice of fabric color, thread, and embroidery to foreground a message that equates the current Social Security system with paganism and blesses Townsendism as God-given (as the other block suggests, "God decrees" the Townsend Plan). The block staunchly rejects the enemies of Townsendism as unchristian and uncivilized. When the quilt was made (1940), the Townsend Plan had achieved several long-fought-over victories. In part due to the leadership's lobbying, there was now an Old-Age and Survivors Insurance hybrid, thanks to the Social Security Amendments—a "limited" move toward "unrestricted old-age pensions."[110] In spite of these moves, Townsend maintained that the system was still making the elderly into paupers, in part because of the inconsistencies between state and federal programs. At the time of the quilt's creation, old-age pensions were still a moving target, never to be achieved: with US entry into World War II the next year, the air was almost completely taken out of the movement, though it persisted for several decades.[111]

The quiltmakers recontextualize a religious appeal in another quilt block located at the top left corner of the quilt, which reads in bold, golden embroidery: "Honor thy father and mother." Because of its position at the top lefthand side of the quilt, and the fairly stark, mostly white space of the layout, this fairly straightforward and familiar message stands out. And yet, the familiarity of the message should not be seen as mere iteration of convention; instead, the block engages difference-in-similarity in order to "sneak in" a fairly radical, disruptive set of political and social beliefs. As discussed in chapter 1, Townsend's plan for American prosperity constituted an ideologically muddled mix of Marxism and a utopian vision based on hope for the future that also called on romanticized notions of family that sought to reestablish "traditional social relations" in the family.[112] One of the aims of the plan was to empower the aged to become less dependent on their children, and so resurrect them to their status as family figureheads who could pass down wisdom and material goods to their children. Restoring honor to the elderly, the movement argued, was the oldsters' right after a lifetime of social service and work; now was the time for the children to take over the reins. However, the Townsend Plan idealized the nuclear family while ignoring changes to the family structure in the United States, including how families were increasingly living in separate communities because of work. The quilt does not include the conclusion of the commandment, which reads "that thy days may be long upon the land which the Lord thy God giveth thee." Although the Townsend Plan was an old-age pension plan, it sought support among the young as well (as we saw in the passionate work of Pearl Burkhalter). As this Bible verse suggests, the Townsend Movement argued that the young had much to gain from both the economic stimulus provided by the plan and the increased independence of the younger generation's parents and grandparents with the pension.

The quiltmakers also cleverly provide a counterargument to anticipate potential skeptics, as seen in the quilt block five blocks below this one. The block reads: "The Townsend Plan Pays As It Goes, Eliminating Cost of Shame Of The Pauper System." Many critics pointed out the impractical nature of the movement, which they said would bankrupt the nation. This quilt block asks what would be costlier: the national shame of a pauper system or a "practical," pay-as-you-go approach to pension reform. The visual and design choices made by the quiltmakers of this block strengthen its claim: "The Townsend Plan" is highlighted in blue thread, with the rest of the quotation neatly embroidered in block letters. The petals are outlined lightly in blue and red, topped by a simple but bold red-and-blue flower. The flower draws attention to the block, which is surrounded by blocks dominated by sponsors whose names are written in yellow embroidery thread. Once again, the quilters have found a way to draw attention to the plan's message, and also to differentiate this particular block from its counterparts: by framing it so that its message is separated from the others in the quilt. The collaborative nature of such a signature quilt project may have meant that many of the blocks were created off site, so the fact that the final product has been framed so that it has coherence points to the skill of its creators. Of the quotations cited by the quiltmakers, one name stands out: the banker J. P. Morgan, who is quoted at the top of the quilt: "Some are too busy to be wise, others are too wise to be busy." The block, uncredited to any particular business or sponsor, was most likely chosen as an add-in by the quiltmakers (as with the blocks previously discussed). The quotation and block foreground, once again, the confusing ideological foundations of the movement.[113] The Morgan quotation also plays with the idea of wisdom, work, and age. Perhaps, the block argues, the nation should listen to the elderly, who have both age and wisdom on their side, but who have not had the time or money to put that wisdom to work for others in their community (the implication is that the Townsend Plan provides the resources for them to participate in such work). Another quilt block, toward the bottom left of the quilt, argues for the ability of the plan to stimulate the economy: "No Man Without an Honorable Job, At Living Wages, Under the Townsend Recovery Plan." In this block, the composers cleverly rework the layout of the block, emphasizing the beauty and practicality of their message by decorating the center of the block with small embroidered flowers as well as, less subtly, dollar signs (the quilt block was sponsored by an individual, "Transfer Geo. A. Tobin," who provides his phone number for interested parties to contact him).

The number of names, places, and businesses from across the country represented on the quilt suggest that the movement continued to have national support—a message that countered the reality on the ground. As the Social Security Act gained traction, the Townsend Plan lost traction, and the national movement eventually gave in to the pressure to focus on more local, state-level pension policy. The quiltmakers purposefully foreground the translocal, even "global" nature of the Townsend Movement, as seen in one quilt block with a globe at the center. Throughout the quilt, Townsend Clubs and individual sponsors include their locations in their flowers, including clubs from Paonia, Colorado; Pierre, South Dakota; Wauconia, Minnesota; Waukegan, Illinois; Lincoln, Nebraska; and other cities in South Dakota (Rapid City and Poykston). The quiltmakers purposefully seek to expand the frame of the quilt by expanding the reach of the fundraising effort across time and space, and so heightening the *ethē* of advocacy and impact of the quilt and its message. The club's organizers must have instructed their sponsors to carefully highlight the places in different-colored thread, so that the audience would understand the plan's reach (individual locations are highlighted in single blocks by alternatives among the red, blue, and gold thread options, sometimes all in the same block).

We can look at the quilt from several different angles: for one, it provides a snapshot of small-town America, a material and visual realization of the people and businesses that made up the "organized elderly" in support of the plan. At the same time, the quilt reveals more than a glimpse into small-town America (embodied, for example, by a kitschy block advertising the local shoe store with an embroidered image of a woman's high-heeled shoe). We can look at the quilt as representative of the intersecting translocal and transmodal threads at work—threads that enabled the Townsend Plan to gain such great popularity in the 1930s and 1940s, and ultimately influence Social Security policy up to the present. The quilt blocks represent the intersection of local and national politics, and the political advocacy of the movement's intersecting appeals to entrepreneurial, religious, and political rhetoric. The amount of organization and labor required to create the quilt is apparent. When we look closely, we can see how carefully and creatively its composers recontextualized the modes and media of the quilt. At the same time, the quilt was not necessarily meant to be beautiful, but rather was intended to serve a larger purpose—as a representation of a collective "we" interested in collaboratively imagining a world where the elderly were not paupers. As a discursive artifact, the quilt makes the argument that the elderly are willing to step aside to let the younger generation take over, if they are taken care of in return. Based on the available evidence, it is likely the quilt was auctioned off as a fundraiser and/or displayed locally. Although the names of women and men appear on the quilt as sponsors, we can assume that the women of the clubs donated the majority of the unpaid time and labor that went into embroidering, sewing, and piecing together the quilt itself.

In *Appropriate[ing] Dress*, Carol Mattingly asks whether it is possible to examine "too many alternative ways of defining rhetoric." "If so," she argues, "I am willing to risk that possibility."[114] In taking that risk, Mattingly has opened doors for other feminist scholars of writing and rhetoric invested in "continu[ing] the search for women's traditions."[115] By focusing on nineteenth-century women's dress and dressmaking, Mattingly was at the forefront of scholars in English studies who have come to recognize the value of studying the multiple media and modes in which women make meaning. As I have argued throughout this chapter, quiltmaking represents a technology that, like dress, "helped to define the struggle for representation and power that is rhetoric."[116] Quilts provide a transmodal literacy practice for those outside the mainstream—whether the impoverished African American women in Alabama or the impoverished elderly supporters of the Townsend Movement—to construct their own discourses and so improve the material conditions of their lives and gain representation in wider social and political contexts.

CONCLUSION

"What Is This Thing You Call a Pen?"

The Courage of Ordinary Americans

No one wants a pen that's going to rat them out. We all want pens that can be used to write anything, and that will stand up for who we are.
—Alexander MacGillivray, general counsel for Twitter

In the days immediately following the election of President Donald J. Trump, many Americans were in a state of shock: how could the nation have elected an unqualified reality television star running on what they saw as a blatantly racist, misogynistic, populist platform?[1] Maureen Dowd's column in *The New York Times* echoed the disbelief of many who had not supported Trump: "It is unthinkable to imagine the most overtly racist candidate—and head of the offensive birther movement—driving in the limousine to the inauguration with the first African-American president."[2] Others responded differently—some with hope that Trump would follow through on his campaign promise to "drain the swamp," and some with recognition rather than surprise at the revelation of the systemic power imbalances and racist discourses underlying the American political, social, and economic system. These divergent reactions led to open discussions in the media exploring what the election meant to specific communities, as when Dre, one of the main characters in the sitcom *Black-ish*, corrects a white colleague who accuses Dre of political apathy, instead pointing out the ways the election saddens him, confirms his experience, and does nothing to change the loyalty he feels to his country.[3] In the years after the 2016 presidential election, the responses still vary, as do the methods of resistance. Some people continue to be paralyzed with shock, fear, and anxiety. Some have retreated further inward, reaching out to friends and family, and choosing to ignore (because they can) the overwhelming news cycle, even as they send thoughts and prayers when some of their worst fears come true. Some have started to fight, to wake up and to listen, attending rallies and marches—both by choice and because they may be faced with deportation and the stripping away of their human rights. And many have continued to resist as they have always done, recontextualizing the available means to adapt to a new social, cultural, and political reality.

The 2016 election thus brought to the fore many of the strategies long used by Americans interested in exercising their First Amendment "right of the people peaceably to assemble" and "to petition the Government for a redress of grievances."[4] As Kathryn Schulz notes in the *New Yorker*, the 2016 election prompted a multitude of Americans to contact their political representatives: when congressional phone lines jammed and email inboxes overflowed, constituents resorted to sending faxes, letters, and even, in some cases, pizza.[5] Others collaborated within and across their communities, finding creative and productive ways of making their voices heard through other outlets, including social media, national and international news outlets, and grassroots organizations in their communities. The response to Trump's election raises important questions about the most effective and efficient means for speaking back to power. How can individuals seeking change effectively engage in resistance in the face of difficult challenges and divisions? Do desperate times call for desperate measures? As Schulz asks in her analysis of the effectiveness of calling Congress: "does it really make a difference?" Though we cannot yet know which response to the current political climate will pay the biggest dividend, given the historical context provided by the case studies in this book, we can recognize the continued power and possibility of the everyday rhetorics of resistance men and women have engaged in across history.

When faced with a desperate problem—poverty, unemployment, racism, ageism, war or the threat of war—the composers in this book responded heroically without resorting to heroic measures. More MacGyver than Marvel superhero, the women featured in this book demonstrate "an extraordinary knack for unconventional problem solving."[6] They chose to look around, assess the situation, gather the existing materials, and solve the problems they faced as best they could, recontextualizing the (extra)ordinary instruments available to them and collaborating with those around them to seek change. Though many of the women in the case studies may, at times, have been desperate, they did not engage in extreme acts of desperation: they acted from a place of (un)familiarity and (dis)comfort, recontextualizing the (un)conventional means available in order to disrupt the status quo in ways that made sense given the affordances of their particular time, place, and space. Their tools were not flashy: they include letter writing, silence, prayer, quiltmaking, and the kinds of everyday social and political activities that take place among friends, families, and neighbors in a community (social gatherings, club meetings, quilt auctions, rummage sales, potlucks, and other promotions and fundraisers). And though we could easily view these composers' everyday activism as futile or inconsequential in the larger historical context, the women in the case studies were empowered to speak out and act in ways that influenced those around them, and had a ripple effect beyond their immediate friends and family. Rather than throwing up their hands at a problem that seemed too big, these women were determined to do something, anything, to improve their lives and the lives of those around them.

Redefining Resistance

In order to recognize everyday rhetorics of resistance, however, we need to broaden and revise our definition of what counts as effective rhetorical resistance. In a discussion of how the keyword *resistance* has been employed in rhetorical studies, Phaedra C. Pezzullo and Ted Striphas identify a variety of applications of the term: resistance as struggle, resistance as taking a stand, and "resistance as rejection, defiance, and the capacity to withstand material and psychological forces."[7] The cultural, social, and ecological contexts in which resistance occurs shape the forms it takes or the choice not to engage in resistance, as resistance is not always the ideal. Although some cultures may promote peace, harmony, and cooperation, or "the path of least resistance," others may value "persistence over resistance, believing that taking a stand may be worthwhile, but not if the short-term risks outweigh long-term survival."[8] Pezzullo and Striphas's discussion highlights the extent to which scholars have approached resistance in binary terms: persistence or resistance, disharmony or harmony, acceptance or refusal, repetition or difference. The case studies in this book disrupt binary approaches to resistance by providing wide-ranging evidence of everyday rhetorics of resistance within and across expected and unexpected means and materials, spaces and places, texts and contexts.

The examples of Pearl Burkhalter, E. P. Gurney, and the Gee's Bend and Townsend quiltmakers demonstrate how letter writing and quiltmaking constitute important but often overlooked acts of resistance: persistence *as* resistance, repetition *as* difference, harmony *as* disharmony, an acceptance of and ability to work within and across the limitations established by the status quo, in order to refute its power. Pearl Burkhalter persisted in writing letter after letter in spite and because of the lack of response she received from her elected officials; in her letters, she both acceded to and strayed from the conventions of letter writing to make her mark on her intended audiences. Gurney spread an activist Quaker message in spite and because of the challenges of access she faced as a nineteenth-century woman, and her persistent promotion of peace and harmony was both radical and revolutionary, though cloaked in a more suitable and acceptable rhetoric of consolation and constraint. The Gee's Bend quilters continued to create art in spite and because of conditions of extreme poverty; their quilts drew upon multiple, sometimes competing, aesthetic traditions, and can be understood as an artistic form of resistance to and recognition of the material conditions of their lives. The Townsendite quilters raised funds in spite and because of a lack of national support for the Townsend Plan, presenting their refusal of the status quo in an acceptable, familiar, ostensibly safe medium and capitalizing on the boundaries of the quilt to represent the appeal of the Townsend message across local, regional, and national contexts.

In these examples, we have seen how even outwardly compliant iterations of the standard, familiar, and normative may hide more activist, disruptive agendas. In line with the translingual approach, I have considered the difference and difference-in-similarity represented in these case studies through the lens of *recontextualization*, which I define as the process by which composers deliberately reform, reinvent, and reconstruct the languages, media, and modes available to them in light of the time, place, and space of their particular practice (their temporal, spatial, and material context). Recontextualization in this framework constitutes an act of resistance with potentially long-term consequences, though in the short term, the effect may be less apparent. Composers' recontextualization of everyday, accessible, ostensibly ordinary means and materials—which could even be associated with taking the "path of least resistance"—in fact contributes to the ongoing sedimentation of linguistic and modal practices which, in turn, may lead to the long-term disruption of dominant linguistic, cultural, social, and political ideologies. In other words, I am a believer in the tortoise over the hare: slow and steady often wins the race, though, at the time, it may be painful to watch and difficult to recognize or appreciate the gains being made.

In the years after the 2016 election, as Americans continue to look for ways to grapple with and take a stand on the issues we believe in, we can learn from these composers' inventive recontextualization of languages, modes, and media in order to voice their experiences and gain a hearing from those in power. The case studies call attention to the value of taking up whatever pen(s) are accessible to us, a problem that transcends history, as seen in an article titled, "What Is This Thing You Call a Pen," in which the general counsel of Twitter, Alexander MacGillivray, claims that "we all want pens that can be used to write anything and that will stand up for who we are." Burkhalter took up her pen as sword, recontextualizing the genre and conventions of the letter handed down to her by Townsend leadership. Burkhalter's passionate exercise of her First Amendment right to petition elected officials for a redress of grievances suggests that the pen enables the writer to wield the power they possess—their vote and the votes of their family, as Burkhalter notes—and to draw attention to the material conditions of their lives, though in ways that may disrupt the conventions of decorum and propriety. Gurney took up the pen in a more peaceful and prayerful, but no less disruptive, manner. Gurney's *Memoir and Correspondence* suggests that her recontextualization of the conventions and traditions of Quaker rhetorical practice (within and across the modes of speech and writing) enabled her to effectively communicate radical messages of equality, peace, and charity to diverse audiences and in diverse contexts. Moreover, the pen can take many forms, as we see in the case of the Gee's Bend and Townsendite quiltmakers, who took up the needle as pen and in the space of a single material object recontextualized within and across multiple modes in order to communicate the particulars of their experiences and collaboratively imagine something better.

The everyday rhetorics of resistance engaged in by the composers in this book demand that we rethink what counts as pen and writing, and that we recognize the creative, resistant potential of the everyday means and materials already on hand. Together, the three case studies point to the inventive ways composers across history have worked within and against the affordances of languages, modes, media, and genres available to them, reframing restrictions as resources and (often subtly) working to disrupt the status quo. Recovering these less known, but longstanding histories of resistance can help generate the radical hope necessary to seek change while also fighting against dangerous and ahistorical understandings of what makes America great.

A Feminist, Translingual, and Transmodal Approach

A translingual and transmodal framework informed by feminist rhetorical practice therefore offers a useful way to recover and reclaim the everyday rhetorics of resistance engaged in by diverse composers across history. The translingual orientation to language and modality provides a through-line for understanding the innovative and disruptive possibilities of composers' recontextualization of language, mode, and medium in these three distinct case studies, and so, I argue, opens up the possibility for applying such a framework to other, diverse case studies in the future. The case studies in this book provide important historical context for translingualism's call to understand difference *as* the norm: the studies illustrate how composers across history have always already engaged in translingual and transmodal literacy practices that disrupt the ideology of a single language or modal norm: composers have always already been reworking, re-forming, and reconstructing within and across language and mode. The distinct nature of the case studies also provides further evidence for the claim that the translingual orientation can be applied to even seemingly monolingual and monomodal composers, compositions, and contexts.

In line with this translingual orientation, feminist historiography and feminist rhetorical practice provide a foundation for recovering and reclaiming the creativity and ingenuity of the women composers I study, whose words and work might otherwise be devalued, overlooked, or lost. My work participates in the long line of feminist scholars who have turned to the archive, the museum, and the footnotes to recover the ordinary—often ephemeral—histories of women's resistance, many of which survive only in incomplete or secondhand accounts. In working across histories, cultures, and contexts, I have sought to practice rhetorical listening and apply the feminist concept of social circulation to my study of the diverse spaces and places where women have engaged in meaning-making. I have connected the dots and filled in the gaps in the archives and records by critically imagining and strategically contemplating how and why these particular women worked with and against the discursive possibilities of the languages, modes, and media available to them in the service of social justice, political reform, and the improvement of their material lives.

Such a framework reveals how Pearl Burkhalter and other Townsendites expressed their displeasure with those in power by making the familiar unfamiliar, and the unfamiliar familiar, recontextualizing the mode of writing and the genre of the complaint letter to reflect their displeasure. Such a framework enables us to reclaim and recognize the resistant possibility of Gurney's recontextualization of Quaker rhetorical traditions to address her audience effectively in light of the particular time, place, and space in which she was speaking. Such a framework also supports theorizing quiltmaking as a discursive social, economic, and political resource for expressing women's experiences to people inside and outside of their communities in ways that can be both extraordinary and ordinary, all at once.

Burkhalter's passionate letters divulge why she and other Townsendites had good reason to be angry about their situation, and help us to understand why the Townsendites chose to recontextualize—and, as a result, change—the genre conventions established by headquarters to voice their anger to those in authority, whether a local or state representative or the president of the United States. Burkhalter made the most of the affordances of the letter to foreground the reality faced by her family and her community, who, she writes, struggled, hoped, and dreamed for the kind of relief provided by a solid pension. Burkhalter's letters—as well as her poems, songs, and journals—represent a brief snapshot of the depth and breadth of the translingual and transmodal literacy practices engaged by Townsendites across the nation, who took up the pen to fight passionately for the cause of pension reform. As the case of Burkhalter and that of the quilters detailed in chapter 3 suggest, although the Townsendites did not always have a great deal of material resources to draw upon, they capitalized upon the resources in their possession.

Gurney called upon the strength of her Quaker belief system to recontextualize prayerful messages of sympathy, consolation, and constraint that appealed to her audiences, no matter the differences in their nationality, class, language, or religious belief. Gurney recontextualized the Quaker rhetorical practice of silence in ways sanctioned by the church, while also using silence to break some of the particular barriers she faced as a woman speaker in the nineteenth century. She also developed a keen sense of *kairos* to connect with her audiences and establish an *ethē* of relation-relating that empowered her to speak and listen across asymmetrical relations of power. Her ability to recontextualize the conventions of ceremonial encounters into memorable exchanges that worked toward the ends of social justice suggests the activist potential of the epideictic.

In Gee's Bend, Alabama, and Mitchell, South Dakota, quiltmakers aggregated their design resources and recontextualized within and across modes (including images, writing, layout) and media (including fabric, thread, words, pictures, and stitches) by engaging in older, but no less radical, transmodal literacy practices. Both the Gee's Bend quiltmakers and the Townsendites reworked the quilt as a space and place for artistic expression and resistance to the status quo. In this way, quilts represent what we might call "evocative objects," "rich sources of inquiry . . . [that] invite us to observe closely, pose questions, forge connections, and anchor ideas in the concrete."[9] In order to understand the depth and breadth of activist work, we must expand the discursive contexts we consider, and reconsider "what counts" as writing and rhetoric, which enables us to better grasp the ways activists across history have shaped larger grassroots movements and fought for the honor, dignity, and quality of life they felt they deserved.

In the introduction, I suggested that one goal of this project was to test out the theory that translingual literacy practices are relevant for all. I asked whether the translingual orientation can be applied to seemingly monolingual and monomodal, multilingual and multimodal, contemporary and historical practices. My analysis supports the relevance of a translingual orientation to understanding the nuances of everyday rhetorics of resistance, including the translingual and transmodal literacy practices that may not appear to engage in more obvious forms of difference. However, I recognize the need to avoid relativizing or essentializing all translingual and transmodal literacy practice as the same. The varied texts, contexts, and composers in these three studies suggest the need for further investigations testing the limits and possibilities of applying a translingual framework to so-called monolingual and monomodal texts; at the same time, these studies suggest the continued need to apply such a framework to more obviously multilingual, multimodal, and transnational texts and contexts. Both paths can support the work of understanding difference as the norm of emergent language practice, shaped by users in conditions of asymmetrical relations of power. Both paths seek to reveal and disrupt the dominant ideologies that impede the agency of composers, who—depending on their particular positionality and (dis)privilege—are very differently situated in relation to the languages, modes, and media they recontextualize. While all users compose in conditions of asymmetrical relations of power, not all users are punished or rewarded in the same ways for the extent to which they are perceived to deviate from the accepted standard and norm. In applying a translingual and transmodal framework to everyday rhetorics of resistance, I am not arguing that recontextualization applies to everyone in the same way; how and why we recontextualize is shaped to a large degree by our positionality and (dis)privilege, and is a function of the particular time, place, and space of our linguistic and modal practices. However, I am arguing that if we can understand these practices as fluid and malleable, and recognize the innovative and constructive ways users have worked within and against the limits of their temporal, spatial, and material contexts, then we can recover and reclaim past and present examples of translingual and transmodal literacy practice, and continue to disrupt the dominance of the single language and modal norm in the future.

The (Extra)Ordinary Antihero

The three case studies in this book suggest that the engine of community activism comes not from the celebrities or heroes we are most familiar with, but from the collective efforts of people who extend themselves in (extra)ordinary ways for the members of their communities, ways often not recognized or valued by those outside their communities. As Paul Feigenbaum writes, "mainstream cultural narratives frequently appropriate historical figures to portray social change as resulting from the singular actions of heroic archetypes rather than from the long-term efforts of many people enduring years of slow, fitful progress. These narratives are not merely historical accounts; they also operate (implicitly or explicitly) as civic educational practices in themselves, limiting perceptions of past activism and narrowly defining what constitutes appropriate civic behavior today."[10] The composers in these studies serve as a counter to the "heroic archetype" that has dominated discussions of activist resistance. Like all good "antiheroes," these composers often put others before themselves, but they also understood their own limits and turned to their communities for support. When singling out individual composers, I also recognize that each operated within a supportive network that provided encouragement, material resources, and mentorship through the ups and downs of the slow, but meaningful activist work Feigenbaum describes as the norm rather than the exception. Burkhalter worked with and for the elderly in her community, both Townsendite supporters and nonsupporters. In her archives, we see her collaborations with Arthur Moore and other Townsendite leaders and club members in Oregon City and beyond. Gurney worked with and for the Society of Friends and, in her travels, always served with a team of fellow ministers. Quiltmaking as a collaborative effort spans time, place, and space, connecting the quiltmakers and their beliefs, values, and ideas in the space of a single object.

Even as the majority of the labor of the rhetors in this book went unrecognized by outsiders for years, the composers themselves and the members of their communities long appreciated the power of their slow, steady work. Though Pearl Burkhalter's efforts have been lost in the narratives and histories of the Townsendites, the archival evidence suggests that her work mattered greatly to her community at the time, who turned to her as a leader and representative, and who labored alongside her to claim their right to a better life. Burkhalter's activism provides an evocative example of how the Townsend Plan inspired the "oldsters" as a constituency to work together and believe in the political power and legitimacy of their own voices. Gurney's *Memoir and Correspondence* acknowledges the power of Gurney's ministry, and how she touched the lives of many in the United States and across the Atlantic, including how her exchanges with Lincoln addressed issues of great importance to her community. In spite of this recognition from within her community, few historians and scholars have taken the time to ask how or why the Quaker minister had such an effect on the president or to consider the larger context of that meeting by studying more closely her years of ministry and activism in and outside of her Quaker community. Though the Gee's Bend quiltmakers have achieved some celebrity and success in recent years, particularly from those outside their community, the women's descriptions of their quiltmaking processes suggest they did not need the validation of outsiders to understand the aesthetic and cultural value of the abstract work-clothes quilts they made for their families and circulated within their families and communities. As in the case of the Gee's Bend quiltmakers, the power of the Townsendite quiltmakers came from the linguistic and modal resources they recontextualized from *within* their community. Though it may seem that it takes a chance meeting with an art dealer, in the case of the Gee's Bend quiltmakers, or a hard-sought interview with a president to bring such everyday rhetorics of resistance to the attention of outsiders, the women's work had value before and beyond these famous or notorious encounters brought their work to the larger public, just as it has value beyond my rendering of it in this book.

The composers in this book imaginatively, persuasively, and persistently communicated their experiences with those around them, detailing with purpose and intent the material conditions of their lives to those inside and outside their communities. In spite of having very little access to and understanding of the newer technologies available to them in the 1930s and 1940s, the Townsendites made the most of the older modes, technologies, and resources with which they were familiar. The Townsendites used the power of the pen to make their suffering and outrage known to their political representatives. They engaged in lobbying by means of letter writing and made their clubs into social and political hubs in their local communities, bringing all their talents and resources to the fight: if they had a farm with land, they painted and put up a homemade billboard to advertise to passers-by; if they had (any) musical talent or ability to entertain, they started a kitchen band; if they could cook, they contributed meals to the rummage sales, auctions, and potluck dinner fundraisers; if they were handy, they made a parade float; if they could sew, they made quilts, pillowcases, or tablecloths to sell. Gurney's decision to present herself with the humility and quietness required of a refined Quaker minister belies the power and forcefulness of her rhetorical approach. At many points in her life and career she refused to be turned away, whether attempting to meet with a royal personage in Europe, the president of the United States, or a gathering of people in Europe or America who had never before heard a woman minister speak. Her power and persistence, though quiet, had a great effect on her audiences and enabled her to communicate a message of extreme peace during wartime. The Gee's Bend quiltmakers have long viewed quilts as objects with multiple possibilities and purposes, both aesthetic and functional, viewing these purposes as constitutive rather than contradictory. Even as the quilts gained fame as artistic objects, and took many of the women with them, the women have reminded themselves and outsiders of the quilts' value as practical objects: to mop with, to warm puppies, to use as throw rugs, to hug and contain children, to clean one's feet, to pad chairs, to protect fruit trees from frost, to wipe up spills, and to use as feminine pads. As poet and quiltmaker Tinnie Pettway writes, the need to make beautiful, practical objects came out of desperate poverty: "Because during that time it's sad to say, that was all those / women had."[11] The women of Mitchell, South Dakota, recognized the political possibility of the quilt as a resource and used the space of the quilt in the same way activists use social media now: to transcend geographic space and cleverly gather resources, and to visualize the support of and momentum behind a movement. The women procured sponsors, represented those sponsors, and, in the process, demonstrated the far-reaching support of the Townsend Plan during a time when many thought the plan was politically dead. The quilt provides a snapshot of the ways the plan brought together actors within and across communities, and the intermingling of political and religious rhetoric in the movement.

If we can reframe our understanding of past activist literacy practices and work against dominant heroic narratives, we can recognize and reclaim the work of composers like the women in these case studies, without romanticizing that work. Their everyday rhetorics of resistance enable a more realistic model for present and future activism.

Everyday Rhetorics of Resistance Then and Now

My application of a translingual and transmodal framework to these particular case studies opens up the possibility for recovering and reclaiming many other historical and contemporary examples of the everyday rhetorics of resistance employed by women and men who recontextualize within and across language, media, and mode for collaborative, activist purposes as part of their daily lives. As we have come to recognize more and more, something as small as a hashtag can spark a revolutionary shift in the cultural conversation. The power of a hashtag comes from its collaborative and representative potential: a hashtag means nothing if it is not taken up in and beyond its original author and circulated in and beyond its original community. #BlackLivesMatter and, more recently, #MeToo and #NeverAgain attest to the impact everyday means and materials can have on the larger social conscience.[12] The power of collective action can force a conversation that brings endemic issues, such as police brutality, sexual harassment and assault, and gun violence, to the foreground, in spite of a longstanding cultural refusal to acknowledge these issues as problems relevant to the majority of Americans. And yet, the dialogue surrounding hashtag movements also points to how quickly a trend or phenomenon can render invisible the larger historical, social, and cultural contexts of a movement, particularly the time and labor of rhetors outside the mainstream who have been actively working for change for years. We saw this problem represented quite starkly with the viral hashtag #MeToo, whose origins were initially attributed to celebrity Alyssa Milano rather than to long-serving women's rights activist Tarana Burke, who had been working for years in the nonprofit world to bring attention to the issue of sexual assault on women and to help survivors of sexual violence.[13] Ironically (but perhaps not surprisingly), though several celebrities and activists associated with the recent sexual harassment allegations were featured as "Silence Breakers" on Time's "Person of the Year" cover, Burke herself was not, though she was cited in the story.

Even as modern composers are amazed by the innumerable opportunities for activism available, the rapidity with which the conversations themselves change—in terms of content, form, and meaning—can be overwhelming. Fortunately, scholars across the disciplines have been working and will continue to work to provide a richer historical context for understanding past and present forms of everyday activism. In particular, historians have sought to transcend partisan politics to uncover the ways composers, during periods of what appears to be activist-stagnation, have participated in local, innovative grassroots organization. For example, historian Michael Stewart Foley counters popular narratives of "civic disengagement and conservative rule" during the 1970s and 1980s by providing evidence of the high levels of political activity and civic engagement. He provides numerous examples of what he calls "front porch politics," arguing that during this period "citizens' engagement originated at their front door—on their porch, stoop, or landing—where they could see one or more ominous forces encroaching" and "were moved to defend their home, heart, and livelihood in circumstances where government had failed to do so."[14] Grassroots activists during this period were quite involved in local and regional issues: "neighborhoods mobilized against toxic waste dumps, young women established battered women's shelters, poor and working families squatted in abandoned housing in declining cities, rust-belt industrial workers took over factories discarded by multi-national corporations."[15] Foley's work, along with scholarship by Clarence Lang on "Black activism" after the civil rights era and by Karissa Haugerberg on conservative women's anti-abortion activism, provide just a few illustrative examples of the gathering momentum of scholarship outside of rhetoric and composition that seeks to counter dominant hero-focused narratives of activism and foreground the work of ordinary people collaboratively recontextualizing the means and materials of their everyday lives to seek change.[16] Foley's argument ultimately takes a pessimistic turn, arguing that Americans "have lost our willingness to step off the front porch and participate in the political life of the nation, at the grass roots, in a fashion that goes beyond partisanship"; however, I argue that the historical examples provided by the case studies in this book turn our attention to the variety of ways the rank and file have engaged and will continue to engage with those in power on the issues they care about, within and across language, culture, media, and mode.

As a field collectively invested in recovering and reclaiming how composers and rhetors across history have engaged with the means available to them to speak back to power, the field of rhetoric and composition provides numerous examples of everyday rhetorics of resistance across history. See, for example, the ongoing work of the feminist scholars cited in the introduction, in addition to recent work by Jessica Enoch, Lindal Buchanan, Carolyn Skinner, Samantha NeCamp, and Alicia Brazeau (to name just a few). Their scholarship recovers the diverse ways women across history have transcended the gendered, apolitical, often limited roles forced upon them in their private, public, and professional lives (mother, teacher, writer, caretaker, doctor) and have adapted (recontextualized) the literacies and resources available in order to engage in more radical work and to seek change.[17] Or see the work of Sonia Arellano, whose dissertation explores how twenty-first-century activists have used the medium of the quilt to represent and fight for the rights of immigrants who have risked or lost their lives migrating to the United States.[18] Or see much of the scholarship in community literacy studies, including work by Diana George and Paula Mathieu, whose analysis of homeless advocacy across several communities offers a revised understanding of public networks that more accurately reflects the practical ways activists compose and circulate public documents using the networks and resources available.[19] Or see Paul Feigenbaum's work, cited throughout this book, which provides several case studies of the progressive activism and practical literacy networks of the Citizenship and Freedom Schools of the 1950s and 1960s; activist educators such as Ken Watson or Robert P. Moses; and the south Florida nonprofit, the Imagination Federation. Or see Stephen Schneider's study of the Highlander Folk School in Tennessee, which uncovers the ways "the folk school's educational programs not only helped oppressed communities recognize the transformative value of their own experiences and traditions but also to develop the various rhetorical strategies needed to agitate for social change."[20] Or see scholarship by Carmen Kynard on the vernacular insurrections that took place as part of the Black Freedom movements.[21] We can learn from composers and rhetors across history who have demonstrated both a faculty for observing the available means of persuasion and an ability to capitalize upon and expand those means in ways that challenge and surpass their limits and possibilities.

In one of the most recent discussions in the field about how composers outside the mainstream speak back to power, Keith Gilyard and Adam Banks draw on Amiri Baraka's idea of the *changing same* as related to jazz music to explore African American rhetorical practice. Quoting Baraka, they write, "What changes is both the means by which oppression does its work as well as the form of the response that African American music takes to address that oppression. What remains the same is both the continual assault on African American freedom in the form of racism as well as the consistent attitude of rebellion in the face of such assault."[22] Like recontextualization, the *changing same* highlights the means by which those outside the mainstream respond to power and, importantly, the systemic nature of oppression. Gilyard and Banks cite Black Twitter as evidence of this work in a twenty-first-century context: it is "built on modes of discourse and persuasive strategies rooted in African-American oral traditions and yet constantly shifting more quickly than software and updated passwords. It operates within fissures of history, ideas, and technologies, and it creates further ruptures or breaks." Recontextualization and the *changing same* suggest the persistently creative strategies by which composers outside the mainstream continue to fight, continue to adopt and adapt tradition and convention, continue to contribute to the ongoing sedimentation of language and modal practice to achieve the goal of social justice. Gilyard and Banks's scholarship—along with the work of many other writers and researchers within and outside our field—suggests the importance of considering the everyday rhetorics of resistance that occur in (un)conventional, (un)familiar, (un)expected, or overlooked places and spaces.

Unfortunately, in spite of the important recovery work occurring within and outside our discipline, many of the cultural conversations surrounding activism and reform continue to reflect a larger cultural obsession with individual achievement, celebrity, and success, such that we often do not have the means to understand or appreciate the everyday rhetorics of resistance engaged in by rhetors outside the spotlight. We overlook the labor of those whose work does not seem to render a particularly interesting result or who might be deemed a failure by their association with a failed social movement or with a nonmainstream religious community, such as Burkhalter and Gurney. We overlook those who engage in less flashy forms of rhetorical labor and so overlook years of activism, and we only acknowledge such work when the rhetor engages with a famous personage, as in the case of Gurney. We define success using the criteria of established outsiders rather than from within the communities themselves, as with the Gee's Bend quiltmakers, and we push outsider frameworks of "what counts as art" onto their quilts in order to understand and value them. We fail to notice the disruptive possibilities of "women's work," including the objects created by and circulated in more social venues, as in the case of the Townsend quilt.

In addition to shifting what counts as meaningful and useful writing, rhetoric, and discourse, we need to shift our understanding of what counts as meaningful social action, including the small acts of everyday resistance engaged in by the rhetors in this book, so that we can recognize the possibility, rather than the impossibility, of contributing to the ongoing work of social change. Small choices can make a big impact, particularly when delivered with intentionality and a consideration of the audience, message, and purpose through recontextualizing the medium, means, and mode. The rhetors and composers in this book broaden the places and spaces of struggle, and the everyday rhetorics of resistance they engage in can, I hope, help us to move beyond traditional notions of rhetorical success to include potential "misunderstanding, miscommunication, disagreement, resistance, and dissent."[23]

In President Barack Obama's speech on the fiftieth anniversary of "Bloody Sunday"—the civil rights march in Selma, Alabama, when six hundred nonviolent protestors were attacked by state troopers—he praised the "courage of ordinary Americans," who, with great bravery, collectively stood together to protest, an act he defines as deeply American and a theme he continues to highlight in his life after office:[24]

> What could more profoundly vindicate the idea of America than plain and humble people—the unsung, the downtrodden, the dreamers not of high station, not born to wealth or privilege, not of one religious tradition but many—coming together to shape their country's course?
>
> What greater expression of faith in the American experiment than this; what greater form of patriotism is there; than the belief that America is not yet finished, that we are strong enough to be self-critical, that each successive generation can look upon our imperfections and decide that it is in our power to remake this nation to more closely align with our highest ideals?

If we take a step back, we might gain hope from recognizing the ongoing political, rhetorical work already taking place in our communities by such ordinary Americans. And we might also see the possibility of the everyday rhetorics of resistance already in our possession and so embolden ourselves and the next generation to see the possibility of community activism and the possibility of recontextualizing languages, media, and modes to improve our lives and the lives of those around us. As Obama said to his audience that day: "You are America. Unconstrained by habits and convention. Unencumbered by what is, and ready to seize what ought to be. For everywhere in this country, there are first steps to be taken, and new ground to cover, and bridges to be crossed." As a field, we should continue to recover and recognize the work of the rhetors and composers who have largely gone unrecognized, and we should push beyond brief moments of recognition to learn more about the contexts of the (un)conventional, (un)constrained, and (un)encumbered everyday rhetorics of resistance they employed to gain a voice and a hearing. To do so is to recognize how ordinary people have taken the "first steps," covered new (and old) ground, and crossed new (and old) bridges. We write letters, call our congressional representatives, make quilts, and engage in often unrecognized forms of activism because we know, as one twenty-first-century complaint letter states, "we speak for millions more."[25] Everyday rhetorics of resistance will always be at the core of grassroots political and social movements, and the temporal-spatial framework provided by translingual literacy practice suggests that those inside and outside of the classroom can recontextualize the resources at their disposal to "collaboratively imagine" the work necessary to improve the material conditions of their lives.

"What is this thing you call a pen?" Anything we want to make of it.

Notes

Introduction

1. Townsend National Recovery Plan, Inc., Records, 1935–45, OHS, MSS 1334; "E. P. Gurney to Abraham Lincoln [September–October 1862] (Seeks interview)," Abraham Lincoln Papers at the Library of Congress, https://www.loc.gov/item/mal4235700/, accessed April 27, 2005; Bendolph quoted in *Gee's Bend: The Women and Their Quilts*, edited by William Arnett and Paul Arnett (Atlanta: Tinwood Books, 2002), 178; "Townsend Plan [quilt]," Wolfsonian–Florida International University Object Collection, accession no. TD1990.122.1, https://digital.wolfsonian.org.

2. Whether or not the story of the letter is true, scholars have begun to make connections between their correspondence and Lincoln's second inaugural address (see chapter 2).

3. For more on the power of objects, particularly documentary photography, to confront injustice, see Christopher Carter, *Rhetorical Exposures: Confrontation and Contradiction in U.S. Social Documentary Photography* (Tuscaloosa: University of Alabama Press, 2015).

4. Victor Villanueva, *Bootstraps* (Urbana, IL: NCTE, 1993), 76. Villanueva defines rhetoric as "the conscious use of language." See also Lloyd Bitzer, "The Rhetorical Situation," *Philosophy and Rhetoric* 1, no. 1 (1968): 1–14. Bitzer defines rhetoric as "a mode of altering reality, not by the direct application of energy to objects, but by the creation of discourse which changes reality through the mediation of thought and action" (4).

5. Paul Feigenbaum, *Collaborative Imagination: Earning Activism through Literacy Education* (Carbondale: Southern Illinois University Press, 2015).

6. Suresh A. Canagarajah, "Introduction," in *Literacy as Translingual Practice: Between Communities and Classrooms*, edited by A. Suresh Canagarajah (New York: Routledge, 2013), 1–10. Canagarajah also uses the term "difference-in-similarity" (4).

7. Canagarajah, "Introduction," 2 (emphasis mine).

8. LuMing Mao, "Redefining Indigenous Rhetoric: From Places of Origin to Translingual Spaces of Interdependence-in-Difference," in *Literacy as Translingual*

Practice, ed. Canagarajah, 47–56; Morris Young, "Neither Asian nor American: The Creolization of Asian American Rhetoric," in *Literacy as Translingual Practice*, ed. Canagarajah, 59–69; Lisa R. Arnold, "'The Worst Part of the Dead Past': Language Attitudes, Policies, and Pedagogies at Syrian Protestant College, 1866–1902," *College Composition and Communication*, 66, no. 2 (2014): 276–300; Nancy Bou Ayash, "Conditions of (Im)Possibility: Postmonolingual Language Representations in Academic Literacies," *College English* 78, no. 6 (2016): 555–77.

9. Bruce Horner, Cynthia Selfe, and Tim Lockridge, "Translinguality, Transmodality, and Difference: Exploring Dispositions, Change in Language, and Learning," *Enculturation Intermezzo*, http://intermezzo.enculturation.net/01/ttd-horner-selfe-lockridge/index.htm; Jody Shipka, "Transmodality in/and Processes of Making: Changing Dispositions and Practice," *College English* 78, no. 3 (2016): 250–57. As I discuss later, in Shipka's discussion of transmodality, she reminds us of the value of "older" technologies.

10. See particularly Canagarajah's edited collection, *Literacy as Translingual Practice*.

11. Barbara Biesecker, "Coming to Terms with Recent Attempts to Write Women into the History of Rhetoric," *Philosophy & Rhetoric* 25, no. 2 (1992): 157; Jacqueline Jones Royster and Gesa E. Kirsch, *Feminist Rhetorical Practices: New Horizons for Rhetoric, Composition, and Literacy Studies* (Carbondale: Southern Illinois University Press, 2012), 60.

12. Carol Mattingly, "Telling Evidence: Rethinking What Counts in Rhetoric," *Rhetoric Society Quarterly* 32, no. 1 (2002): 105.

13. Mattingly, "Telling Evidence," 104; Faith Kurtyka, "'Get Excited People!' Gendered Acts of Literacy in a Social Sorority," *Literacy in Composition Studies*, 3, no. 2 (2015): 22–43; Faith Kurtyka, "We're Creating Ourselves Now: Crafting as Feminist Rhetoric in a Social Sorority," *Peitho Journal* 18, no. 2 (2016): 25–44. Kurtyka's scholarship on the rhetorical work of sorority women also takes up the idea of engaging with those who do not "fit neatly" into the field's conception of valued and valuable rhetorical work.

14. Mattingly, "Telling Evidence," 102.

15. Quoted in Mattingly, "Telling Evidence," 99–100.

16. Mattingly, "Telling Evidence," 99–100.

17. Royster and Kirsch, *Feminist Rhetorical Practices*, 100.

18. Maureen Daly Goggin, "Introduction: Threading Women," in *Women and the Material Culture of Needlework and Textiles, 1750–1950*, edited by Maureen Daly Goggin and Beth Fowkes Tobin (Surrey, UK: Ashgate, 2009), 4.

19. See Carol Mattingly, *Appropriate[ing] Dress: Women's Rhetorical Style in Nineteenth-Century America* (Carbondale: Southern Illinois University Press, 2002); Goggin and Tobin, eds., *Women and the Material Culture of Needlework and Textiles*; Rosalyn Collings Eves, "A Recipe for Remembrance: Memory and Identity in African-American Women's Cookbooks," *Rhetoric Review* 24, no. 3 (2005): 280–97; Elaine Showalter, *Sister's Choice: Tradition and Change in American Women's Writing: The Clarendon Lectures 1989* (Oxford: Clarendon Press, 1989); Goggin, "Introduction: Threading Women," 1–10.

20. Goggin, "Introduction: Threading Women," 4.

21. Heather Pristash, Inez Schaechterle, and Sue Carter Wood, "The Needle as the Pen: Intentionality, Needlework, and the Production of Alternate Discourses of

Power," in *Women and the Material Culture of Needlework and Textiles,* ed. Goggin and Tobin, 27.

22. Pristash, Schaechterle, and Wood, "The Needle as the Pen," 13.

23. Feigenbaum, *Collaborative Imagination*, 40, 20.

24. "Read Oprah Winfrey's Rousing Golden Globes Speech," *CNN*, January 10, 2018, https://www.cnn.com/2018/01/08/entertainment/oprah-globes-speech-transcript/index.html.

25. Amisha Padnani and Jessica Bennett, "Overlooked," *New York Times*, March 8, 2018, https://www.nytimes.com/interactive/2018/obituaries/overlooked.html. The "Overlooked" series provides an activist counternarrative by asking the newspaper's readers to write in and nominate the less noted, but no less notable, people who should have been commemorated.

26. Charlotte Hogg, "Sorority Rhetorics as Everyday Epideictic," *College English* 80, no. 5 (2018): 423–48. Hogg points this out in her analysis of sorority rhetorics as what she calls "everyday epideictic."

27. Feigenbaum, *Collaborative Imagination*, 20.

28. Krista Ratcliffe, *Rhetorical Listening: Identification, Gender, Whiteness* (Carbondale: Southern Illinois University Press, 2005).

29. Throughout this project, I situate the temporal-spatial orientation of the translingual approach in relation to discussions of materiality and modality in composition. In an earlier piece on the recontextualization of the Gee's Bend quiltmakers, I discussed the recontextualization at work in the quilts (implicitly rooted in a translingual framework) in relation to material-rhetorical practice. See Jay Jordan, "Material Translingual Ecologies," *College English* 77, no. 4 (2005): 364–82. Jordan brings together translingual and object-oriented rhetorical approaches to materiality in his scholarship.

30. Jacqueline Jones Royster, "Academic Discourses or Small Boats on a Big Sea," in *ALT DiS: Alternative Discourse and the Academy*, edited by Christopher Schroeder, Helen Fox, and Patricia Bizzell (Portsmouth, NH: Boynton/Cook-Heinemann, 2002), 25.

31. Jennifer Sinor, *The Extraordinary Work of Ordinary Writing: Annie Ray's Diary* (Iowa City: University of Iowa Press, 2002), 5.

32. Sinor, *Extraordinary Work*, 7.

33. Vanessa Kraemer Sohan, "Relocalized Listening: Responding to All Student Texts from a Translingual Starting Point," in *Reworking English in Rhetoric and Composition: Global Discussion of Interrogations, Local Interventions*, edited by Bruce Horner and Karen Kopelson (Carbondale: Southern Illinois University Press, 2014); Vanessa Kraemer Sohan, "Thinking Differently about Language Difference: Relocalized Listening," PhD diss., University of Louisville, 2011; Alastair Pennycook, *Language as a Local Practice* (New York: Routledge, 2010). In defining the aims and goals of my framework, I draw on my framing in "Relocalized Listening," particularly the introduction to that chapter (191–95), and in my dissertation. See note 95, below, for a discussion of my choice of recontextualization *versus* relocalization.

34. Vershawn Ashanti Young and Aja Y. Martinez, with Julie Anne Naviaux, "Introduction: Code-Meshing as World English," in *Code-Meshing as World English: Pedagogy, Policy, Performance*, edited by Vershawn Ashanti Young and Aja Y. Martinez, with Julie Anne Naviaux (Urbana, IL: NCTE, 2011), xix–xxxi. See their work for more on the ideological nature of Standard Written English (SWE).

35. Committee on CCCC Language Statement, "Students' Right to Their Own

Language," *College Composition and Communication* 25, no. 3 (1974): 1–18; Bruce Horner and John Trimbur, "English-Only and U.S. College Composition," *College Composition and Communication* 53, no. 4 (2002): 594–630; Bruce Horner and Min-Zhan Lu, *Representing the "Other": Basic Writers and the Teaching of Basic Writing* (Urbana, IL: NCTE, 1999); Jacqueline Jones Royster, "When the First Voice You Hear Is Not Your Own," *College Composition and Communication* 47, no. 1 (1996): 29–40. The publication of the "Students' Rights to Their Own Language" document is often heralded as the start of such discussions, though scholars within and outside the field had been discussing such issues for years, particularly with the advent of the open-admissions movement. The translingual approach builds on Horner and Trimbur's work on the predominance of English Only as an ideology in US composition, Min-Zhan Lu and Bruce Horner's scholarship on basic writing and error, and Royster's work listening to and recovering the voices of African American woman rhetoricians.

36. Missy Watson and Rachel Shapiro, "Clarifying the Multiple Dimensions of Monolingualism: Keeping Our Sights on Language Politics," *Composition Forum* 38 (2018), http://compositionforum.com/issue/38/monolingualism.php#note1. I refer to *Standard Academic English (*SAE) throughout, though scholars also refer to Standard Written English (SWE), and Edited American English, among other appellations. In their discussion of the continued dominance of monolingual ideologies inside and outside the academy, Watson and Shapiro follow in the footsteps of Rosina Lippi-Green by marking their chosen designation (*Standardized English) with an asterisk in order to deny the term its mythological power.

37. Patricia Bizzell, "The Intellectual Work of 'Mixed' Forms of Academic Discourses," in *ALT DiS*, ed. Schroeder, Fox, and Bizzell, 1–10; A. Suresh Canagarajah, *Translingual Practice: Global Englishes and Cosmopolitan Relations* (New York: Routledge, 2013); Peter Elbow, *Vernacular Eloquence: What Speech Can Bring to Writing* (Oxford: Oxford University Press, 2012); Sidney I. Dobrin, "A Problem with Writing (about) 'Alternative' Discourse," in *ALT DiS*, ed. Schroeder, Fox, and Bizzell, 45–56; Keith Gilyard, *Voices of the Self: A Study of Language Competence* (Detroit: Wayne State University Press, 1991); Carmen Kynard, "'New Life in This Dormant Creature': Notes on Social Consciousness, Language, and Learning in a College Classroom," in *ALT Dis*, ed. Schroeder, Fox, and Bizzell, 31–44; Min-Zhan Lu, "Living-English Work," *College English* 68, no. 6 (2006): 605–18; Min-Zhan Lu, "Metaphors Matter: Transcultural Literacy," *JAC: A Journal of Composition Theory* 29, no. 1–2 (2009): 285–93; Min-Zhan Lu, "Professing Multiculturalism: The Politics of Style in the Contact Zone," in Horner and Min-Zhan Lu, *Representing the "Other"*; LuMing Mao, "Re-Clustering Traditional Academic Discourse," in *ALT Dis*, ed. Schroeder, Fox, and Bizzell, 112–25; Malea Powell, "Listening to Ghosts: An Alternative (Non)Argument," in *ALT DiS*, ed. Schroeder, Fox, and Bizzell, 11–22; Paul Kei Matsuda, "Alternative Discourses: A Synthesis," in *ALT DiS*, ed. Schroeder, Fox, and Bizzell, 191–96; Royster, "Academic Discourses"; Geneva Smitherman, *Word from the Mother: Language and African Americans* (New York: Routledge, 2006); Villanueva, *Bootstraps*; Vershawn Ashanti Young, *Your Average Nigga: Performing Race, Literacy, and Masculinity* (Detroit: Wayne State University Press, 2007); David Wallace, *Compelled to Write: Alternative Rhetoric in Theory and Practice* (Logan: Utah State University Press, 2011). This scholarship includes work on topics as diverse as "basic" writers and writing, multiculturalism, L2/ESL/ELL writers and writing, bilingual-

ism, multilingualism, cultural rhetorics, comparative rhetorics, African American Vernacular Englishes, code-switching, and code-meshing. The scholars who have engaged in such work within the field are too many to name, but these are some of the most prominent and oft-cited scholars.

38. Bruce Horner, Min-Zhan Lu, Jacqueline Jones Royster, and John Trimbur, "Opinion: Language Difference in Writing: Toward a Translingual Approach," *College English* 73, no. 3 (2011): 303–21.

39. Horner, Lu, Royster, and Trimbur, "Opinion," 311.

40. Horner, Lu, Royster, and Trimbur, "Opinion," 303. See the following for definitions of translingual approaches to writing and translingualism: Bruce Horner, Samantha NeCamp, and Christiane Donahue, "Toward a Multilingual Composition Scholarship: From English Only to a Translingual Norm," *College Composition and Communication* 63, no. 2 (2011): 269–300; A. Suresh Canagarajah, "Multilingual Strategies of Negotiating English: From Conversation to Writing," *JAC* 29, nos. 1–2 (2009): 17–48; A. Suresh Canagarajah, "Translanguaging in the Classroom: Emerging Issues for Research and Pedagogy," *Applied Linguistics Review* 2 (2011): 1–28; A. Suresh Canagarajah, "World Englishes as Code-Meshing," afterword, in *Code-Meshing as World English*, ed. Young and Martinez, 273–81.

41. Horner, NeCamp, and Donahue, "Toward a Multilingual Composition Scholarship," 287; Horner, Lu, Royster, and Trimbur, "Opinion," 305.

42. For an excellent visual representation of the differences between translingual, multilingual, and monolingual approaches, see Horner, NeCamp, and Donahue, "Toward a Multilingual Conposition Scholarship," 287.

43. Horner, Lu, Royster, and Trimbur, "Opinion," 305.

44. Horner, Lu, Royster, and Trimbur, "Opinion," 310.

45. Canagarajah, "Introduction," 4.

46. Lu, "Metaphors," 290–91.

47. Vanessa Kraemer Sohan, "Working English(es) as Rhetoric(s) of Disruption," *JAC* 29, nos. 1–2 (2009): 270–76. I make the connection between this orientation to language practice and listening in "Working Englishes." See also Canagarajah, "Introduction," 5. Canagarajah also recognizes the importance of rhetorical listening.

48. Ratcliffe, *Rhetorical Listening*, 1. In my previous work, I have connected the translingual approach with rhetorical listening. See Sohan, "Relocalized Listening," 193. Canagarajah also makes this connection in his introduction to *Literacy as Translingual Practice*, 5.

49. Rebecca Lorimer Leonard, "Writing across Languages: Developing Rhetorical Attunement," in *Translingual Literacy Practice*, ed. Canagarajah, 162–68; Rebecca Lorimer Leonard, "Multilingual Writing as Rhetorical Attunement," *College English* 76, no. 3 (2014): 227–47. Leonard uses the term *rhetorical attunement* to describe her subjects' dispositions toward language and literacy practice.

50. Canagarajah, "Introduction," 1.

51. Horner, Selfe, and Lockridge, "Translinguality, Transmodality."

52. Horner, Selfe, and Lockridge, "Translinguality, Transmodality," 6.

53. Horner, Selfe, and Lockridge, "Translinguality, Transmodality," 10 (emphasis mine).

54. Min-Zhan Lu and Bruce Horner, "Translingual Literacy, Language Difference, and Matters of Agency," *College English* 75, no. 6 (2013): 582–607; Canagarajah, "Introduction," 1–10; Bruce Horner and Karen Kopelson, eds., *Reworking English*

in Rhetoric and Composition: Global Interrogations, Local Interventions (Carbondale: Southern Illinois University Press, 2014); Dwight Atkinson et al., "Clarifying the Relationship between L2 Writing and Translingual Writing: An Open Letter to Writing Studies Editors and Organization Leaders," *College English* 77, no. 4 (2015): 383–86; Keith Gilyard, "The Rhetoric of Translingualism," *College English* 78, no. 3 (2016): 284–89; Carrie Kilfoil, "Beyond the 'Foreign' Language Requirement: From a Monolingual to a Translingual Ideology in Rhetoric and Composition Graduate Education," *Rhetoric Review* 34, no. 5 (2015): 426–44.

55. Dylan B. Dryer, "Appraising Translingualism," *College English* 78, no. 3 (2016): 274–83; Rebecca Lorimer Leonard and Rebecca Nowacek, "Transfer and Translingualism," *College English* 78, no. 3 (2016): 258–64.

56. Anis Bawarshi, "Beyond the Genre Fixation: A Translingual Perspective on Genre," *College English* 78, no. 3 (2016): 244.

57. Carolyn Miller, "Genre as Social Action," *Quarterly Journal of Speech* 70 (1984): 151–67; Bawarshi, "Beyond the Genre Fixation," 244.

58. Bawarshi, "Beyond the Genre Fixation," 246. Bawarshi writes that such an approach enables "students and instructors to examine the meanings and relations conditioned by genres as well as to open up genre actions to new *interplays* of possible meanings and linguistic relations" (245).

59. Bawarshi, "Beyond the Genre Fixation," 246.

60. Bawarshi, "Beyond the Genre Fixation."

61. Bawarshi, "Beyond the Genre Fixation," 245, 247.

62. Bawarshi, "Beyond the Genre Fixation," 247.

63. Laura Gonzales, *Sites of Translation: What Multilinguals Can Teach Us about Digital Writing and Rhetoric* (Ann Arbor: University of Michigan Press, 2018); Laura Gonzales, "Multimodality, Translingualism, and Rhetorical Genre Studies," *Composition Forum* 31 (2015), http://compositionforum.com/issue/31/multimodality.php; Bawarshi, "Beyond the Genre Fixation," 247.

64. Gonzales, "Multimodality," n.p.

65. Jody Shipka, "Transmodality," 250–57; Jody Shipka, *Toward a Composition Made Whole* (Pittsburgh: University of Pittsburgh Press, 2011).

66. Shipka, "Transmodality," 252.

67. Shipka, "Transmodality," 252–53.

68. Vanessa Kraemer Sohan, "'But a Quilt Is More': Recontextualizing the Discourse(s) of the Gee's Bend Quilts," *College English* 77, no. 4 (2015): 294–316.

69. Min-Zhan Lu and Bruce Horner, "Introduction: Translingual Work," *College English* 78, no. 3 (2016), 214.

70. Christiane Donahue, "'Internationalization' and Composition Studies: Reorienting the Discourse," *College Composition and Communication* 61, no. 2 (2009): 212–43.

71. Ayash, "Conditions of (Im)Possibility"; Arnold, "'The Worst Part of the Dead Past'"; Lisa Arnold, "An Imagined America: Rhetoric and Identity during the First Student Rebellion in the Arab World," *College English* 78, no. 6 (2016): 578–601.

72. Atkinson et al., "Clarifying the Relationship," 383–86. L2 scholars have argued that the translingual approach damages the field's understanding of multilingual pedagogy and overlooks years of L2 scholarship on language, identity, and writing.

73. Villanueva, *Bootstraps*, xii.

74. See, for example, Horner and Trimbur, "English-Only," 594–630. And, more recently, Steven Alvarez, "Official American English Is Best," in *Bad Ideas about Writing*, edited by Cheryl Ball and Drew M. Loewe (Morgantown: West Virginia University Libraries, 2017), 93–98; Watson and Shapiro, "Clarifying," n.p.; Anjali Pattanayak, "There Is One Correct Way of Writing and Speaking," in *Bad Ideas*, ed. Ball and Loewe, 82–87.

75. Lu and Horner, "Translingual Literacy," 585.

76. "Anti-hero," Google Dictionary, accessed October 3, 2018.

77. Lu and Horner, "Translingual Literacy," 597.

78. Lu and Horner, "Translingual Literacy," 588.

79. Lilia Bartolomae, "The Recontextualized Language Patterns of Fluent English and Spanish Bilingual Students in Academic Discourse Situations," PhD diss., Stanford University, 1991, 1.

80. Bartolomae, "Recontextualized Language Patterns" (emphasis mine).

81. Carol Berkenkotter, "Genre Systems at Work: DSM-IV," *Written Communication* 18, no. 3 (2001), 328.

82. Jeff Bezemer and Gunther Kress, "Writing in Multimodal Texts: A Social Semiotic Account of Designs for Learning," *Written Communication* 25, no. 2 (2008): 166–95; Jeff Bezemer and Gunther Kress, *Multimodality, Learning, and Communication: A Social Semiotic Frame* (London: Routledge, 2016). The former provides an earlier version of the framework discussed in the latter.

83. Bezemer and Kress, *Multimodality, Learning, and Communication*, 75 (emphasis mine).

84. Bezemer and Kress, "Writing in Multimodal Texts," 171.

85. Bezemer and Kress, "Writing in Multimodal Texts," 171–72.

86. Bezemer and Kress, "Writing in Multimodal Texts," 173.

87. Bezemer and Kress, "Writing in Multimodal Texts," 77–78.

88. Bezemer and Kress, *Multimodality*, ix.

89. Bezemer and Kress, *Multimodality*, 5–6. Horner, Selfe, and Lockridge, "Translinguality, Transmodality," 15 and 37. In their work on transmodality, Horner, Selfe, and Lockridge point to Kress's scholarship.

90. Bezemer and Kress, "Writing in Multimodal Texts," 172.

91. Bezemer and Kress, "Writing in Multimodal Texts," 173–74. Bezemer and Kress connect the terms "genre" and "frame": "Genres are the semiotic obverse of the social event. They are realized at the textual level; every text has a generic form. Each of these frames/genres defines text in terms of activity, of social relations of participants in an event, and in terms of the use of modes and media. Frames operate at any level: Whatever the semiotic entity is, it requires a frame" (173). They differentiate between composition and design, preferring the term "design," which they define as rhetorical and social (175). Although I can see their purpose and intent in calling such multimodal work "design," I employ "composition" throughout the text, as I aim to define the agents in these studies as writers/composers, in spite of the diverse mediums in which they compose, write, or design. Design can help us see the agency of their compositions; however, I like the term "composing" for its general appeal and its particular connection to writing as a discursive practice. Bruce Horner, *Rewriting Composition: Terms of Exchange* (Carbondale: Southern Illinois University Press, 2016); Jody Shipka, *Toward a Composition Made Whole*.

92. Bezemer and Kress, *Multimodality*, 4.

93. Claire Kramsch, "The Traffic in Meaning: A Response to Mary Louise Pratt," *Asia-Pacific Journal of Teacher Education* 26, no. 1 (2006): 81–86.

94. Kramsch, "The Traffic in Meaning," 103.

95. Pennycook, *Language as a Local Practice*, 34. Pennycook uses "relocalization" to describe the process, so as "to move beyond the notion of 'context' and instead engage with a notion of locality that includes theories of space and movement as part of a new way of thinking about how we relate to place" (35). I employ "recontextualization" instead of "relocalization" throughout this text in order to more clearly situate my work in relation to interdisciplinary discussions on recontextualization and recent discussions of translingual approaches to writing, which continue to use "recontextualization" to describe the composers' inventive use of difference and difference-in-repetition across time, place, and space. While I agree that time, place, and location must be taken into consideration, for the purposes of my project, I do not think a new term (relocalization) is necessary to remind us of the temporal-spatial framework of language practice. In my earlier work on "relocalized listening," I connected the idea of relocalization to recent discussions of rhetorical listening by Krista Ratcliffe and others, a move I also make in relation to recontextualization in this project.

96. Pennycook, *Language as a Local Practice*. Bizzell, "Intellectual Work," 3–4. Bizzell draws on Deepika Bahri to critique the notion of hybridity as overly simplistic and not reflective of the power relations. I also prefer not to view the work of the composers in these case studies as linguistic or modal "hybridity," since this would suggest that the different elements can be separated or pulled apart.

97. Pennycook, *Language as a Local Practice*, 40.

98. Pennycook, *Language as a Local Practice*, 42; Lu and Horner, "Translingual Literacy," 589, 591–92. Lu and Horner provide more detail of the theoretical underpinnings of recontextualization and fertile mimesis, including its use by Judith Butler.

99. Pennycook, *Language as a Local Practice*, 10.

100. Pennycook, *Language as a Local Practice*, 42.

101. Pennycook, *Language as a Local Practice*, 41, 13.

102. Jan Blommaert, *The Sociolinguistics of Globalization* (Cambridge: Cambridge University Press, 2010). Similarly, Blommaert (2) outlines a "theory of changing language in a changing society" that defines language as a mobile resource that changes as it travels through time and space—imagined as made up of horizontal space (spanning neighborhoods, regions, and countries) and vertical space (social, cultural, and political indexical distinctions). "Mobility," in Blommaert's model, "is therefore a trajectory through different stratified, controlled and monitored spaces in which language 'gives you away'" (6). Pennycook, Blommaert, Canagarajah, and others provide us with a view of language as a set of mobile resources and practices that shift and change depending on the context of their use.

103. Lu and Horner, "Translingual Literacy," 585.

104. Lu and Horner, "Translingual Literacy," 592.

105. Judith Butler, *Excitable Speech: A Politics of the Performative* (New York: Routledge, 1997), 147, quoted in Lu and Horner, "Translingual Literacy," 592. Lu and Horner also draw on the work of Anthony Giddens on "structuration" to explain the productive potential of such seeming reproductions, or recontextualizations (587–89).

106. Lu and Horner, "Translingual Literacy," 595.

107. Canagarajah, "Introduction," 5–6.
108. Canagarajah, "Introduction," 6.
109. Canagarajah, "Introduction."
110. LuMing Mao, "Introduction: Searching for the Way: Between the Whats and Wheres of Chinese Rhetoric," *College English* 72, no. 4 (2010), 332.
111. LuMing Mao, "Introduction."
112. Rachel Griffo, "Recontextualizing Composition Studies: Translingual Practice, Representation, and an Enacted Methodology," PhD diss., Indiana University of Pennsylvania, 2015.
113. Elaine Richardson, "'To Protect and Serve': African American Female Literacies," *College Composition and Communication* 53, no. 4 (2002), 680.
114. Lu and Horner, "Translingual Literacy," 591.
115. Royster and Kirsch, *Feminist Rhetorical Practices*, 20.
116. Royster and Kirsch, *Feminist Rhetorical Practices*, 79.
117. Royster and Kirsch, *Feminist Rhetorical Practices*, 71.
118. Royster and Kirsch, *Feminist Rhetorical Practices*, 72–73.
119. Royster and Kirsch, *Feminist Rhetorical Practices*, 75.
120. Royster and Kirsch, *Feminist Rhetorical Practices*, 21.
121. Royster and Kirsch, *Feminist Rhetorical Practices*, xi.
122. Royster and Kirsch, *Feminist Rhetorical Practices*, 61.
123. Suzanne Bordelon, "'Private Letters' for Public Audiences: The Complexities of Ethos in Louise Clappe's *The Shirley Letters from the California Mines, 1851–1852*," *Rhetoric Review* 37, no. 1 (2018): 78.
124. Bordelon, "'Private Letters,'" 78–79.
125. Kathleen J. Ryan, Nancy Myers, and Rebecca Jones, eds., *Rethinking Ethos: A Feminist Ecological Approach to Rhetoric* (Carbondale: Southern Illinois University Press, 2016).
126. Ryan, Myers, and Jones, eds., *Rethinking Ethos,* 111.
127. Royster and Kirsch, *Feminist Rhetorical Practices*, 100.
128. Royster and Kirsch, *Feminist Rhetorical Practices*, 100.
129. Royster and Kirsch, *Feminist Rhetorical Practices*, 101.
130. Anne Ruggles Gere, "Kitchen Tables and Rented Rooms: The Extracurriculum of Composition," *College Composition and Communication* 45, no. 1 (1994): 76, 80.
131. Gere, "Kitchen Tables," 86.
132. Gere, "Kitchen Tables," 85.
133. Gere, "Kitchen Tables," 85. See Gere's brief discussion of white women's clubs in the period from 1880 to the 1920s.
134. Gere, "Kitchen Tables," 89.
135. Nancy Welch, "Living Room: Teaching Public Writing in a Post-Publicity Era," *College Composition and Communication* 56, no. 3 (2005): 474 (some emphasis mine).
136. Sinor, *Extraordinary Work*, 10.
137. John Trimbur, quoted in Paula Mathieu and Diana George, "*Not* Going It Alone: Public Writing, Independent Media, and the Circulation of Homeless Advocacy," *College Composition and Communication* 61, no. 1 (2009): 131.
138. Feigenbaum, *Collaborative Imagination*, 52, citing Paul Rogat Loeb's idea of the perfect standard.

Chapter 1

1. Abraham Holtzman, *The Townsend Movement: A Political Study* (New York: Octagon Books, 1975), 35; John Steele Gordon, "Dr. Townsend's Crusade," *American Heritage* 52, no. 7 (2001): 49; Edwin Amenta, *When Movements Matter: The Townsend Plan and the Rise of Social Security* (Princeton, NJ: Princeton University Press, 2006), 1, 35; Jesse George Murray, ed., *New Horizons (An Autobiography) By Dr. Francis E. Townsend* (Chicago: J. L. Stewart Publishing Co., 1943), 137–40. Townsend's autobiography reproduces the "original" letter, but revises the original figure of $150 to $200, the figure Townsend and his co-founder later settled upon.

2. Murray, *New Horizons*, 138–39; Amenta, *When Movements Matter*, 35. Amenta writes that the original figure was $150, which was later changed by Townsend in his autobiography to $200.

3. Murray, *New Horizons*, 138.

4. Murray, *New Horizons*, 33–36.

5. Amenta, *When Movements Matter*, 36, 61.

6. Amenta, *When Movements Matter*, 61.

7. Holtzman, *Townsend Movement*, 50–51. Though the Townsend leadership claimed millions of Townsendite followers, Holtzman (49) corrects this as a stark exaggeration, presenting evidence of paid club membership from 1938 to 1953, which indicates that at its height in 1939, the movement only claimed 761,624 *paid* members. See also Amenta, *When Movements Matter*, 1. Amenta (3) provides evidence of the movement's immense impact on the elderly: "Townsend clubs claimed nearly a fifth of Americans over sixty years old, 2 million altogether, a size never reached by any organization in the civil rights or women's movement, and the Townsend Plan was raising funds at a more rapid clip than the Democratic Party."

8. I follow Holtzman in capitalizing Townsend Movement throughout, though Amenta very purposefully refers to the movement as the Townsend Plan throughout his text.

9. Amenta, *When Movements Matter*, 4. He notes that sociologists call this the state of being "biographically available."

10. Deborah Brandt, *Literacy in American Lives* (Cambridge: Cambridge University Press, 2001). Brandt (19) defines literacy sponsors as "any agents, local or distant, concrete or abstract, who enable, support, teach, and model, as well as recruit, regulate, suppress, or withhold, literacy—and gain advantage by it in some way. Just as the ages of radio and television accustomed us to having programs brought to us by various commercial sponsors, it is useful to think about who or what underwrites occasions of literacy learning and use."

11. A note on my methodology: I visited the Oregon Historical Society (OHS) archives April 6–9, 2016, where I accessed 2 cubic feet (two boxes) of materials (MSS 1334, Townsend National Recovery Plan, Inc., Records). The materials included letters and other correspondence, newspaper clippings, bulletins, membership lists, campaign materials, and Townsend pamphlets and books. Also included were club manuals, speaker's manuals, scrapbooks, convention materials, identification cards and badges, notebooks, diaries, journals, financial records from 1936 to 1944, pins, photographs, meeting minutes from 1936 to 1944, diaries, and other ephemera from the Townsend Clubs active in Oregon. In addition to Pearl Burkhalter's archive, there were a variety of records related to local clubs and more de-

tailed records of local club leaders Elmer J. and M. Ethel Greenwood. I photographed 112 weekly issues of the *TNW* plus Official Club Bulletins, dating from February 7, 1936, to December 14, 1940 (the archives include issues through May 31, 1958). I was also able to view a film reel produced by Townsend national headquarters, described as "[a] record of Francis E. Townsend's 1935 visit to Eastern Oregon to promote his plan for national economic recovery. Preceded by footage from another source depicting women working in factories with an examination of the effects of industrial automation." At the time, I was unable to access the sound records available in the archives.

I read straight through the first thirty-four issues of the *TNW* included in the archive, then read one issue per month, often backtracking when finding references to previous articles in issues I may have skipped. As I read, I initially coded each article into one of several categories: literacy, advocacy, bureaucracy, materiality, social, multimodality, advertisements, voice/voicing. As I coded, I became most interested in and found the most evidence in the categories of literacy and materiality, and so began to consider how the Townsend Movement served as a literacy sponsor that both encouraged its followers to work within and across diverse modes, media, and genres, and suppressed them from doing so. As I read, I also coded a variety of subpurposes, media, and modes, and I found that the newspaper served a diverse set of purposes for its audience of mostly elderly Townsendite faithful. These included advertising innumerable products both related and unrelated to the movement (ranging from Townsend books and pamphlets to questionable medical cures for bowel impaction) that readers could buy and/or sell to raise money for and promote the movement (while also making a little money themselves); educating readers on the Townsend Plan's official (but often changing) positions on national and local political, policy, and economic debates; modeling and promoting the particular ways Townsendites should read, write, and speak about the movement in their clubs and local communities; modeling and promoting fundraising efforts by individuals and clubs; advertising and promoting national drives related to letter writing, fundraising, and particular elections and bills being pushed by the movement; entertaining readers with successful examples (both serious and silly) of the extreme passion and dedication of Townsendites across the United States; and promoting the plan's appeal to a variety of audiences, including and especially youth as well as the aged. As I began to focus more closely on the kinds of activist literacies sponsored by the Townsend Plan and its clubs, I identified in particular the material literacies promoted by club members (especially women), the Townsend literature and how it circulated within and outside the cubs, the letter-writing campaigns, and the visual education and technological literacies promoted by the movement. For the purposes of this chapter, I focus on the letter-writing campaigns as a form of activist literacy, though (as this note suggests) the *TNW* provides a remarkable (though very biased) snapshot of the political, economic, and social lives of Townsendites across the nation.

12. Royster and Kirsch, *Feminist Rhetorical Practices*, 101.

13. Arthur Schlesinger, *The Age of Roosevelt: The Politics of Upheaval* (Boston: Houghton Mifflin, 1960), 29.

14. Schlesinger, *The Age of Roosevelt*, 29.

15. Schlesinger, *The Age of Roosevelt*, 29.

16. Schlesinger, *The Age of Roosevelt*, 7. On the "old lower-middle classes," see

Sam Tanenhaus, "What Do This Season's Books Tell Us about the Election?" *New York Times,* June 20, 2016, https://www.nytimes.com/2016/06/26/books/review/. Tanenhaus is quoting Schlesinger.

17. Richard L. Neuberger and Kelley Loe, *An Army of the Aged: A History and Analysis of the Townsend Old Age Pension Plan* (Caldwell, ID: Caxton Printers, 1936; rpt., New York: DaCapo Press, 1973), 67–78. According to Neuberger and Loe, and the *TNW*, some Townsendites even went so far as to create imaginary budgets and asked business owners to provide them with loans against the Townsend Plan's eventual passage.

18. Tanenhaus, "What Do This Season's Books Tell Us."

19. Quoted in Tanenhaus, "What Do This Season's Books Tell Us."

20. "Representative Brewster Sees in Townsend Plan Way to Give Balanced Budget to Nation," *TNW*, July 4, 1938, 31, OHS. All references to the *TNW* come from the collection of the OHS in Portland.

21. Holtzman, *Townsend Movement*, 41–43.

22. Holtzman, *Townsend Movement.*

23. Holtzman, *Townsend Movement* (emphasis mine).

24. Holtzman, *Townsend Movement*, 35.

25. Amenta, *When Movements Matter*, 43, 50; Holtzman, *Townsend Movement*, 41–42.

26. Amenta, *When Movements Matter*, 45.

27. Holtzman, *Townsend Movement*, 41–42.

28. Steven Bret Burg, "The Gray Crusade: The Townsend Movement Old Age Politics and the Development of Social Security," PhD diss., University of Wisconsin–Madison, 1999, 136.

29. Amenta, *When Movements Matter*, 42–43.

30. Amenta, *When Movements Matter*, 48; Burg, "Gray Crusade," 3.

31. Amenta, *When Movements Matter*, 39–40. Townsend and Clements changed the $150 monthly pension to $200 for political reasons during the first year of the plan's existence; however, that same number was subsequently dropped as it became a political liability in later years, and there was eventually an attempt to deny the $200 figure was ever a major part of the plan, even by Townsend himself. The same evolution occurred with the plan's funding mechanism: between 1933 and 1935, the initial "federal retail sales tax" to fund the pension was changed to a "transaction sales tax" and then simply a "transaction tax" in order to increase the plan's popular political appeal.

32. Amenta, *When Movements Matter*, 120. Supportive legislation was often stymied in the Ways & Means Committee or brought to the floor for a quick, unsuccessful vote without debate (120–24).

33. Neuberger and Loe, *An Army of the Aged.*

34. Amenta, *When Movements Matter*, 56.

35. Amenta, *When Movements Matter*, 48–49.

36. Amenta, *When Movements Matter*, 117; Holtzman, *Townsend Movement*, 49–54.

37. Burg, "Gray Crusade," 243.

38. Amenta, *When Movements Matter*, 117; quoted in Burg, "Gray Crusade," 243–44, and Holtzman, *Townsend Movement*, 48.

39. Amenta, *When Movements Matter*, 119. Amenta challenges the assertion that

most members were newly unemployed and impoverished by the Great Depression, as Townsend himself had been when he started the movement.

40. Amenta, *When Movements Matter*, 119.

41. Amenta, *When Movements Matter*, 119.

42. "Mandate" [voter polling/interviewing/petitioning], *TNW* insert, n.d.

43. Schlesinger, *Age of Roosevelt*, 40–41. Schlesinger remains ambivalent, though he acknowledges the positive effect of the Townsend Plan on Roosevelt's Social Security policy. He identifies the movement as one of many symptoms of the "politics of upheaval" of FDR's presidency, a symptom that possibly influenced the Social Security Act. Holtzman, *Townsend Movement*, 87. Holtzman also acknowledges the plan's impact on federal Social Security policy.

44. Amenta, *When Movements Matter*, 206–8.

45. Neuberger and Loe, *Army of the Aged*, 12.

46. There are some gaps in the run of the newspapers in the OHS; for example, the archive includes only one issue from 1937.

47. Club Manual, 26–27, OHS.

48. "Speak Softly!" *TNW*, February 13, 1939, 6. The editorial cautions against negative messaging and asks club members to read one another's letters before sending.

49. Murray, *New Horizons*, 131.

50. Official bulletins were later published in the *TNW*, too, but in 1936 the bulletins were published separately as flyers meant to be read aloud at club meetings.

51. See Burg, "Gray Crusade," 241–42, on the power of ladies' auxiliaries. See also "Townsend Plan Merit Told by Georgia Girl," *TNW*, April 27, 1940, 4; "Student Wins Montana Club's Essay Contest," *TNW*, February 13, 1939, 10; "Arizona Clubs Sponsor School Essay Contest," *TNW*, December 16, 1939, 3; "Tennessee Essay Contest Prizes Given Students," *TNW*, May 18, 1940, 11. The *TNW* often reported on movement-sponsored essay-writing contests for young people in local schools. In order to counter the reality of the movement's ongoing struggle to get young people as actively involved as their elderly counterparts, the paper included numerous reports of young people's work in the Townsend Club scene and in essay contests (in which the younger generation wrote essays proclaiming their support of the plan). See "Cue from Women (Evansville, Ind., *Courier*)," *TNW*, May 18, 1940, 7. The reprinted piece discussed the changing role of women in politics and noted the surprise in Congress at the organized writing campaigns by women. "Mostly" the women demonstrate "understanding" and "clear arguments," and their activism suggests that "women in politics" could be a positive trend. The Postmaster-General himself believes women in politics to be a good thing, and women's activism suggests they "take their civic duties seriously" and are interested in "study[ing] public affairs from both partisan and non-partisan angles" (a not-so-subtle acknowledgment of the stereotype that women are dominated by their emotions or by the will of others). The article's inclusion in the *TNW* suggests that the work of women advocating for the Townsend Plan reflected a larger trend, one that countered the general culture's surprise at women's contributions. Although the clubs' activities were still mostly divided by gender, women became more and more central to the clubs and their activities as the movement progressed.

52. "Official Bulletin No. 72," February 7, 1936, OHS.

53. "Official Bulletin No. 74," February 21, 1936, OHS.

54. "Club in Oregon Gives Townsend Facts to Paper," *TNW*, May 11, 1940, 11. The *TNW* praised the club for countering its local paper's account of the "dwindling" of club membership by citing statistics of the club's growth, under the header "How They Dwindle." See also "Official Club Bulletin No. 73: Again Caution," *TNW*, February 6, 1939, 5; "Official Club Bulletin No. 76," *TNW*, February 27, 1939, 5.

55. "A Personal Request," *TNW*, October 3, 1938, 1; "Official Club Bulletin No. 59: Don't Write Letters," *TNW*, October 31, 1938.

56. "Official Club Bulletin No. 75," February 28, 1936, OHS (emphasis in original).

57. Amenta, *When Movements Matter*, 98. Amenta notes the level of vitriol may have come, in part, from the fact that many Townsendites "did not distinguish between the potential friends of old-age benefits but not of the McGroarty bill, or not yet, and the enemies of old-age benefits generally."

58. Amenta, *When Movements Matter*, 85, 90, 93, 94, 189, for more on letter-writing campaigns and specific legislative efforts.

59. "Speak Softly!" *TNW*, February 13, 1939, 6. The editors write that they have heard directly from "resentful" members of Congress about the Townsendites' "threatening and abusive letters"—letters that have put off those who had an open mind about the current Townsend legislation under consideration, H.R. 2. Adopting the tone of a disappointed parent, the editors write that such letters are "certainly . . . not a general practice among Townsend club members," especially since Townsend members have been repeatedly "cautioned . . . to write respectfully and in a friendly tone when urging support of Townsend legislation." Letter writers must avoid threats and coercion, and instead should strive to reflect the legislation itself by remaining "rational, humane," "reasonable," "kindly," and "patient." Members are told that this "matter is of utmost importance" and are told to discuss their letters freely at club meetings, "from the platform" and "from the floor." Clubs are asked to provide "competent aid . . . to Club members who feel they need help in writing to their Representatives and Senators, and every letter written should show that the writer feels that full measure of respect to which the high position held by the Senator or Representative is entitled." Encouraged "to convince rather than alienate," members are told again, "Speak softly!" The editors draw on President Theodore Roosevelt's oft-cited maxim to imply that if the Townsendites can learn to speak softly in their letters, the editors and the organization will carry a big stick for them.

60. "Letters Urging Enactment Flood Rep. Dowell's Office," *TNW*, April 24, 1939, 9 (emphasis mine).

61. "The Honor Roll," *TNW*, April 20, 1940, 13; "Letters Urging Enactment Flood Rep. Dowell's Office," *TNW*, April 24, 1939, 9; "See Townsend Influence in Article by *Chicago Daily News* Columnist," *TNW*, January 23, 1939, 3. "The Honor Roll," "The Open Forum," and other regular columns touted the grassroots political and social activities of individuals and clubs.

62. "Would Have Clubs Deluge Congressmen with Demands," TNW, January 30, 1939, 8. One Townsendite suggests clubs elect a "Corresponding Committee," made up of three to five people, to deluge members of Congress with letters and remind them "that hundreds of thousands of Americans are watching to see how he'll vote on the Townsend measure. We'd get action."

63. "See Townsend Influence in Article by *Chicago Daily News* Columnist," *TNW*, January 23, 1939, 3.

64. "Sen. Nye Endorses Plan," *TNW*, September 5, 1938, 1, 3.

65. "Sen. Nye Endorses Plan," *TNW*, September 5, 1938,1.

66. "Sen. Nye Endorses Plan," *TNW*, September 5, 1938, 1.

67. "Editors Realize Townsend Voters Sway Elections," *TNW*, October 10, 1938, 11; "Editors of Small Papers See Merit in Townsend Plan," *TNW*, October 10, 1939, 12. Clubs depended on local newspapers and editors to tout the plan to their communities, and the *TNW* repeatedly celebrates the role of the "editors of small town dailies and weeklies" who—unlike the "metropolitan press," which has ignored or reluctantly acknowledged the sway of the Townsend Plan—"are in the forefront of the fight to make the elders of the nation Prosperity Agents" and who realize "the political sway of Townsend voters."

68. "The Honor Roll," *TNW*, May 18, 1940, 11.

69. "The Townsend Forum: Reaches Many with Column," February 27, 1939, 9.

70. "Official Club Bulletin No. 111: Announcement of Meetings," *TNW*, November 24, 1939, 10.

71. Staff Correspondent, "Memphis Man Sees Townsend Plan as Sound Philosophy," *TNW*, October 3, 1939, 11.

72. Staff Correspondent, "Memphis Man Sees Townsend Plan as Sound Philosophy," *TNW*, October 3, 1939, 11.

73. Old Age Revolving Pensions, Ltd., to Pearl Burkhalter, February 19, 1936, "Townsend Club—Correspondence to Mrs. P. Burkhalter 1936–1943," MS 1334-1, OHS.

74. Old Age Revolving Pensions, Ltd., to Pearl Burkhalter, February 19, 1936.

75. Harrisburg, Oregon, Club No. 1 to West Linn Club No. 1, February 10, 1936, "Townsend Club—Correspondence to Mrs. P. Burkhalter 1936–1943," MS 1334-1, OHS.

76. Harrisburg, Oregon, Club No. 1 to West Linn Club No. 1, February 10, 1936.

77. "Charter or Permit of the Townsend National Recovery Plan, Inc.," March 16, 1937, "Townsend Club—Bulletins 1936," MS 1334-1, OHS. The certificate is framed in green and embellished with Townsend's image in the upper lefthand corner and lists Pearl Burkhalter as president and Mrs. Laura Priesler as club secretary.

78. Ryan et al., *Rethinking Ethos*, 23.

79. Ryan et al., *Rethinking Ethos*, 23.

80. "Official Bulletin—Special," March 13, 1936, "Townsend Club—Bulletins 1936," MSS 1334-1, OHS.

81. Pearl Burkhalter to Congressman McNary [handwritten note/draft], "Townsend Club—Correspondence from Mrs. Pearl Burkhalter, 1939–1945," MSS 1334-1, OHS; Louis Resnick to Mr. and Mrs. Burkhalter, March 27, 1936, "Townsend Club—Correspondence to Mrs. P. Burkhalter 1936–1943," OHS.

82. Pearl Burkhalter to Congressman McNary [handwritten draft/note], April 12, 1936, "Townsend Club—Correspondence from Mrs. Pearl Burkhalter 1939–1945," MSS 1334-1, OHS.

83. Charles McNary to Pearl Burkhalter, April 20, 1936, "Townsend Club—Correspondence to Mrs. Pearl Burkhalter 1936–1943," MS 1334-1, OHS.

84. James William Bryan to Pearl Burkhalter, April 3, 1936, "Townsend Club—Correspondence from Mrs. Pearl Burkhalter 1939–1945," MSS 1334-1, OHS.

85. Though the brief responses Burkhalter received from McNary's and Resnick's offices were addressed to "Mr. and Mrs. Burkhalter," based on her handwritten notes

and other letters in the archives, it is clear that Pearl Burkhalter took it upon herself to write the response to Resnick.

86. Louis Resnick to Mr. and Mrs. Burkhalter, March 27, 1936 [handwritten notes by Burkhalter on front and back of Resnick letter], "Townsend Club—Correspondence to Mrs. P. Burkhalter 1936–1943," OHS.

87. Louis Resnick to Mr. and Mrs. Burkhalter, March 27, 1936 [handwritten notes by Burkhalter on front and back of Resnick letter]. I have chosen to present the archival documents as written, without correcting minor errors of spelling or calling them out with the use of "sic," though I have included a few bracketed notations to add context or enhance readability.

88. "Write Congressman without Delay," *TNW*, May 11, 1940, 1. The article implores Townsendites to write, but asks them to be courteous, to ask for a specific action, and to demand a response.

89. Aja Y. Martinez, "A Plea for Critical Race Theory Counterstory: Stock Story versus Counterstory Dialogues concerning Alejandra's 'Fit' in the Academy," *Composition Studies* 42, no. 2 (2014): 33–55; Victor Villanueva, "*Memoria* Is a Friend of Ours: On the Discourse of Color," *College English* 67, no. 1 (2004): 9–19.

90. Pearl Burkhalter to President Roosevelt, September 23, 1940, "Townsend Club—Correspondence from Mrs. Pearl Burkhalter 1939–1945," MSS 1334-1, OHS.

91. Pearl Burkhalter to President Roosevelt, September 23, 1940.

92. Note that it is quite difficult to differentiate between commas and periods in the typed correspondence in Burkhalter's files.

93. Pearl Burkhalter to Representative [unnamed], April 19, 1939, "Townsend Club—Correspondence from Mrs. Pearl Burkhalter 1939–1945," MSS 1334-1, OHS.

94. Pearl Burkhalter to Representative [unnamed], April 19, 1939.

95. Pearl Burkhalter to Representative [unnamed], April 19, 1939.

96. Amenta, *When Movements Matter*, 203. The shift from a national to a state agenda focused on Old-Age Assistance (OAA) programs came about in part due to the start of World War II (along with a round of new failures on the national level). Amenta also cites the continued popularity of the plan in Oregon in the 1940s and the push for the "Little Townsend Plan" in 1946 (208).

97. Horner, Selfe, and Lockridge, "Translinguality, Transmodality," 18.

98. Pearl Burkhalter to Charles McNary, March 16, 1939, "Townsend Club—Correspondence from Mrs. Pearl Burkhalter 1939–1945," MSS 1334-1, OHS.

99. Pearl Burkhalter to Charles McNary, March 16, 1939.

100. Amenta, *When Movements Matter*, 148.

101. Arthur Moore to Pearl Burkhalter, September 6, 1941, "Townsend Club—Correspondence to Mrs. Burkhalter from Arthur Moore [ARYE organization director]," MSS 1334-1, OHS; Arthur Moore to Owen Buckbee (treasurer, Oregon City Club), May 14, 1942, "Townsend Club—Correspondence to Mrs. Burkhalter from Arthur Moore," MSS 1334-1, OHS.

102. Arthur Moore to Pearl Burkhalter, July 2, 1939, "Townsend Club—Correspondence to Mrs. Burkhalter from Arthur Moore," MSS 1334-1, OHS.

103. Arthur Moore to Pearl Burkhalter, September 5, 1939, "Townsend Club—Correspondence to Mrs. Burkhalter from Arthur Moore," MSS 1334-1, OHS.

104. Pearl Burkhalter, "Townsend Club—Letters to the Editor—Newspaper Clippings by Pearl Burkhalter," MSS 1334-1, OHS.

105. Pearl Burkhalter, "Townsend Club—Letters to the Editor—Newspaper Clippings by Pearl Burkhalter," August 8, 1937, MSS 1334-1, OHS.

106. Pearl Burkhalter, "Relief and Pensions," January 29, 1939, "Townsend Club—Letters to the Editor—Newspaper Clippings by Pearl Burkhalter," MSS 1334-1, OHS.

107. Pearl Burkhalter, "People's Forum: Assail Legislature," March 15, 1940, "Townsend Club—Letters to the Editor—Newspaper Clippings by Pearl Burkhalter," MSS 1334-1, OHS.

108. Pearl Burkhalter, "People's Forum: Assail Legislature," March 15, 1940.

109. Pearl Burkhalter, "People's Forum: Need Charity Here," December 16, 1939, "Townsend Club—Letters to the Editor—Newspaper Clippings by Pearl Burkhalter," MSS 1334-1, OHS; Pearl Burkhalter, "Charity Begins at Home, Editor, *The Enterprise*," May 17, 1941, "Townsend Club—Letters to the Editor—Newspaper Clippings by Pearl Burkhalter," MSS 1334-1, OHS.

110. Pearl Burkhalter, "Charity Begins at Home, Editor, *The Enterprise*," May 17, 1941, "Townsend Club—Letters to the Editor—Newspaper Clippings by Pearl Burkhalter," MSS 1334-1, OHS.

111. Pearl Burkhalter, "Could Add to Beauty," n.d., "Townsend Club—Letters to the Editor—Newspaper Clippings by Pearl Burkhalter," MSS 1334-1, OHS.

112. Pearl Burkhalter, "People's Forum: Editor, *The Enterprise*, 'Again I have to . . . ,'" October 31, 1941, "Townsend Club—Letters to the Editor—Newspaper Clippings by Pearl Burkhalter," MSS 1334-1, OHS.

113. Pearl Burkhalter, "People's Forum: Editor, *The Enterprise*, 'Again I have to . . . ,'" October 31, 1941.

114. Pearl Burkhalter, "People's Forum: Editor, *The Enterprise*, 'Again I have to . . . ,'" October 31, 1941.

115. Pearl Burkhalter, "People's Forum: Editor, *The Enterprise*, 'Please allow me . . . ,'" n.d. [c. 1941], "Townsend Club—Letters to the Editor—Newspaper Clippings by Pearl Burkhalter," MSS 1334-1, OHS.

116. Pearl Burkhalter, "People's Forum: Editor, *The Enterprise*, 'The only way . . . ,'" n.d. [c. 1941], "Townsend Club—Letters to the Editor—Newspaper Clippings by Pearl Burkhalter," MSS 1334-1, OHS.

117. Pearl Burkhalter, "People's Forum: Editor, *The Enterprise*, 'The only way . . . ,'" n.d. [c. 1941].

118. Pearl Burkhalter, "Censures Working Mothers," n.d., "Townsend Club—Letters to the Editor—Newspaper Clippings by Pearl Burkhalter," MSS 1334-1, OHS.

119. Pearl Burkhalter, "Censures Working Mothers," n.d.

120. Pearl Burkhalter, "Censures Working Mothers," n.d.

121. Pearl Burkhalter, "Editor, *The Enterprise*, 'The Human Side,'" n.d., "Townsend Club—Letters to the Editor—Newspaper Clippings by Pearl Burkhalter," MSS 1334-1, OHS.

122. Pearl Burkhalter, "Editor, *The Enterprise*, 'The Human Side,'" n.d.

123. Pearl Burkhalter, "Editor, *The Enterprise*, 'The Human Side,'" n.d.

124. Pearl Burkhalter, "Editor, *The Enterprise*, 'The Human Side,'" n.d.

125. Pearl Burkhalter, "Editor, *The Enterprise*, 'The Human Side,'" n.d.

126. Arthur Moore to Secretary of Sponsoring Committee, January 30, 1940, "Townsend Club—Letters Miscellaneous, 1936–1943," MSS 1334-1, OHS; Arthur Moore, Receipt, February 11, 1940, "Townsend Club—Finances Receipts & Expenditures, 1936–1942," MSS 1334-1, OHS.

127. Arthur Moore, Receipt Monmouth Herald, "Townsend Club—Finances Receipts & Expenditures, 1936–1942," MSS 1334-1, OHS.

128. George Nelson to Pearl Burkhalter, Secretary, "Operating Report," March

25, 1939, "Townsend Club—Correspondence to Mrs. P. Burkhalter 1936–1943," MSS 1334-1, OHS.

129. OARP, Inc., to Pearl Burkhalter, September 3, 1936, "Townsend Club—Correspondence to Mrs. P. Burkhalter 1936–1943," OHS.

130. "Speaker's Manual 1935," MS 1334-1, OHS. A speaker's manual in the archives serves as both a guidebook and a scrapbook for another local leader in the Oregon Townsend Movement, E. J. Greenwood, whose work for the movement also included establishing a periodical for publishing texts (fiction and nonfiction) by local Townsendites. The guidebook includes "The Art of Making a Speech," and sample speeches.

131. "2nd National Townsend Convention," "Townsend Club—Meeting Minutes 1936 Convention Notes 1937," MS 1334-1, OHS.

132. "2nd National Townsend Convention."

133. "Townsend Club—Townsend Campaign Songs and Pledges," MS 1334-1, OHS.

134. Though I do not have the time to explore the arts here, Townsendites composed, performed, and distributed plays inspired by members' stories and utopian dreams of a life post–Townsend Plan (many included a before-and-after-the-Townsend-Plan story arc).

135. Mrs. D. Juttner to Pearl Burkhalter [handwritten note], "Townsend Club—Correspondence to Mrs. P. Burkhalter 1936–1943," MS 1334-1, OHS.

136. "How Does Our ARYE Club Grow," "Townsend Club—Townsend Campaign Songs and Pledges," MS 1334-1, OHS.

137. "How Does Our ARYE Club Grow," "Townsend Club—Townsend Campaign Songs and Pledges," MS 1334-1, OHS.

138. "Cock*Eyed World," "Townsend Club—Townsend Campaign Songs and Pledges," MS 1334-1, OHS.

139. "To Our Townsend Secretaries," "Townsend Club—Townsend Campaign Songs and Pledges," MS 1334-1, OHS. Though Burkhalter does not sign her name to many of these documents, the handwriting is consistent and the signed letters throughout the file folders indicate they came from her archive.

140. Andrea A. Lunsford and Lisa Ede, "Representing Audience: 'Successful' Discourse and Disciplinary Critique," *College Composition and Communication* 47, no. 2 (1996): 173–74.

141. Lunsford and Ede, "Representing Audience," 174.

142. Ryan et al., "Rethinking *Ethos*," 25.

143. Pearl Burkhalter to Clyde S. Shaw, February 21, 1940, "Townsend Club-Correspondence from Mrs. Pearl Burkhalter 1936–1945," MS 1334-1, OHS.

Chapter 2

1. "Emancipation Proclamation," Abraham Lincoln Papers at the Library of Congress, https://memory.loc.gov/ammem/alhtml/almintr.html, accessed July 8, 2017. Lincoln had been waiting to announce the proclamation since mid-July, when he first circulated a draft among his secretaries of navy and war and his cabinet. They convinced him to hold off announcing until the Union could claim a much-needed victory, which did not come until Antietam.

2. William Robinson, ed., *The Annual Monitor for 1883 or Obituary of the*

Members of the Society of Friends in Great Britain and Ireland for the Year 1882 (London: Barrett Sons & Co., 1882), 173. According to Robinson, her delegation included a friend from Baltimore, James Carey, and one or two other female Quakers. See Richard Mott, ed., *Memoir and Correspondence of E. P. Gurney* (Philadelphia: J. B. Lippincott & Co., 1884), 307. According to Mott, she was accompanied by John M. Whitall, Hannah B. Mott, and Carey.

3. William Wistar Comfort, "Quaker Visitors to American Presidents in the Nineteenth Century," *Bulletin of Friends' Historical Association* 38, no. 2 (1949): 72; George B. Johnson, "The Quakerism of Abraham Lincoln," *Bulletin of Friends Historical Association* 28, no. 2 (1939): 63. Quaker scholars cite the encounter as the "best-known of Quaker visits to Lincoln," who, they also note, claimed some Quaker ancestry himself. Henry J. Cadbury, "Briefer Notices," *Quaker History* 55, no. 2 (1966): 122–26; David Elton Trueblood, *Abraham Lincoln: Theologian of American Anguish* (New York: Harper & Row, 1973). Cadbury cites Trueblood, who argues that Lincoln's response to Gurney "is parallel to his 'Meditation on the Divine Will' and to his Second Inaugural" (125). Margaret Hope Bacon, *Mothers of Feminism: The Story of Quaker Women in America* (San Francisco: Harper & Row, 1986). Bacon is one of the few scholars to cite Gurney outside of her encounters with Lincoln.

4. Robinson, *Annual Monitor*, 178.

5. Mott, *Memoir*, 322; Daniel Bassuk, "The Missing Quaker Letter," *Friends Journal*, February 1, 1987, 16. A Quaker and religious studies scholar, Bassuk cites Lincoln scholar F. Lauriston Bullard, among others, to corroborate Mott's claim that Gurney's letter was in Lincoln's pocket on April 14, 1865. Bacon, *Mothers of Feminism*, 122. Bacon writes that despite extensive research, she has found no evidence for the letter being in Lincoln's pocket. See also "Artifacts of Assassination," American Treasures of the Library of Congress: Memory Gallery B, http://www.loc.gov/exhibits/treasures/tr11b.html#obj54, accessed April 27, 2008. The Library of Congress exhibit further undermines the legend; its display of the contents of Lincoln's pockets at the time of his assassination does not include the letter.

6. Daniel Bassuk, *Abraham Lincoln and the Quakers*, Pendle Hill Pamphlet No. 273 (Wallingford, PA: Pendle Hill Publishing, 1987), 13.

7. Cheryl Glenn, *Unspoken: A Rhetoric of Silence* (Carbondale: Southern Illinois University Press, 2004); Ratcliffe, *Rhetorical Listening*.

8. Karlyn Kohrs Campbell, *Man Cannot Speak for Her: A Critical Study of Early Feminist Rhetoric*, 2 vols. (New York: Greenwood Press, 1989), 1:1.

9. Campbell, *Man Cannot Speak*.

10. Sheila Wright, "Gaining a Voice: An Interpretation of Quaker Women's Writing, 1740–1850," *Quaker Studies* 8, no. 1 (2003): 40.

11. Bacon, *Mothers of Feminism*, 1.

12. Bacon, *Mothers of Feminism*, 33–34.

13. Patricia Bizzell and Bruce Herzberg, eds., *The Rhetorical Tradition: Readings from Classical Times to the Present*, 2nd ed. (Boston: Bedford / St. Martin's, 2001), 749; Karlyn Kohrs Campbell, "Pluralism in Rhetorical Criticism: The Case of Lucretia Mott's 'Discourse on Woman,'" *Rhetoric Society Quarterly* 25 (1995): 7; Joy Ritchie and Kate Ronald, eds. *Available Means: An Anthology of Women's Rhetoric(s)* (Pittsburgh: University of Pittsburgh Press, 2001). Campbell and other feminist historiographers have sought to recover the contributions of early Quaker feminist rhetoricians, such as Margaret Fell, Angelina and Sarah Grimké, Lucretia Coffin Mott,

Abby Kelley Foster, Amy Post, and others. Quaker women's rhetoric is anthologized in collections, including Bizzell and Herzberg's *Rhetorical Traditions*, Campbell's *Man Cannot Speak*, and Joy S. Ritchie and Kate Ronald, eds., *Available Means: An Anthology of Women's Rhetoric(s)* (Pittsburgh: University of Pittsburgh Press, 2001), among others. See also Mattingly, *Appropriate[ing] Dress*; Jane Donawerth, *Conversational Rhetoric: The Rise and Fall of a Women's Tradition 1600–1900* (Carbondale: Southern Illinois University Press, 2012). Quaker women's work has also been included in studies by Mattingly, Donawerth, and many others, and has been the focus of journal articles too numerous to list here, but notably including a *Rhetoric Society Quarterly* special issue devoted to Lucretia Coffin Mott's "Discourse on Woman" (1995).

14. Bizzell and Herzberg, *Rhetorical Tradition*, 989; Jami Carlacio, "'Ye Knew Your Duty, But Ye Did It Not': The Epistolary Rhetoric of Sarah Grimké," *Rhetoric Review* 21, no. 3 (2002): 247–63; Campbell, "Pluralism," 7. In addition to writing in support of abolition, women were often forced to defend their right to speak.

15. Robinson, *Annual Monitor*, 153. Gurney was said to be "an engaging child." Mott, *Memoir*, 7, 13, 14. She was schooled at home, then at a Philadelphia school run by Elizabeth Cox, and when she was eleven, at Friends' Boarding School in Westtown, Pennsylvania, where she studied "very happily" for several years. She was forced to leave at fourteen to help care for her ill father (she did not return after his death in 1816). She is described as having a quick, if sometimes impulsive, personality and was encouraged by her teachers to pursue friendships and correspondence with her classmates, activities seen as "promot[ing] the ready expression of their feelings" (7–8). Elizabeth Kimball, "Commonplace, Quakers, and the Founding of Haverford School," *Rhetoric Review* 30, no. 4 (2011): 377–78. Gurney's Quaker education most likely focused on the importance of "truth, the experimental, and the useful"; she would have had very little, if any, rhetorical instruction, something that had explicitly been rejected by William Penn and others in favor of a more experiential educational approach (373).

16. Mott, *Memoir*, 198. One of the most instrumental of these friendships was her relationship with Hannah C. Backhouse, "a valuable minister from England" whom she met in 1830 and remained close to until Backhouse's death in 1850.

17. Tony Seaton, "Travel and Touring in England by Elite Quaker, Industrial Families in the Long Century: The Journeys of Mary-Anne Schimmelpenninck (Née Galton) of Birmingham (1778–1856)," *Quaker Studies* 20, no. 1 (2015): 120. Eliza met J. J. Gurney when traveling to England to meet Backhouse in 1836. The Gurneys "were wealthy and influential, of high culture, and remarkable for piety and devotion, many of them prominent in the Society of Friends" (61).

18. Mott, *Memoir*, 61. As mistress of the household, Gurney was afforded additional material resources but was also under some pressure "to act with the holy consistency befitting a Christian minister, under circumstances to which her previous experience afforded little, if any parallel." Gurney references this pressure in a letter to a friend, in which she describes her "vast responsibilities" as potentially "overwhelming," were it not for "the grace of our Lord Jesus Christ." Larry H. Ingle, *Quakers in Conflict: The Hicksite Reformation* (Knoxville: University of Tennessee Press, 1986), xiii; Bacon, *Mothers of Feminism*, 92. Following the doctrinal split between reformists and orthodox Quakers in 1827, the orthodox J. J. Gurney became a divisive figure in the United States and the United Kingdom. In the United States, mostly rural, "Hicksite" Quakers (so called after Quaker Elias Hicks) sought to main-

tain individualistic, quietist traditions, the "primacy of the Christ within the believer over the Christ of the Bible," and the freedom to speak out at meetings without fear of discipline. Ingle, *Quakers in Conflict*, xiv, 14; Bacon, *Mothers of Feminism*, 92. Orthodox evangelicals like J. J. Gurney represented the more urban, elite, wealthy, and powerful Quakers, who wanted to turn outward, "break from the past," and develop a more structured and organized church based on a dogmatic formal reading of the Bible as *the* Word of God. Bacon, *Mothers of Feminism*, 94–95. In J. J. Gurney's travels in the United States during 1837 (following his voyage there with Eliza), he preached an evangelical theology of adherence to scripture and led numerous revivals, which led to another split within Orthodox Quakers, the Wilburite-Gurneyite split of 1845.

19. Mott, *Memoir*, 72–73.

20. Mott, *Memoir*, 72–73.

21. Mott, *Memoir*, 37.

22. Mott, *Memoir*, 39.

23. Bacon, *Mothers of Feminism*, 32.

24. Bacon, *Mothers of Feminism*, 32.

25. Wright, "'Gaining a Voice,'" 37–38.

26. Wright, "'Gaining a Voice,'" 38.

27. Mott, *Memoir*, 37–38.

28. Mott, *Memoir*, 39 (emphasis mine).

29. Bacon, *Mothers of Feminism*, 32.

30. Howard Brinton, *A Guide to Quaker Practice,* Pendle Hill Pamphlet No. 20 (Philadelphia: Pendle Hill, 1955), 56.

31. Brinton, *Guide*, 49–53.

32. Brinton, *Guide*, 53.

33. Bacon, *Mothers of Feminism*, 96. Despite Fry's being one of the best known of the prison reformers, Bacon reports that she "had mixed feelings about women carrying out public roles and often wished she could be more retiring."

34. Mott, *Memoir*, 56–57.

35. Mott, *Memoir*, 263.

36. Phillip Sipiora, "Introduction: The Ancient Concept of *Kairos*," in *Rhetoric and Kairos: Essays in History, Theory, and Praxis*, edited by Phillip Sipiora and James S. Baumlin (Albany: State University of New York Press, 2002), 1.

37. James L. Kinneavy, "*Kairos* in Classical and Modern Rhetorical Theory," in *Rhetoric and Kairos*, ed. Sipiora and Baumlin, 58.

38. Kinneavy, "*Kairos* in Classical," 61.

39. Carolyn R. Miller, "Foreword," in *Rhetoric and Kairos*, ed. Sipiora and Baumlin, xi.

40. Miller, "Foreword," xii–xiii.

41. William C. Trapani and Chandra A. Maldonado, "*Kairos*: On the Limits to Our (Rhetorical) Situation," *Rhetoric Society Quarterly* 48, no. 3 (May 2018): 278–86.

42. Brinton, *Guide*, 16.

43. Brinton, *Guide*, 19–20.

44. Campbell, *Man Cannot Speak*, 1:11.

45. Brinton, *Guide*, 20.

46. Amelie Frost Benedikt, "On Doing the Right Thing at the Right Time: Towards an Ethics of *Kairos*," in *Rhetoric and Kairos*, ed. Sipiora and Baumlin, 233.

47. Kinneavy, "*Kairos* in Classical," 71. The third being good will.

48. Joy S. Ritchie and Kate Ronald, "Introduction: A Gathering of Rhetorics," in *Available Means*, ed. Ritchie and Ronald, xxii.
49. Ritchie and Ronald, "Introduction."
50. Ritchie and Ronald, "Introduction," xviii.
51. Kathleen J. Ryan, Nancy Myers, and Rebecca Jones, "Introduction: Identifying Feminist Ecological *Ethē*," in *Rethinking Ethos*, ed. Ryan, Myers, and Jones, 6.
52. Ryan, Myers, and Jones, "Introduction," 3.
53. Ryan, Myers, and Jones, "Introduction," 11.
54. Mott, *Memoir*, 86.
55. Mott, *Memoir*, 86.
56. Mott, *Memoir*, 86–87.
57. Mott, *Memoir*, 88.
58. Michael P. Graves, "One Friend's Journey," *Rhetoric and Public Affairs* 7, no. 4 (2004): 518. See Howard Brinton on the distinction between "threshing meetings" and "opportunities" as two forms of Quaker ministry (*Guide*, 24–25).
59. Glenn, *Unspoken*, xi.
60. Brinton, *Guide*, 17 (emphasis mine).
61. Brinton, *Guide*, 90.
62. Brinton, *Guide*, 90–91.
63. Brinton, *Guide*, 92 (emphasis mine).
64. Benedikt, "On Doing the Right Thing," 230.
65. Mott, *Memoir*, 92.
66. Mott, *Memoir*, 94–95.
67. Mott, *Memoir*, 93.
68. Mott, *Memoir*.
69. Mott, *Memoir*, 85.
70. Mott, *Memoir*, 289.
71. Mott, *Memoir*, 126.
72. Mott, Memoir, 127.
73. Benedikt, "On Doing the Right Thing," 226.
74. Mott, *Memoir*, 128.
75. Mott, *Memoir*, 129.
76. Mott, *Memoir*, 130.
77. Aristotle, *Rhetoric* 1415b14–20. Quoted in Kinneavy, "*Kairos* in Classical," 73.
78. Glenn, *Unspoken*, 9.
79. Mott, *Memoir*, 130.
80. Margaret D. Zulick and Michael Leff, "Time and the 'True Light' in Lucretia Mott's 'Discourse on Woman,'" *Rhetoric Society Quarterly* 25 (1995): 20–31. See also David Henry, "Text in Context: Lucretia Mott's 'Discourse on Woman,'" *Rhetoric Society Quarterly* 25 (1995): 11–19.
81. Mott, *Memoir*, 276.
82. Mott, *Memoir*, 104.
83. Mott, *Memoir*, 105.
84. Mott, *Memoir*, 106.
85. Mott, *Memoir*, 113.
86. Mott, *Memoir*, 117.
87. Mott, *Memoir*, 263.
88. Mott, *Memoir*, 263.

89. Mott, *Memoir*, 263.
90. Mott, *Memoir*, 263–64.
91. Mott, *Memoir*, 265.
92. Mott, *Memoir*, 266.
93. Mott, *Memoir*, 272–73.
94. Mott, *Memoir*, 272–73.
95. Mott, *Memoir*, 272–73.
96. Mott, *Memoir*, 277–78.
97. Mott, *Memoir*, 278.
98. Mott, *Memoir*, 274.
99. Mott, *Memoir*, 281–84.
100. Hugh Barbour and J. William Frost, *The Quakers* (Richmond, IN: Friends United Press, 1988). Though "some 'Orthodox' Quakers of 1828 were socially conservative, many Orthodox Quakers were liberal reformers, active in service programs, hospitals, prisons, and even against slavery." Barbour and Frost (193–94) hold up J. J. Gurney as "the best model" for such work, noting his travel in America and the West Indies, and his publication of "an open letter to Henry Clay" proposing the end of slavery in the West Indies and America. Gurney continued to promote abolition in Washington, DC, and Barbour and Frost argue (194) that he employed "liberal methods, based on sympathy and persuasion, [which] were typical also of his sister Elizabeth Fry's work for women prisoners, and other reform work by English and 'Orthodox' Friends."
101. Mott, *Memoir*, 307.
102. Barbour and Frost, *The Quakers*, 197.
103. Margaret Hope Bacon, *The Quiet Rebels: The Story of the Quakers in America* (Philadelphia: New Society Publishers, 1985), 116.
104. Bacon, *Quiet Rebels,* 116.
105. Bacon, *Quiet Rebels*, xiv, xvii; Barbour and Frost, *The Quakers*, 197.
106. Bacon, *Quiet Rebels*, 117; Barbour and Frost, *The Quakers*, 198.
107. Barbour and Frost, *The Quakers*, 198.
108. Bacon, *Quiet Rebels*, 117.
109. Barbour and Frost, *The Quakers*, 198.
110. Mott, *Memoir*, 307.
111. E. P. Gurney, "E. P. Gurney [October 26, 1862] (Copy of Interview with Abraham Lincoln)," Abraham Lincoln Papers at the Library of Congress, https://www.loc.gov/item/mal1870500/, accessed April 27, 2005. The Lincoln Papers date the interview October 26, 1862, though a footnote to her letter requesting the interview suggests the exact date is unknown. Mott, *Memoir*, 308–15. Gurney's memoir quotes an unnamed delegation member's description of the interview.
112. Though I refer to all versions of the interview, I depend most heavily on the reproduction in Gurney's memoir, which is the longest and seems most consistent in style and tone with Gurney's writing and speech in the rest of her correspondence. Part of the inconsistency between the memoir's version and the Lincoln Papers version is the ordering of the conclusion of the speech. Although the two versions agree on the message, tone, and even most of the content, the Lincoln Papers version is more straightforward in its rendering, while the memoir is more in line with the speaking style associated with Quaker rhetorical practice.
113. Robinson, *Annual Monitor*, 173.

114. Robinson, *Annual Monitor*, 173. Braithwaite provides context for the timing by obliquely referencing the Union surrender at the Battle of Harpers Ferry and subsequent "victory" at Antietam, as well as Lincoln's call for increased troops. "1862 Battle of Harpers Ferry," National Park Service, https://www.nps.gov/hafe/learn/historyculture/1862-battle-of-harpers-ferry.htm, accessed November 20, 2017.

115. "The Proclamation," *National Republican*, September 30, 1862, Primary Documents of American History, Library of Congress Chronicling America: Historic American Newspapers, http://www.loc.gov/rr/program/bib/ourdocs/EmanProc.html, accessed October 10, 2017.

116. Edwin J. Bronner, "Articles in Quaker Periodicals" *Quaker History* 52, no. 2 (1963): 118–19.

117. Joshua Wolfshank, "Lincoln's Great Depression," *Atlantic*, October 2005, https://www.theatlantic.com/magazine/archive/2005/10/lincolns-great-depression/304247/, accessed September 9, 2017.

118. Robinson, *Annual Monitor*, 173.

119. Robinson, *Annual Monitor*, 173.

120. E. P. Gurney, [October 26, 1862] (Copy of Interview); Robinson, *Annual Monitor*, 173.

121. Mott, *Memoir*, 306; Brinton, *Guide*, 56.

122. Bacon, *Mothers of Feminism*, 95. Due to their wealth, power, and privilege, J. J. Gurney and other orthodox Quakers were more likely to be influenced by Victorian mores regarding gender (in)equality than were their more radical Hicksite counterparts. And J. J. Gurney seemed to hold contradictory views about the status of women: he both defended women's "right to preach under the direct leading of the spirit" and "warned that they must not usurp authority over men, as the apostle Paul had said."

Gurney's life's work potentially complicates how we think about the roles and purposes of consolation and sentimentality in nineteenth-century women's writing. She also composed and edited poetry and prose, including E. P. Kirkbride Gurney, *Heart Utterances at Various Periods of a Chequered Life* (unpublished), HathiTrust Digital Library, accessed on January 10, 2018, http://hdl.handle.net/2027/nyp.334330666-155; *Heart Utterances of a Chequered Life* (unknown publication date, most likely after her death); E. P. Gurney, *The Garland: Selections from Various Authors by E. P. Gurney* (Philadelphia: Porter and Coates, 1879), HathiTrust Digital Library, accessed on January 10, 2018, https://babel.hathitrust.org. Gurney compiled her own and others' poetry in *The Garland*. Mary Louise Kete, *Sentimental Collaborations: Mourning and Middle-Class Identity in Nineteenth-Century America* (Durham: Duke University Press, 2000). It is possible to argue, following Kete, that Gurney's poetry and other writing reinforce community ties by affirming sentimentalism's utopian promise, but I would argue that Gurney's literary output also functions to reaffirm the Quaker belief in the divine-human bond that becomes the foundation for the inter-human bonds and reform efforts she engages in later in life.

123. Mott, *Memoir*, 302–6. In a letter to Gurney, her friend Thomas Evans writes of how important and precious her friendship has been and underscores the importance of her messages of consolation to him, while also acknowledging the labor involved in Gurney's continued work. He urges her to continue her ministry as "messenger of consolation," even if she may not feel up to the challenge (she had expressed some frustration to him with her role as a host of local Quaker meetings).

124. Mott, *Memoir*, 309 (emphasis mine).

125. See Chaïm Perelman and Lucy Olbrechts-Tyteca, *The New Rhetoric: A Treatise on Argumentation*, translated by John Wilkinson and Purcell Weaver (Notre Dame, IN: University of Notre Dame Press, 1969), 53, on community values. See also Dale L. Sullivan, "The Ethos of Epideictic Encounter," *Philosophy and Rhetoric* 26 (1993): 113–33. Sullivan suggests that the purposes of epideictic rhetoric are supported by the rhetor's *ethos*, which he defines (118) as having five characteristics: reputation, vision, authority, good reason, and "consubstantiality with the audience."

126. The much briefer version of her speech included in her obituary says, "She then proceeded to assure him of the deep sympathy which in common with the members of her own religious Society, and indeed with every true-hearted citizen of the United States, she had felt for the President in his arduous duties" (174). Robinson, *Annual Monitor*.

127. E. P. Gurney, [October 26, 1862] (Copy of Interview).

128. *Oxford English Dictionary* (*OED*), Florida International University Libraries, s.v. "sympathy."

129. Michael L. Birkel, *A Near Sympathy: The Timeless Quaker Wisdom of John Woolman* (Richmond, IN: Friends United Press, 2003), xiii.

130. *OED*, s.v. "sympathy."

131. "With Malice toward None: The Abraham Lincoln Bicentennial Exhibition: Frederick Douglass Describing Lincoln," Library of Congress, https://www.loc.gov/exhibits/lincoln/ext/al0177.html?loclr=blogtea, accessed December 1, 2017. See also Cheryl Lederle and Bernice Ramirez, "Frederick Douglass on Abraham Lincoln: The Writer and Abolitionist Remembers the President in Library of Congress Primary Sources," Library of Congress, Teaching with the Library of Congress, February 7, 2013, https://blogs.loc.gov/teachers/2013/02; Frederick Douglass, "Oration in Memory of Abraham Lincoln, April 14, 1876," TeachingAmericanHistory.org, accessed December 1, 2017, http://teachingamericanhistory.org/library/document/oration-in-memory-of-abraham-lincoln/. The ambivalent position of the abolitionists toward Lincoln was voiced most memorably by Frederick Douglass, whose opinions were valued by Lincoln during Lincoln's lifetime, but who delivered an epideictic speech of praise and blame on the eleventh anniversary of Lincoln's assassination, April 14, 1876 (at the dedication of the Emancipation [or Freedmen's] Memorial in Washington, DC), in which he criticized Lincoln as "pre-eminently the white man's president."

132. David M. Timmerman, "Epideictic Oratory," in *Encyclopedia of Rhetoric: Communication from Ancient Times to the Information Age*, edited by Theresa Enos (New York: Routledge, 1996), 229.

133. For "difficult and puzzling," see Laurent Pernot, *Epideictic Rhetoric: Questioning the Stakes of Ancient Praise* (Austin: University of Texas Press, 2015), vii. For "most problematic" and a catchall, see George A. Kennedy, ed., *Aristotle* On Rhetoric*: A Theory of Civic Discourse*, 2nd ed. (New York: Oxford University Press, 2007). For definition, see Timmerman, "Epideictic Oratory." See also Arthur Walzer, "*Epideictic Rhetoric: Questioning the Stakes of Ancient Praise*, by Laurent Pernot," *Rhetoric Society Quarterly* 46, no. 5 (2016): 1–5.

134. Kennedy, *Aristotle*, 20.

135. Kennedy, *Aristotle*, 21. For conflict and tension, see Perelman and Olbrechts-Tyteca, *The New Rhetoric*, 51. For sociopolitical impact, see Pernot, *Epideictic Rhetoric*, 85.

136. Cynthia Miecznikowski Sheard, "The Public Value of Epideictic Rhetoric,"

College English 58, no. 7 (1996): 765–94. See also Charlotte Hogg on the epideictic as a tool for everyday feminist rhetorical work: "Sorority Rhetorics as Everyday Epideictic," *College English* 80, no. 5 (2018): 423–48.

137. Sheard, "Public Value," 771.

138. Mott, *Memoir*, 25–30, 357–58; Robinson, *Annual Monitor*, 167.

139. Pernot, *Epideictic*, 99. Pernot writes, "Epideictic orators therefore shape awareness and develop a vision of the world," an aim that verges on the utopian. For Quaker peace testimony, see "A Declaration from the Harmless and Innocent People of God, Called Quakers," Quaker.org, http://www.quaker.org/peaceweb/pdecla07.html, accessed January 10, 2018. See also Peter Brock's chapter, "The Quakers in the Civil War," in his *Pioneers of a Peaceable Kingdom: The Quaker Peace Testimony from the Colonial Era to the First World War* (Princeton, NJ: Princeton University Press, 1968): 273–339, www.jstor.org/stable/j.ctt13x0z5p.10.

140. Bassuk, *Abraham Lincoln and the Quakers*, 5–6. Bassuk details David S. Keiser's research into Lincoln's genealogy, which confirms Lincoln's Quaker ancestry.

141. Michael Barram, "Isaiah 58:1–12," *Interpretation: A Journal of Bible & Theology* 69, no. 4 (2015): 460–62.

142. Barram, "Isaiah 58:1–12," 461.

143. Brock, *Pioneers of a Peaceable Kingdom*, xi.

144. Sheard, "Public Value," 770. In discussing idealization, Sheard cites N. Loraux, T. Poulakos, and D. Sullivan.

145. Sheard, "Public Value," xii.

146. Brock, *Pioneers of a Peaceable Kingdom*, 277: Brock juxtaposes Gurney's rhetoric with the "militant anti-militarist propaganda of Ann Branson."

147. Brock, *Pioneers of a Peaceable Kingdom*, xii (emphasis mine).

148. Mott, *Memoir*, 312.

149. Mott, *Memoir*, 308: "And then to see the tears run down the cheeks of our honored President as E. P. Gurney solemnly addressed him! I cannot possibly describe the impressive scene."

150. E. P. Gurney, [October 26, 1862] (Copy of Interview).

151. Robinson, *Annual Monitor*, 175.

152. Robinson, *Annual Monitor*, 175–76.

153. Abraham Lincoln, "Meditation on the Divine Will," in *The Collected Works of Abraham Lincoln*, 9 vols., edited by Roy P. Basler (New Brunswick, NJ: Rutgers University Press, 1953), 5:403–4.

154. Timmerman, "Epideictic Oratory," 231.

155. Abraham Lincoln, "Reply to Emancipation Memorial Presented by Chicago Christians of All Denominations," in *Collected Works*, ed. Basler, 5:419–21; John Burt, *Lincoln's Tragic Pragmatism* (Cambridge, MA: Harvard University Press, 2013), 675–76. Burt quotes this episode in his discussion of Lincoln's disgust with many of the clergymen he encountered.

156. Trueblood, *Abraham Lincoln: Theologian*, 5. Quaker theologian Trueblood suggests that because Gurney and her fellow Quakers did not visit Lincoln "to criticize or to offer unasked advice" but "to give spiritual support to one who sorely needed it, the President responded with unusual warmth [. . .] sharing with them in both silence and prayer," 43. See also Bassuk on *Abraham Lincoln* on Lincoln claiming "honesty and long silences" as part of his Quaker heritage.

157. "E. P. Gurney to Abraham Lincoln, Tuesday, August 18, 1863 (Support)"

and "Benjamin Tatham to Isaac Newton, Friday, October 28, 1864 (Cover letter; charges against officer)," both in Abraham Lincoln Papers at the Library of Congress, https://www.loc.gov/item/mal2569300/ and https://www.loc.gov/item/mal3767800/, accessed April 27, 2005.

158. "E. P. Gurney to Abraham Lincoln, Tuesday, August 18, 1863 (Support)." See also Lincoln, *Collected Works*, ed. Basler, 7:332–33.

159. Sullivan, "Ethos of Epideictic Encounter," 118.

160. Sheard, "Public Value," 781.

161. Cambridge Dictionary, "May," Cambridge Dictionary English Grammar Today, http://dictionary.cambridge.org/grammar/british-grammar/modals-and-modality/may, accessed October 30, 2017.

162. Psalm 20:1–2; Isaiah 9: 7 (KJV). Gurney refers to both passages in her letter.

163. "E. P. Gurney to Abraham Lincoln," Tuesday, August 18, 1863 (Support). A note in the Library of Congress Lincoln Papers states: "On July 15, shortly after the Union victories at Gettysburg and Vicksburg, Lincoln set aside Thursday, August 6 as 'a day for National Thanksgiving, Praise and Prayer.'" See also Lincoln, *Collected Works*, ed. Basler, 6:332–33.

164. Abraham Lincoln, "Proclamation of Thanksgiving, July 15, 1863," in *Collected Works*, ed. Basler, 6:333.

165. Rietveld, "Reviewed Work," 79. Samuel W. Calhoun and Lucas E. Morel, "Abraham Lincoln's Religion: The Case for His Ultimate Belief in a Personal, Sovereign God" *Journal of the Abraham Lincoln Association* 33, no. 1 (2012): 38–74. www.jstor.org/stable/41342666. Joseph R. Fornieri, "Lincoln's Theology of Labor," in *Lincoln and Liberty: Wisdom for the Ages* ed. by Lucas E. Morel (Lexington: University Press of Kentucky, 2014): 207–22.

166. Burt, *Lincoln's Tragic Pragmatism*, 678.

167. Burt, *Lincoln's Tragic Pragmatism*, 678.

168. Abraham Lincoln, "Abraham Lincoln to E. P. Gurney, Sunday, September 04, 1864 (Reply to Gurney's Letter of August 8)," Abraham Lincoln Papers at the Library of Congress, https://www.loc.gov/item/mal3590700/, accessed April 5, 2005.

169. E. P. Gurney, "E. P. Gurney to Abraham Lincoln, Thursday, September 08, 1864 (Reply to Lincoln's Letter of September 4)," Abraham Lincoln Papers at the Library of Congress, https://www.loc.gov/item/mal3605300/, accessed April 7, 2005.

170. 1 John 5:4 (KJV) (emphasis mine).

171. Hebrews 11:1 (KJV): "Now faith is the substance of things hoped for, the evidence of things not seen."

172. Mott, *Memoir*, 371.

173. Bassuk, *Abraham Lincoln*, 9–10.

Chapter 3

1. Quoted in Arnett, "Gee's Bend: The Architecture of the Quilt," 37 (Mensie Lee Pettway); Arnett and Arnett, *Gee's Bend: The Women and Their Quilts*, 104 (Annie Mae Young); "Townsend Plan [quilt]," Wolfsonian–Florida International University Object Collection, accession no. TD1990.122.1, https://digital.wolfsonian.org.

2. Mary Rose Williams, "A Reconceptualization of Protest Rhetoric: Women's Quilts as Rhetorical Forms," *Women's Studies in Communication* 17, no. 2 (1994): 20–44; Cheryl B. Torsney and Judy Elsley, "Introduction," in *Quilt Culture: Tracing*

the Pattern, edited by Cheryl B. Torsney and Judy Elsley (Columbia: University of Missouri Press, 1994), 10; Carole Blair and Neil Michel, "The AIDS Memorial Quilt and the Contemporary Culture of Public Commemoration," *Rhetoric & Public Affairs* 10, no. 4 (2007): 595–626; Beverly Gordon and Laurel Horton, "Turn-of-the-Century Quilts: Embodied Objects in a Web of Relationships," in *Women and the Material Culture of Needlework and Textiles*, ed. Goggin and Tobin, 109; Liz Rohan, "I Remember Mama: Material Rhetoric, Mnemonic Activity, and One Woman's Turn-of-the-Twentieth-Century Quilt," *Rhetoric Review* 23, no. 4 (2004): 368–87; Marsha MacDowell, "Native Quiltmaking: History, Traditions, and Studies," in *Women and the Material Culture of Needlework and Textiles*, ed. Goggin and Tobin, 146; Sonia Christine Arellano, "Quilting the Migrant Trail: Rhetorical Text(iles) and Rehumanizing Narratives," PhD diss., University of Arizona, 2017. Arellano's powerful work provides further evidence for the power of quiltmaking as rhetorical resistance.

3. Maureen Daly Goggin, "Visual Rhetoric in Pens of Steel and Inks of Silk: Challenging the Great Visual/Verbal Divide," in *Defining Visual Rhetorics*, edited by Charles A. Hill and Marguerite Helmers (Mahwah, NJ: Lawrence Erlbaum, 2004), 90–91.

4. Maureen Daly Goggin, "Stitching a Life in 'Pen of Steele and Silken Inke': Elizabeth Parker's *Circa* 1830 Sampler," in *Women and the Material Culture of Needlework and Textiles*, ed. Goggin and Tobin, 37.

5. Pristash, Schaechterle, and Wood, "The Needle as the Pen," 27.

6. Pristash, Schaechterle, and Wood, "The Needle as the Pen," 14 (emphasis in original).

7. Paul Prior and Jody Shipka, "Chronotopic Lamination: Tracing the Contours of Literate Activity," in *Writing Selves / Writing Societies: Research from Activity Perspectives*, edited by Charles Bazerman and David R. Russell (Fort Collins, CO: WAC Clearinghouse, 2003), n.p.

8. Goggin, "Visual Rhetoric," 90.

9. Goggin, "Visual Rhetoric," 90.

10. John Dixon Hunt, "The Sign of the Object," in *History from Things: Essays on Material Culture*, edited by Steven Lubar and W. David Kingery (Washington, DC: Smithsonian Institution Press, 1993), 297.

11. Malea Powell, "Listening to Ghosts: An Alternative (Non)Argument," in *ALT DiS*, ed. Schroeder, Fox, and Bizzell, 12 (emphasis in original).

12. Arnett and Arnett, "On the Map," in *Gee's Bend*, ed. Arnett and Arnett, 36; Alvia Wardlaw, "Introduction: The Quilts of Gee's Bend," in *Gee's Bend*, ed. Arnett and Arnett, 10.

13. William Arnett, "Gee's Bend: The Architecture of the Quilt," in *Gee's Bend: The Architecture of the Quilt*, edited by Paul Arnett, Joanne Cubbs, and Eugene W. Metcalf (Atlanta: Tinwood Books, 2006), 10.

14. Michael Kimmelman, "Art Review: Jazzy Geometry, Cool Quilters," *New York Times*, November 29, 2002, http://www.nytimes.com/2002/11/29/arts/art-review-jazzy-geometry-cool-quilters.html.

15. Michael Kimmelman, "Art/Architecture: The Year in Review—the Critics/10 Moments; Richter, and Cloth, Were Abundant," *New York Times*, December 29, 2002, http://www.nytimes.com/2002/12/29/arts/art-architecture-year-review-critics-10-moments-richter-cloth-were-abundant.html.

16. Lisa Gray, "Made in Gee's Bend: The Alabama Quilters Return to the Houston Museum That Launched Their Art Careers," *Houston Chronicle*, June 11, 2006, http://www.chron.com/entertainment/article/Made-in-Gee-s-Bend-1895640.php.

17. Jane Livingston, "Reflections on the Art of Gee's Bend," in *Gee's Bend*, ed. Arnett and Arnett, 55; Joanne Cubbs, "A History of the Work-Clothes Quilt," in *Gee's Bend: The Architecture*, ed. Arnett, Cubbs, and Metcalf, 76–77.

18. Bruce Horner, "Traditions and Professionalization: Reconceiving Work in Composition," *College Composition and Communication* 51, no. 3 (2000): 389.

19. Lu and Horner, "Translingual Literacy," 585.

20. Lu and Horner, "Translingual Literacy," 585, 597.

21. Lu and Horner, "Translingual Literacy," 590.

22. Lu and Horner, "Translingual Literacy," 584.

23. Richardson, "'To Protect and Serve,'" 680.

24. Richardson, "'To Protect and Serve,'" 680.

25. Lu and Horner, "Translingual Literacy," 584.

26. Peter Marzio, "Foreword," in *Gee's Bend*, ed. Arnett and Arnett, 9.

27. Richardson, "'To Protect and Serve,'" 680.

28. Richardson, "'To Protect and Serve,'" 678.

29. Livingston, "Reflections," in *Gee's Bend*, ed. Arnett and Arnett, 58.

30. Cubbs, "A History of the Work-Clothes Quilt," in *Gee's Bend: The Architecture of the Quilts*, ed. Arnett, Cubbs, and Metcalf, 74–75.

31. Nancy Callahan, *The Freedom Quilting Bee: Folk Art and the Civil Rights Movement* (Tuscaloosa: University of Alabama Press, 1987), 18. The FQB was established during the civil rights movement by Father Francis X. Walter, a young Episcopalian priest who, like Arnett, came into the community, "discovered" the abstract, colorful quilts, and worked with the women of Gee's Bend to sell them to a larger audience (3–30). Callahan notes that it is important to differentiate between the FQB and the Gee's Bend quilters. See Nancy Callahan, "Freedom Quilting Bee," in *Encyclopedia of Alabama*, Alabama Humanities Foundation, last updated April 24, 2015, http://www.encyclopediaofalabama.org/article/h-1628, accessed June 13, 2014. While some of the quilters "belonged to both groups," they are not one and the same.

32. Livingston, "Reflections," 57.

33. Mary Lee Bendolph, "Mama's Song," in *Gee's Bend: The Architecture of the Quilt*, ed. Arnett, Cubbs, and Metcalf, 176.

34. Anna C. Chave, "Dis/Cover/ing the Quilts of Gee's Bend, Alabama," *Journal of Modern Craft* 1, no. 2 (2008): 227.

35. William Arnett, "Gee's Bend: The Architecture," 37. Louisiana P. Bendolph, "A New Generation of 'Housetops,'" in *Gee's Bend: The Architecture of the Quilt*, ed. Arnett, Cubbs, and Metcalf, 194.

36. *Why Quilts Matter: History, Art & Politics*, DVD, Kentucky Quilt Project, 2011.

37. Cuesta Benberry, *Always There: The African-American Presence in American Quilts* (Louisville: Kentucky Quilt Project, 1992); Shelly Zegart, "Myth and Methodology: Shelly Zegart Unpicks African-American Quilt Scholarship," *Selvedge* 21 (2008): 48–56. Mazloomi is interviewed in the DVD *Why Quilts Matter*.

38. Benberry, *Always There*, 15.

39. Benberry, *Always There*, 16.

40. On "Africanisms," see Maude Southwell Wahlman, *Signs and Symbols: African Images in African-American Quilts* (New York: Studio Books, 1993); Eli Leon, *Accidentally on Purpose: The Aesthetic Management of Irregularities in African Textiles and African-American Quilts* (Davenport, IA: Figge Art Museum, 2006). For quilting as a tool used by slaves on the underground railroad, see Jacqueline L. Tobin and Raymond G. Dobard, *Hidden in Plain View: A Secret Story of Quilts and the Underground Railroad* (Columbia: University of Missouri Press, 1994). For an initial critique of the Tobin and Dobard text, see Leigh Fellner, "The Quilt Code—The Other Side," *Quilter's World* 29, no. 5 (2007): 14–16. For more on how to interpellate the mythology of the underground railroad and quilting, see Heather D. Russell, "Quilted Discourse: Writing and Resistance in African Atlantic Narratives," in *Stitching Resistance: Women, Creativity, and Fiber Arts*, edited by Marjorie Agosín (Kent, UK: Solis Press, 2014).

41. Mazloomi quoted in *Why Quilts Matter*.

42. Recontextualization also points to the limits of similar discussions of difference and "alternativity" in composition.

43. Suresh A. Canagarajah, "Afterword: World Englishes as Code-Meshing," in *Code-Meshing as World English: Pedagogy, Policy, Performance*, edited by Vershawn Ashanti Young and Aja Y. Martinez (Urbana, IL: NCTE, 2011), 276.

44. The photograph is discussed and pictured in *Gee's Bend*, ed. Arnett and Arnett, 64.

45. Arnett, "Gee's Bend," in *Gee's Bend: The Architecture*, ed. Arnett, Cubbs, and Metcalf, 17.

46. Arnett, "Gee's Bend," in *Gee's Bend: The Architecture*, ed. Arnett, Cubbs, and Metcalf, 17.

47. Arnett, "Gee's Bend," in *Gee's Bend: The Architecture*, ed. Arnett, Cubbs, and Metcalf, 17.

48. Carl Fleischhauer and Beverly W. Brannan, eds., *Documenting America, 1935–1943* (Berkeley: University of California Press, 1988), 147–48.

49. *Why Quilts Matter*.

50. Callahan, *Freedom Quilting Bee*, 18.

51. Callahan, *Freedom Quilting Bee*, 178.

52. Callahan, *Freedom Quilting Bee*, 116.

53. Callahan, *Freedom Quilting Bee*, 181.

54. Livingston, "Reflections," 58.

55. Loretta P. Bennett, "Dinah, Sally, Tank, Mother, and Me," in *Gee's Bend: The Architecture*, ed. Arnett, Cubbs, and Metcalf, 162.

56. John Beardsley, "Freedom Quilting Bee," in *Gee's Bend*, ed. Arnett and Arnett, 182.

57. Young quoted in Beardsley, "Freedom Quilting Bee," 184, and in *Gee's Bend*, ed. Arnett and Arnett, 366.

58. Beardsley, "Freedom Quilting Bee," 184–85.

59. A photograph of Nettie Young's Basket Weave quilt can be found at http://www.soulsgrowndeep.org/artist/nettie-young/work/basket-weave-freedom-quilting-bee-name-crazy-quilt. A photograph of Candis Pettway's Coat of Many Colors quilt can be found at http://www.soulsgrowndeep.org/artist/candis-pettway/work/coat-many-colors-quilting-bee-name.

60. Beardsley, "Freedom Quilting Bee," 184.

61. Lu and Horner, "Translingual Literacy," 598.
62. Beardsley, "Freedom Quilting Bee," 184.
63. Arnett and Arnett, eds., *Gee's Bend*, 46.
64. Chave, "Dis/Cover/ing the Quilts," 244.
65. Chave, "Dis/Cover/ing the Quilts," 235.
66. Ratcliffe, *Rhetorical Listening*.
67. bell hooks, *Yearning: Race, Gender, and Cultural Politics* (Cambridge, MA: South End Press, 1990), 115.
68. hooks, *Yearning*, 116.
69. hooks, *Yearning*, 118.
70. hooks, *Yearning*, 117.
71. hooks, *Yearning*, 121.
72. hooks, *Yearning*, 120.
73. hooks, *Yearning*, 120.
74. hooks, *Yearning*, 43, 42.
75. Arnett and Arnett, eds., *Gee's Bend*, 81–83; Arnett, Cubbs, and Metcalf, eds., *Gee's Bend: The Architecture*, 177.
76. M. Bendolph, "Mama's Song," in *Gee's Bend*, ed. Arnett and Arnett, 179.
77. Mihaly Csikszentmihalyi, "Why We Need Things," in *History from Things: Essays on Material Culture*, ed. Steven Lubar and W. David Kingery (Washington, DC: Smithsonian Books, 1993), 23.
78. Arnett, Cubbs, and Metcalf, eds., *Gee's Bend: The Architecture*, 74.
79. Wardlaw, "Introduction: The Quilts," in *Gee's Bend*, ed. Arnett and Arnett, 10; Arnett, "Gee's Bend," 21–24.
80. Chave, "Dis/Cover/ing the Quilts," 240.
81. Chave, "Dis/Cover/ing the Quilts," 240.
82. Ratcliffe, *Rhetorical Listening*, 17.
83. Gray, "Made in Gee's Bend"; Bob Johnson, "Internationally Acclaimed Quilter Claims Fraud in Lawsuit Seeking Share of Quilts' Profits," *Daily Herald*, June 6, 2007, http://www.heraldextra.com/business/internationally-acclaimed-quilter-claims-fraud-in-lawsuit-seeking-share-of/; Chave, "Dis/Cover/ing the Quilts," 221–54.
84. Bob Johnson, "Suits Brought by Rural Alabama Quilters Resolved," *Associated Press*, August 25, 2008, accessed May 15, 2011; Glenn McNatt, "Controversy Blankets Gee's Bend Community," *Chicago Tribune*, June 29, 2007, http://articles.chicagotribune.com/2007-07-29/news/0707260758_1_william-arnett-mr-arnett-quilts; Ben Raines, "Gee's Bend: A Fight for Rights," *Mobile Register* (Alabama), June 15, 2007, accessed May 15, 2011.
85. Bernard Herman, "The Quilts of Gee's Bend: How Great Art Gets Lost," *Journal of Modern Craft* 2, no. 1 (2009): 9–15.
86. "Topic: Gee's Bend Quilts in Smithsonian," Artisan's Square, Simple Machines Forum, updated October 17, 2006, accessed May 15, 2011, http://artisanssquare.com/sg_classic/index.php?topic=916.0.
87. "Topic: Gee's Bend Quilts in Smithsonian."
88. "Quilts from Gee's Bend," CraftBanter.com, Jelsoft Enterprises, updated December 31, 2004, accessed May 15, 2011, http://www.craftbanter.com/showthread.php?t=36051.
89. Sally Anne Duncan, "From Cloth to Canvas: Reinventing Gee's Bend Quilts in the Name of Art," *Museum Anthropology* 28, no. 1 (2005): 19–34.

90. Royster, "When the First Voice You Hear Is Not Your Own," 35.

91. Royster, "When the First Voice You Hear Is Not Your Own," 38.

92. "Another Potlucker," *TNW*, September 5, 1938, 8. One Townsendite wrote to explain how to organize a potluck or a picnic (an example of the tacit knowledge the Townsendites had probably never explicitly written down before, much less in a national forum). He or she explained that they charge 35 cents to those who don't bring a dish, and 25 cents to those who do.

93. "Townsend Plan Quilt."

94. "$20 Donation," *TNW*, July 25, 1938, 10; "Quilt Brings $86," *TNW*, July 4, 1938, 14; "$20 is donated," *TNW*, July 4, 1938, 23.

95. "Texas Club's Activities for 1938 Are Summarized," *TNW*, October 31, 1938, 14.

96. "Woman of 75 Finds Way to Help Plan," *TNW*, February 17, 1940, 2.

97. "Brockton, Mass. Sale of This Quilt" [photo], *TNW*, July 4, 1938, 23.

98. "Makes Novel Quilt," *TNW*, June 16, 1939, 6.

99. Brea Barthel, "The AIDS Quilt as a Rhetorical Artifact: Intentional Reshaping of *Ethos*," in *Rhetoric in the Vortex of Cultural Studies: Proceedings of the Fifth Biennial Rhetoric Society of American Conference*, edited by Arthur Walzer and Laurie Ward Gardner (Minneapolis: Burgess, 1992), 187.

100. Barthel, "The AIDS Quilt," in *Rhetoric in the Vortex*, ed. Walzer and Gardner, 187.

101. Blommaert, *The Sociolinguistics of Globalization*. See also Nedra Reynolds, *Geographies of Writing: Inhabiting Places and Encountering Difference* (Carbondale: Southern Illinois University Press, 1997). Pennycook, *Language as a Local Practice*.

102. Blommaert, *Sociolinguistics of Globalization*, 5.

103. "Townsend Plan [quilt]."

104. "South Dakota Rally," *TNW*, May 11, 1940, 3; "J. E. Owens' Wife Back from Wales," *TNW*, May 18, 1940, 9.

105. Arellano, "Quilting the Migrant Trail." Arellano offers an important look at quilting as activism.

106. Amenta, *When Movements Matter*, 55.

107. "Townsend Club Manual 1937," pamphlet (Chicago: Townsend National Recovery Plan, Inc., 1937), "Townsend Club—Campaign Booklets—The Townsend Plan," OHS. A love of music, hymns, and group singalongs can be seen throughout the Townsend literature and in the archives. According to the section of the Townsend Club Manual titled "Order of Business for Clubs, Conventions, and Board Meetings," each gathering should include as the third order of business the singing of "America," followed by the recitation of the Pledge of Allegiance; meetings closed with the "Townsend Pledge" (24). See also "Townsend Club—Townsend Campaign Songs and Pledges," OHS. The songbook from the second national convention, held in Cleveland (1936), opens with a message "To the Townsend Family" emphasizing the collaborative nature of the songs and noting that the contents "have been freely offered by the authors and are gratefully acknowledged," though not all authors are known. Townsend lyrics were set to well-known patriotic and popular songs and hymns, including "Onward Christian Soldiers," "The Battle Hymn of the Republic," "Marching through Georgia," "Auld Lang Syne," "America," "America the Beautiful," "The Battle Cry of Freedom," "Old-Time Religion," and "Over There," among others.

108. "An Open Letter to Representative Dies," *TNW*, February 17, 1940, 3.

109. "Open Letter to Representative Dies."
110. Amenta, *When Movements Matter*, 194.
111. Amenta, *When Movements Matter*, 196.
112. Amenta, *When Movements Matter*, 43.
113. Amenta, *When Movements Matter*, 45.
114. Mattingly, *Appropriate[ing] Dress*, 3.
115. Mattingly, *Appropriate[ing] Dress*, 2.
116. Mattingly, *Appropriate[ing] Dress*, 4.

Conclusion

1. The title and epigraph come from MacGillivray's comments about "the social media giant's legal efforts to protect the privacy of its users." *Above the Law*, October 8, 2012, https://abovethelaw.com/2012/10/quote-of-the-day-what-is-this-thing-you-call-a-pen/

2. Maureen Dowd, "Absorbing the Impossible," *New York Times*, November 9, 2016, https://www.nytimes.com/2016/11/09/opinion/.

3. Sameer Rao, "This 'Black-ish' Scene Perfectly Captures Many Black Americans' Reaction to the Election," *Colorlines*, January 12, 2017, https://www.colorlines.com/articles/black-ish-scene-perfectly-captures-many-black-americans-reaction-election.

4. Quoted in Kathryn Schulz, "What Calling Congress Achieves," *New Yorker*, March 6, 2017, https://www.newyorker.com/magazine/2017/03/06/what-calling-congress-achieves, accessed June 6, 2017.

5. Schulz, "What Calling Congress Achieves."

6. Glenn Whipp. "MacGyver's Pop Cultural Hold on Us," *LA Times*, May 16, 2010, http://articles.latimes.com/2010/may/16/entertainment/la-ca-macgyver-20100516. In popular culture, the word "MacGyver" has come to mean "to solve a problem using only the tools at hand." See Afterbuzz TV Network, "MacGyver," Apple Inc., https://itunes.apple.com/us/podcast/macgyver-reviews-after-show/, accessed June 13, 2018.

7. Phaedra C. Pezzullo and Ted Striphas, "Resistance: Taking a Stand, Struggling to Matter," *Rhetoric Society Quarterly* 48, no. 3 (2018): 311.

8. Pezzullo and Striphas, "Resistance," 312.

9. Doug Hesse, Nancy Sommers, and Kathleen Blake Yancey, "Evocative Objects: Reflections on Teaching, Learning, and Living in Between," *College English* 74, no. 4 (2012): 325; Sherry Turkle, ed., *Evocative Objects: Things We Think With* (Cambridge, MA: MIT Press, 2007).

10. Feigenbaum, *Collaborative Imagination*, 33.

11. Tinnie Pettway, *Gee's Bend Experience: Poems and Tidbits about Life by Quilter Tinnie Pettway* (Alberta, AL: That's Sew Gee's Bend, 2008), 19–20. In her poetry collection, Pettway describes the value of the quilts in "Our Quilt Value," listing the ways the women have used and reused the quilts over the years. Pettway juxtaposes the list of practical uses for the quilts with the buses, planes, cities, and sights the quiltmakers experienced when the Gee's Bend phenomenon took off: "These quilts are taking us everywhere, doing things we / never done / When we drive up crowds cheer and stare / We even dined and sop with millionaires!"

12. Julie Nelson, "'Out of the Mountain of Despair a Stone of Hope': Black Twitter and Rhetorics of Hope," presentation, Rhetoric Society of America Conference, May 30–June 3, 2018.

13. Stephanie Zacharek, Eliana Dockterman, and Haley Sweetland Edwards, "Person of the Year: The Silence Breakers," *Time*, December 18, 2017.

14. Michael Stewart Foley, *Front Porch Politics* (New York: Hill & Wang, 2013), 5.

15. Teresa Welsh, "A Forgotten Era of Activism," *U.S. News and World Report,* November 21, 2013, https://www.usnews.com/opinion/articles/2013/11/21/the-forgotten-era-of-grassroots-american-activism-in-the-70s-and-80s, accessed June 15, 2018.

16. Clarence Lang, *Black America in the Shadow of the Sixties: Notes on the Civil Rights Movement, Neoliberalism, and Politics* (Ann Arbor: University of Michigan Press, 2015); Karissa Haugeberg, *Women against Abortion: Inside the Largest Moral Reform Movement of the Twentieth Century* (Urbana: University of Illinois Press, 2017).

17. Jessica Enoch, *Refiguring Rhetorical Education: Women Teaching African American, Native American, and Chicano/a Students, 1865–1911* (Carbondale: Southern Illinois University Press, 2008); Lindal Buchanan, *Rhetorics of Motherhood* (Carbondale: Southern Illinois University Press, 2013); Carolyn Skinner, *Women Physicians and Professional Ethos in Nineteenth-Century America* (Carbondale: Southern Illinois University Press, 2014); Samantha NeCamp, *Adult Literacy and American Identity: The Moonlight Schools and Americanization Programs* (Carbondale: Southern Illinois University Press, 2014); Alicia Brazeau, *Circulating Literacy: Writing Instruction in American Periodicals, 1880–1910* (Carbondale: Southern Illinois University Press, 2016).

18. Arellano, "Quilting the Migrant Trail."

19. Mathieu and George, "*Not* Going It Alone."

20. Stephen A. Schneider, *You Can't Padlock an Idea: Rhetorical Education at the Highlander Folk School, 1932–1961* (Columbia: University of South Carolina Press, 2014), 2.

21. Carmen Kynard, *Vernacular Insurrections: Race, Black Protest, and the New Century in Composition-Literacies Studies* (Albany: State University of New York Press, 2013).

22. Keith Gilyard and Adam J. Banks, *On African-American Rhetoric* (New York: Routledge, 2018), 7.

23. Lunsford and Ede, "Representing Audience," 174.

24. Maya Rhodan, "Transcript: Read Full Text of President Barack Obama's Speech in Selma," *Time,* March 7, 2015, http://time.com/3736357/barack-obama-selma-speech-transcript/; Barack Obama and David Letterman, interview, "My Next Guest Needs No Introduction," interview, Netflix, accessed January 14, 2017. In his first sit-down interview after his presidency, Obama emphasized the theme of the power of ordinary Americans coming together to engage in collective action and protest.

25. Banks et al., "Just Another Angry Black Man? An Open Letter from Penn State Faculty, Staff and Graduate Students on Nolan Richardson's Firing," *Black Issues in Higher Education* 19, no. 4 (April 11, 2002): 68.

Bibliography

Archival Sources

Abraham Lincoln Papers: Series 1, General Correspondence, 1833–1916, Library of Congress, Washington, DC

Gurney, Eliza P. "E. P. Gurney [October 26, 1862] (Copy of Interview with Abraham Lincoln)." https://www.loc.gov/item/mal1870500/. Accessed April 27, 2005.

Gurney, Eliza P. "E. P. Gurney to Abraham Lincoln, Thursday, September 08, 1864 (Reply to Lincoln's Letter of September 4)." https://www.loc.gov/item/mal3605300/. Accessed April 7, 2005.

Gurney, Eliza P. "E. P. Gurney to Abraham Lincoln, Tuesday, August 18, 1863 (Support)." https://www.loc.gov/item/mal2569300/. Accessed April 27, 2005.

Lincoln, Abraham. "Abraham Lincoln to E. P. Gurney, Sunday, September 04, 1864 (Reply to Gurney's Letter of August 8)." https://www.loc.gov/item/mal3590700/. Accessed April 5, 2005.

Tatham, Benjamin. Letter to Isaac Newton, Friday, October 28, 1864 [cover letter; charges against officer]. https://www.loc.gov/item/mal3767800/. Accessed April 27, 2005.

Abraham Lincoln Papers: Series 2, General Correspondence, 1858–64, Library of Congress, Washington, DC

Gurney, Eliza P. "E. P. Gurney to Abraham Lincoln, [September–October 1862] (Seeks interview)." https://www.loc.gov/item/mal4235700/. Accessed April 27, 2005.

Oregon Historical Society (OHS) Archives, Portland, OR

Townsend National Recovery Plan, Inc., Records [Manuscript], 1935–45. MSS 1334.

Townsend Club—Bulletins 1936.

Townsend Club—Campaign Booklets—The Townsend Plan.

Townsend Club—Correspondence to Mrs. Burkhalter from Arthur Moore.
Townsend Club—Correspondence to Mrs. P. Burkhalter, 1936–43.
Townsend Club—Correspondence from Mrs. Pearl Burkhalter, 1939–45.
Townsend Club—Finances—Receipts & Expenditures, 1936–42.
Townsend Club—Letters—Miscellaneous, 1936–43.
Townsend Club—Letters to the Editor—Newspaper Clippings by Pearl Burkhalter.
Townsend Club—Meeting Minutes 1936, Convention Notes 1937.
Townsend Club—Townsend Campaign Songs and Pledges.

Townsend National Weekly (TNW). Los Angeles, CA: Old Age Revolving Pensions, 1935–58.
The Townsend Plan. Motion picture. MI 01371.

Wolfsonian–Florida International University Object Collection, Miami, FL

"Townsend Plan" [quilt]. Accession number TD1990.122.1. https://digital.wolfsonian.org/WOLF014858/00001.

Secondary Sources

Afterbuzz TV Network. "MacGyver." Apple Inc. https://itunes.apple.com/us/podcast/macgyver-reviews-after-show/. Accessed June 13, 2018.

Alvarez, Steven. "Official American English Is Best." In *Bad Ideas about Writing*, edited by Cheryl Ball and Drew M. Loewe, 93–98. Morgantown: West Virginia University Libraries, 2017.

Amenta, Edwin. *When Movements Matter: The Townsend Plan and the Rise of Social Security*. Princeton, NJ: Princeton University Press, 2006.

Applegarth, Risa. "Working with and Working for: Ethos and Power in Women's Writing." In *Rethinking Ethos: A Feminist Ecological Approach to Rhetoric*, edited by Kathleen J. Ryan, Nancy Myers, and Rebecca Jones, 216–36. Carbondale: Southern Illinois University Press, 2016.

Arellano, Sonia Christine. "Quilting the Migrant Trail: Rhetorical Text(iles) and Rehumanizing Narratives." PhD diss., University of Arizona, 2017.

Arnett, William. "Gee's Bend: The Architecture of the Quilt." In *Gee's Bend: The Architecture of the Quilt*, edited by Paul Arnett, Joanne Cubbs, and Eugene W. Metcalf, 8–65. Atlanta: Tinwood Books, 2006.

Arnett, William, and Paul Arnett, eds. *Gee's Bend: The Women and Their Quilts*. Atlanta: Tinwood Books, 2002.

Arnold, Lisa R. "An Imagined America: Rhetoric and Identity during the First Student Rebellion in the Arab World." *College English* 78, no. 6 (2016): 578–601.

———. "'The Worst Part of the Dead Past': Language Attitudes, Policies, and Pedagogies at Syrian Protestant College, 1866–1902." *College Composition and Communication* 66, no. 2 (2014): 276–300.

"Artifacts of Assassination." *American Treasures of the Library of Congress: Memory Gallery B*. http://www.loc.gov/exhibits/treasures/tr11b.html#obj54. Accessed April 27, 2008.

Atkinson, Dwight, et al. "Clarifying the Relationship between L2 Writing and Translingual Writing: An Open Letter to Writing Studies Editors and Organization Leaders." *College English* 77, no. 4 (2015): 383–86.

Ayash, Nancy Bou. "Conditions of (Im)Possibility: Postmonolingual Language Representations in Academic Literacies." *College English* 78, no. 6 (2016): 555–77.

Bacon, Margaret Hope. *Mothers of Feminism: The Story of Quaker Women in America*. San Francisco: Harper & Row, 1986.

———. *The Quiet Rebels: The Story of the Quakers in America*. Philadelphia: New Society Publishers, 1985.

Baker, Jean. "Varieties of Religious Experience: Abraham and Mary Lincoln." In *Lincoln Revisited: New Insights from the Lincoln Forum*, edited by John Y. Simon et al., 105–16. New York: Fordham University Press, 2007. www.jstor.org/stable/j.ctt13x0bmq.10.

Banks, Adam, et al. "Just Another Angry Black Man? An Open Letter from Penn State Faculty, Staff and Graduate Students on Nolan Richardson's Firing." *Black Issues in Higher Education* 19, no. 4 (April 11, 2002): 68.

Barbour, Hugh, and J. William Frost. *The Quakers*. Richmond, IN: Friends United Press, 1988.

Barnett, Scot. "Toward an Object-Oriented Rhetoric: A Review of Tool-Being: Heidegger and the Metaphysics of Objects and Guerrilla Metaphysics: Phenomenology and the Carpentry of Things by Graham Harman." *Enculturation* 7 (2010). http://enculturation.net/toward-an-object-oriented-rhetoric.

Barram, Michael. "Isaiah 58:1–12." *Interpretation: A Journal of Bible & Theology* 69, no. 4 (2015): 460–62.

Barthel, Brea. "The AIDS Quilt as a Rhetorical Artifact: Intentional Reshaping of *Ethos*." In *Rhetoric in the Vortex of Cultural Studies: Proceedings of the Fifth Biennial Rhetoric Society of American Conference*, edited by Arthur Walzer and Laurie Ward Gardner, 183–92. Minneapolis: Burgess, 1992.

Bartolomae, Lilia. "The Recontextualized Language Patterns of Fluent English and Spanish Bilingual Students in Academic Discourse Situations." PhD diss., Stanford University, 1991.

Bassuk, Daniel. *Abraham Lincoln and the Quakers*. Pendle Hill Pamphlet No. 273. Wallingford, PA: Pendle Hill Publishing, 1987.

———. "The Missing Quaker Letter." *Friends Journal*, February 1, 1987, 16.

Bawarshi, Anis. "Beyond the Genre Fixation: A Translingual Perspective on Genre." *College English* 73, no. 3 (2016): 243–49.

Beardsley, John. "Freedom Quilting Bee." In *Gee's Bend: The Women and Their Quilts*, edited by William Arnett and Paul Arnett, 178–85. Atlanta: Tinwood Books, 2002.

Benberry, Cuesta. *Always There: The African-American Presence in American Quilts*. Louisville: Kentucky Quilt Project, 1992.

Bendolph, Louisiana P. "A New Generation of 'Housetops.'" In *Gee's Bend: The Architecture of the Quilt*, edited by Paul Arnett, Joanne Cubbs, and Eugene W. Metcalf, 188–205. Atlanta: Tinwood Books, 2006.

Bendolph, Mary Lee. "Mama's Song." In *Gee's Bend: The Architecture of the Quilt*, edited by Paul Arnett, Joanne Cubbs, and Eugene W. Metcalf, 172–87. Atlanta: Tinwood Books, 2006.

Benedikt, Amelie Frost. "On Doing the Right Thing at the Right Time: Towards an Ethics of *Kairos*." In *Rhetoric and Kairos: Essays in History, Theory, and Praxis*, edited by Phillip Sipiora and James S. Baumlin, 226–35. Albany: State University of New York Press, 2002.

Bennett, Loretta P. "Dinah, Sally, Tank, Mother, and Me." In *Gee's Bend: The Archi-*

tecture of the Quilt, edited by Paul Arnett, Joanne Cubbs, and Eugene W. Metcalf, 157–71. Atlanta: Tinwood Books, 2006.

Berkenkotter, Carol. "Genre Systems at Work: DSM-IV." *Written Communication* 18, no. 3 (2001): 326–49.

Berry, Patrick W., Gail E. Hawisher, and Cynthia L. Selfe, eds. *Transnational Literate Lives in Digital Times*. Logan, UT: Computers and Composition Digital Press / Utah State University Press, 2012. eBook, http://ccdigitalpress.org/transnational/.

Bezemer, Jeff, and Gunther Kress. "Writing in Multimodal Texts: A Social Semiotic Account of Designs for Learning." *Written Communication* 25, no. 2 (2008): 166–95.

Biesecker, Barbara. "Coming to Terms with Recent Attempts to Write Women into the History of Rhetoric." *Philosophy & Rhetoric* 25, no. 2 (1992): 140–61.

Birkel, Michael L. *A Near Sympathy: The Timeless Quaker Wisdom of John Woolman*. Richmond, IN: Friends United Press, 2003.

Bishop, Wendy, ed. *Elements of Alternate Style: Essays on Writing and Revision*. Portsmouth, NH: Heinemann, 1997.

Bitzer, Lloyd. "The Rhetorical Situation." *Philosophy and Rhetoric* 1, no. 1 (1968): 1–14.

Bizzell, Patricia. "Feminist Methods of Research in the History of Rhetoric: What Difference Do They Make?" *Rhetoric Society Quarterly* 30, no. 4 (2000): 5–17.

———. "The Intellectual Work of 'Mixed' Forms of Academic Discourses." In *ALT DiS: Alternative Discourses and the Academy*, edited by Christopher Schroeder, Helen Fox, and Patricia Bizzell, 1–10. Portsmouth, NH: Boynton/Cook-Heinemann, 2002.

Bizzell, Patricia, and Bruce Herzberg, eds. *The Rhetorical Tradition: Readings from Classical Times to the Present*. 2nd ed. Boston: Bedford / St. Martin's, 2001.

Blair, Carole. "Contemporary U.S. Memorial Sites as Exemplars of Rhetoric's Materiality." In *Rhetorical Bodies*, edited by Jack Selzer and Sharon Crowley, 16–57. Madison: University of Wisconsin Press, 1999.

Blair, Carole, and Neil Michel. "The AIDS Memorial Quilt and the Contemporary Culture of Public Commemoration." *Rhetoric & Public Affairs* 10, no. 4 (2007): 595–626.

Blommaert, Jan. *The Sociolinguistics of Globalization*. Cambridge: Cambridge University Press, 2010.

Bordelon, Suzanne. "Complexities of Ethos in Louise Clappe's *The Shirley Letters from the California Mines, 1851–1852*." *Rhetoric Review* 37, no. 1: 77–89.

Brandt, Deborah. *Literacy in American Lives*. Cambridge: Cambridge University Press, 2001.

Brandt, Deborah, and Katie Clinton. "Limits of the Local: Expanding Perspectives on Literacy as a Social Practice." *Journal of Literacy Research* 34, no. 3 (2002): 337–56.

Brazeau, Alicia. *Circulating Literacy: Writing Instruction in American Periodicals, 1880–1910*. Carbondale: Southern Illinois University Press, 2016.

Bridwell-Bowles, Lillian. "Discourse and Diversity: Experimental Writing within the Academy." *College Composition and Communication* 43, no. 3 (1992): 349–68.

Brinton, Howard. *A Guide to Quaker Practice*. Pamphlet No. 20. Philadelphia: Pendle Hill, 1955.

Brock, Peter. *Pioneers of a Peaceable Kingdom: The Quaker Peace Testimony from the Colonial Era to the First World War*. Princeton, NJ: Princeton University Press, 1968.

Bronner, Edwin J. "Articles in Quaker Periodicals." *Quaker History* 52, no. 2 (1963): 118–19.

Browne, Francis F., ed. *The Every-Day Life of Lincoln (1886)*. Lincoln: University of Nebraska Press, 1995.

Buchanan, Lindal. *Rhetorics of Motherhood*. Carbondale: Southern Illinois University Press, 2013.

Burg, Steven Bret. "The Gray Crusade: The Townsend Movement Old Age Politics and the Development of Social Security." PhD diss., University of Wisconsin–Madison, 1999.

Burt, John. *Lincoln's Tragic Pragmatism*. Cambridge, MA: Harvard University Press, 2013.

Cadbury, Henry J. "Briefer Notices." *Quaker History* 55, no. 2 (1966): 122–26. www.jstor.org/stable/41946518.

Calhoun, Samuel W., and Lucas E. Morel. "Abraham Lincoln's Religion: The Case for His Ultimate Belief in a Personal, Sovereign God." *Journal of the Abraham Lincoln Association* 33, no. 1 (2012): 38–74. www.jstor.org/stable/41342666.

Callahan, Nancy. "Freedom Quilting Bee." In *Encyclopedia of Alabama*, Alabama Humanities Foundation. Updated April 24, 2015. http://www.encyclopediaofalabama.org/article/h-1628. Accessed June 13, 2014.

———. *The Freedom Quilting Bee: Folk Art and the Civil Rights Movement*. Tuscaloosa: University of Alabama Press, 1987.

Campbell, Karlyn Kohrs. "Biesecker Cannot Speak for Her Either." *Philosophy & Rhetoric* 26, no. 2 (1993): 153–59.

———. *Man Cannot Speak for Her: A Critical Study of Early Feminist Rhetoric*. 2 vols. New York: Greenwood Press, 1989.

———. "Pluralism in Rhetorical Criticism: The Case of Lucretia Mott's 'Discourse on Woman.'" *Rhetoric Society Quarterly* 25 (1995): 1–10.

Canagarajah, A. Suresh. "Afterword: World Englishes as Code-Meshing." In *Code-Meshing as World English: Pedagogy, Policy, Performance*, edited by Vershawn Ashanti Young and Aja Y. Martinez, 273–81. Urbana, IL: NCTE, 2011.

———. "Introduction." In *Literacy as Translingual Practice: Between Communities and Classrooms*, edited by A. Suresh Canagarajah, 1–10. New York: Routledge, 2013.

———, ed. *Literacy as Translingual Practice: Between Communities and Classrooms*. New York: Routledge, 2013.

———. "Multilingual Strategies of Negotiating English: From Conversation to Writing." *JAC: A Journal of Composition Theory* 29, nos. 1–2 (2009): 17–48.

———. "Translanguaging in the Classroom: Emerging Issues for Research and Pedagogy." *Applied Linguistics Review* 2 (2011): 1–28.

———. *Translingual Practice: Global Englishes and Cosmopolitan Relations*. New York: Routledge, 2013.

———. "World Englishes as Code-Meshing." Afterword. In *Code-Meshing as World English: Pedagogy, Policy, Performance*, edited by Vershawn Ashanti Young and Aja Y. Martinez, 273–81. Urbana, IL: NCTE, 2011.

Carlacio, Jami. "'Ye Knew Your Duty, But Ye Did It Not': The Epistolary Rhetoric of Sarah Grimké." *Rhetoric Review* 21, no. 3 (2002): 247–63. https://doi.org/10.1207/S15327981RR2103_3.

Carter, Christopher. *Rhetorical Exposures: Confrontation and Contradiction in U.S. Social Documentary Photography*. Tuscaloosa: University of Alabama Press, 2015.

Cavitch, Max. *American Elegy: The Poetry of Mourning from the Puritans to Whitman*. Minneapolis: University of Minnesota Press, 2007.

Chase, Paul. "Questions and Their Answers." *TNW*, January 16, 1939, 7.

Chave, Anna C. "Dis/Cover/ing the Quilts of Gee's Bend, Alabama." *Journal of Modern Craft* 1, no. 2 (2008): 221–54.

Comfort, William Wistar. "Quaker Visitors to American Presidents in the Nineteenth Century." *Bulletin of Friends' Historical Association* 38, no. 2 (1949): 72.

Committee on CCCC Language Statement. "Students' Right to Their Own Language." *College Composition and Communication* 25, no. 3 (1974): 1–18.

Cope, Bill, and Mary Kalantzis, eds. *Multiliteracies: Literacy Learning and the Design of Social Futures*. London: Routledge, 2000.

Csikszentmihalyi, Mihaly. "Why We Need Things." In *History from Things: Essays on Material Culture*, edited by Steven Lubar and W. David Kingery, 20–29. Washington, DC: Smithsonian Books, 1993.

Cubbs, Joanne. "A History of the Work-Clothes Quilt." In *Gee's Bend: The Architecture of the Quilt*, edited by Paul Arnett, Joanne Cubbs, and Eugene W. Metcalf, 76–77. Atlanta: Tinwood Books, 2006.

"A Declaration from the Harmless and Innocent People of God, Called Quakers." Quaker.org. http://www.quaker.org/peaceweb/pdecla07.html. Accessed January 10, 2018.

Deneen, Patrick J. *Democratic Faith*, Princeton, NJ: Princeton University Press, 2005.

Dobrin, Sidney I. "A Problem with Writing (about) 'Alternative' Discourse." In *ALT DiS: Alternative Discourses and the Academy*, edited by Christopher Schroeder, Helen Fox, and Patricia Bizzell, 45–56. Portsmouth, NH: Boynton/Cook-Heinemann, 2002.

Donahue, Christiane. "'Internationalization' and Composition Studies: Reorienting the Discourse." *College Composition and Communication* 61, no. 2 (2009): 212–43.

Donawerth, Jane. *Conversational Rhetoric: The Rise and Fall of a Women's Tradition 1600–1900*. Carbondale: Southern Illinois University Press, 2012.

———. "Women's Reading Practices in Seventeenth-Century England: Margaret Fell's *Women's Speaking Justified*." *Sixteenth Century Journal* 27, no. 4 (2006): 985–1005.

Douglass, Frederick. "Oration in Memory of Abraham Lincoln, April 14, 1876." TeachingAmericanHistory.org. http://teachingamericanhistory.org/library/document/oration-in-memory-of-abraham-lincoln/. Accessed December 1, 2017.

Dowd, Maureen. "Absorbing the Impossible." *New York Times*, November 9, 2016. https://www.nytimes.com/2016/11/09/opinion/.

Dryer, Dylan B. "Appraising Translingualism." *College English* 78, no. 3 (2016): 274–83.

Duncan, Sally Anne. "From Cloth to Canvas: Reinventing Gee's Bend Quilts in the Name of Art." *Museum Anthropology* 28, no. 1 (2005): 19–34.

"1862 Battle of Harpers Ferry." National Park Service. https://www.nps.gov/hafe/learn/historyculture/1862-battle-of-harpers-ferry.htm. Accessed November 20, 2017.

Elbow, Peter. *Vernacular Eloquence: What Speech Can Bring to Writing*. Oxford: Oxford University Press, 2012.

"Emancipation Proclamation." Abraham Lincoln Papers at the Library of Congress. https://memory.loc.gov/ammem/alhtml/almintr.html. Accessed July 8, 2017.

Enoch, Jessica. *Refiguring Rhetorical Education: Women Teaching African American,*

Native American, and Chicano/a Students, 1865–1911. Carbondale: Southern Illinois University Press, 2008.

Eves, Rosalyn Collings. "A Recipe for Remembrance: Memory and Identity in African-American Women's Cookbooks." *Rhetoric Review* 24, no. 3 (2005): 280–97.

Feigenbaum, Paul. *Collaborative Imagination: Earning Activism through Literacy Education*. Carbondale: Southern Illinois University Press, 2015.

Fellner, Leigh. "The Quilt Code—The Other Side." *Quilter's World* 29, no. 5 (2007): 14–16.

Fleischhauer, Carl, and Beverly W. Brannan, eds. *Documenting America, 1935–1943*. Berkeley: University of California Press, 1988.

Foley, Michael Stewart. *Front Porch Politics*. New York: Hill & Wang, 2013.

Fornieri, Joseph R. "Lincoln's Theology of Labor." In *Lincoln and Liberty: Wisdom for the Ages*, edited by Lucas E. Morel, 207–22. Lexington: University Press of Kentucky, 2014. www.jstor.org/stable/j.ctt9qhm08.14.

Fulwiler, Toby. *College Writing: A Personal Approach to Academic Writing*. 3rd ed. Portsmouth, NH: Heinemann, 2002.

Gee, James Paul. "Semiotic Social Spaces and Affinity Spaces from *The Age of Mythology* to Today's Schools." In *Beyond Communities of Practice: Language, Power, and Social Context*, edited by David Barton and Karin Tusting, 214–32. Cambridge: Cambridge University Press, 2005.

Gere, Anne Ruggles. "Kitchen Tables and Rented Rooms: The Extracurriculum of Composition." *College Composition and Communication* 45, no. 1 (1994): 75–92.

Gilyard, Keith. "The Rhetoric of Translingualism." *College English* 78, no. 3 (2016): 284–89.

———. *Voices of the Self: A Study of Language Competence*. Detroit: Wayne State University Press, 1991.

Gilyard, Keith, and Adam J. Banks. *On African-American Rhetoric*. New York: Routledge, 2018.

Glenn, Cheryl. "Comment: Truth, Lies, and Method: Revisiting Feminist Historiography." *College English* 62, no. 3 (2000): 387–89.

———. *Rhetoric Retold: Regendering the Tradition from Antiquity through the Renaissance*. Carbondale: Southern Illinois University Press, 1997.

——— *Unspoken: A Rhetoric of Silence*. Carbondale: Southern Illinois University Press, 2004.

Goggin, Maureen Daly. "Introduction: Threading Women." In *Women and the Material Culture of Needlework and Textiles, 1750–1950*, edited by Maureen Daly Goggin and Beth Fowkes Tobin, 1–10. Burlington, VT: Ashgate, 2009.

———. "Stitching a Life in 'Pen of Steele and Silken Inke': Elizabeth Parker's *Circa* 1830 Sampler." In *Women and the Material Culture of Needlework and Textiles, 1750–1950*, edited by Maureen Daly Goggin and Beth Fowkes Tobin, 31–50. Burlington, VT: Ashgate, 2009.

———. "Visual Rhetoric in Pens of Steel and Inks of Silk: Challenging the Great Visual/Verbal Divide." In *Defining Visual Rhetorics*, edited by Charles A. Hill and Marguerite Helmers, 87–110. Mahwah, NJ: Lawrence Erlbaum, 2004.

Goggin, Maureen Daly, and Beth Fowkes Tobin, eds. *Women and the Material Culture of Needlework and Textiles, 1750–1950*. Burlington, VT: Ashgate, 2009.

Gonzales, Laura. "Multimodality, Translingualism, and Rhetorical Genre Studies." *Composition Forum* 31 (2015). http://compositionforum.com/issue/31/multimodality.php.

———. *Sites of Translation: What Multilinguals Can Teach Us about Digital Writing and Rhetoric*. Ann Arbor: University of Michigan Press, 2018.

Gordon, Beverly, and Laurel Horton. "Turn-of-the-Century Quilts: Embodied Objects in a Web of Relationships." In *Women and the Material Culture of Needlework and Textiles, 1750–1950*, edited by Maureen Daly Goggin and Beth Fowkes Tobin, 93–110. Burlington, VT: Ashgate, 2009.

Gordon, John Steele. "Dr. Townsend's Crusade." *American Heritage* 52, no. 7 (2001): 49.

Graves, Michael P. "One Friend's Journey." *Rhetoric and Public Affairs* 7, no. 4 (2004): 513–23. https://doi.org/10/1353/rap.2005/0026.

Gray, Lisa. "Made in Gee's Bend: The Alabama Quilters Return to the Houston Museum That Launched Their Art Careers." *Houston Chronicle*, June 11, 2006. http://www.chron.com/entertainment/article/Made-in-Gee-s-Bend-1895640.php.

Griffo, Rachel. "Recontextualizing Composition Studies: Translingual Practice, Representation, and an Enacted Methodology." PhD diss., Indiana University of Pennsylvania, 2015.

Guelzo, Allen C. "Abraham Lincoln and the Doctrine of Necessity." *Journal of the Abraham Lincoln Association* 18, no. 1 (1997): 57–81. www.jstor.org/stable/20148949.

Gurney, Eliza P. Kirkbride. *The Garland: Selections from Various Authors by E. P. Gurney*. Philadelphia: Porter & Coates, 1879.

———. *Heart Utterances at Various Periods of a Chequered Life*. Unpublished. HathiTrust Digital Library. http://hdl.handle.net/2027/nyp.334330666-155. Accessed January 10, 2018.

Haltunnen, Karen. *Confidence Men and Painted Women: A Study of Middle-Class Culture in America, 1830–1870*. New Haven, CT: Yale University Press, 1986.

Harrison, Kimberly. *The Rhetoric of Rebel Women: Civil War Diaries and Confederate Persuasion*. Carbondale: Southern Illinois University Press, 2013.

Haugeberg, Karissa. *Women against Abortion: Inside the Largest Moral Reform Movement of the Twentieth Century*. Urbana: University of Illinois Press, 2017.

Hedges, Elaine. "Quilts and Women's Culture." *Radical Teacher* 100 (2014): 10–14.

Helmers, Marguerite, and Charles A. Hill, eds. *Defining Visual Rhetorics*. Mahwah, NJ: Lawrence Erlbaum, 2004.

Henry, David. "Text in Context: Lucretia Mott's 'Discourse on Woman.'" *Rhetoric Society Quarterly* 25 (1995): 11–19.

Herman, Bernard. "The Quilts of Gee's Bed: How Great Art Gets Lost." *Journal of Modern Craft* 2, no. 1 (2009): 9–15.

Hesse, Doug, Nancy Sommers, and Kathleen Blake Yancey. "Evocative Objects: Reflections on Teaching, Learning, and Living in between." *College English* 74, no. 4 (2012): 325–50.

Highsmith, Carol M., photographer. *Gee's Bend, Alabama*. Photograph. April 5, 2010. https://www.loc.gov/item/2010639030/.

Hogg, Charlotte. "Sorority Rhetorics as Everyday Epideictic." *College English* 80, no. 5 (2018): 423–48.

Holland, Matthew S. "A Model of Civic Charity." In *Bonds of Affection: Civic Charity and the Making of America—Winthrop, Jefferson, and Lincoln*. Washington, DC: Georgetown University Press, 2007.

Holtzman, Abraham. *The Townsend Movement: A Political Study*. New York: Octagon Books, 1975.

hooks, bell. *Yearning: Race, Gender, and Cultural Politics*. Cambridge, MA: South End Press, 1990.

Horner, Bruce. *Rewriting Composition: Terms of Exchange*. Carbondale: Southern Illinois University Press, 2016.

———. "Traditions and Professionalization: Reconceiving Work in Composition." *College Composition and Communication* 51, no. 3 (2000): 366–98.

Horner, Bruce, and Karen Kopelson, eds. *Reworking English in Rhetoric and Composition: Global Interrogations, Local Interventions*. Carbondale: Southern Illinois University Press, 2014.

Horner, Bruce, and Min-Zhan Lu. *Representing the "Other": Basic Writers and the Teaching of Basic Writing*. Urbana, IL: NCTE, 1999.

Horner, Bruce, Min-Zhan Lu, Jacqueline Jones Royster, and John Trimbur. "Opinion: Language Difference in Writing: Toward a Translingual Approach." *College English* 73, no. 3 (2011): 303–21.

Horner Bruce, Samantha NeCamp, and Christiane Donahue. "Toward a Multilingual Composition Scholarship: From English Only to a Translingual Norm." *College Composition and Communication* 63, no. 2 (2011): 269–300.

Horner, Bruce, Cynthia Selfe, and Tim Lockridge. "Translinguality, Transmodality, and Difference: Exploring Dispositions, Change in Language, and Learning." *Enculturation Intermezzo*. http://intermezzo.enculturation.net/01/ttd-horner-selfe-lockridge/index.htm.

Horner, Bruce, and John Trimbur. "English-Only and U.S. College Composition." *College Composition and Communication* 53, no. 4 (2002): 594–630.

Hunt, John Dixon. "The Sign of the Object." In *History from Things: Essays on Material Culture*, edited by Steven Lubar and W. David Kingery, 293–98. Washington, DC: Smithsonian Institution Press, 1993.

Indivisible. "How Your Member of Congress Thinks and How to Use that to Save Democracy." https://indivisible.org/resource/how-your-member-congress-thinks-and-how-use-save-democracy. Accessed June 18, 2018.

Ingle, Larry H. *Quakers in Conflict: The Hicksite Reformation*. Knoxville: University of Tennessee Press, 1986.

Jarratt, Susan. "Comment: Rhetoric and Feminism: Together Again." *College English* 62 (2000): 390–93.

———. *Rereading the Sophists: Classical Rhetoric Refigured*. Carbondale: Southern Illinois University Press, 1991.

Johnson, Bob. "Internationally Acclaimed Quilter Claims Fraud in Lawsuit Seeking Share of Quilts' Profits." *Daily Herald*, June 6, 2007. http://www.heraldextra.com/business/internationally-acclaimed-quilter-claims-fraud-in-lawsuit-seeking-share-of/.

———. "Suits Brought by Rural Alabama Quilters Resolved." Associated Press, August 25, 2008. https://www.foxnews.com/printer_friendly_wires/2008Aug25/0,4675,GeeapossBendQuilts,00.html. Accessed May 15, 2011.

Johnson, George B. "The Quakerism of Abraham Lincoln." *Bulletin of Friends Historical Association* 28, no. 2 (1939): 63–67.

Jordan, Jay. "Material Translingual Ecologies." *College English* 77, no. 4 (2005): 364–82.

Kennedy, George A., ed. *Aristotle* On Rhetoric*: A Theory of Civic Discourse*. 2nd ed. New York: Oxford University Press, 2007.

Kete, Mary Louise. *Sentimental Collaborations: Mourning and Middle-Class Identity in Nineteenth-Century America*. Durham, NC: Duke University Press, 2000.

Kilfoil, Carrie. "Beyond the 'Foreign' Language Requirement: From a Monolingual to a Translingual Ideology in Rhetoric and Composition Graduate Education." *Rhetoric Review* 34, no. 5 (2015): 426–44.

Kimball, Elizabeth. "Commonplace, Quakers, and the Founding of Haverford School." *Rhetoric Review* 30, no. 4 (2011): 377–78.

Kimmelman, Michael. "Art/Architecture: The Year in Review—The Critics/10 Moments; Richter, and Cloth, Were Abundant." *New York Times*, December 29, 2002. http://www.nytimes.com/2002/12/29/arts/art-architecture-year-review-critics-10-moments-richter-cloth-were-abundant.html.

———. "Art Review: Jazzy Geometry, Cool Quilters." *New York Times*, November 29, 2002. http://www.nytimes.com/2002/11/29/arts/art-review-jazzy-geometry-cool-quilters.html.

Kinneavy, James L. "*Kairos* in Classical and Modern Rhetorical Theory." In *Rhetoric and Kairos: Essays in History, Theory, and Praxis*, edited by Phillip Sipiora and James S. Baumlin, 58–76. Albany: State University of New York Press, 2002.

Kraemer, Vanessa. "Letters to Lincoln: The Epideictic Rhetoric of Eliza P. Gurney." MA thesis, University of Louisville, 2006.

Kramsch, Claire. "The Traffic in Meaning: A Response to Mary Louise Pratt." *Asia-Pacific Journal of Teacher Education* 26, no. 1 (2006): 81–86.

Kress, Gunther R. *Multimodality: A Social Semiotic Approach to Contemporary Communication*. London: Routledge, 2010.

Kurtyka, Faith. "'Get Excited People!' Gendered Acts of Literacy in a Social Sorority." *Literacy in Composition Studies*, 3, no. 2 (2015): 22–43.

———. "We're Creating Ourselves Now: Crafting as Feminist Rhetoric in a Social Sorority." *Peitho Journal* 18, no. 2 (2016): 25–44.

Kynard, Carmen. "'New Life in This Dormant Creature': Notes on Social Consciousness, Language, and Learning in a College Classroom." In *ALT DiS: Alternative Discourses and the Academy*, edited by Christopher Schroeder, Helen Fox, and Patricia Bizzell, 112–25. Portsmouth, NH: Boynton/Cook-Heinemann, 2002.

———. *Vernacular Insurrections: Race, Black Protest, and the New Century in Composition-Literacies Studies*. Albany: State University of New York Press, 2013.

Lang, Clarence. *Black America in the Shadow of the Sixties: Notes on the Civil Rights Movement, Neoliberalism, and Politics*. Ann Arbor: University of Michigan Press, 2015.

Lederle, Cheryl, and Bernice Ramirez. "Frederick Douglass on Abraham Lincoln: The Writer and Abolitionist Remembers the President in Library of Congress Primary Sources." Library of Congress, Teaching with the Library of Congress. February 7, 2013. https://blogs.loc.gov/teachers/2013/02.

Leon, Eli. *Accidentally on Purpose: The Aesthetic Management of Irregularities in African Textiles and African-American Quilts*. Davenport, IA: Figge Art Museum, 2006.

Leonard, Rebecca Lorimer. "Multilingual Writing as Rhetorical Attunement." *College English* 76, no. 3 (2014): 227–47.

———. "Writing across Languages: Developing Rhetorical Attunement." In *Literacy as Translingual Practice: Between Communities and Classrooms*, edited by A. Suresh Canagarajah, 162–68. New York: Routledge, 2013.

Leonard, Rebecca Lorimer, and Rebecca Nowacek. "Transfer and Translingualism." *College English* 78, no. 3 (2016): 258–64.

Lincoln, Abraham. "Meditation on the Divine Will." In *The Collected Works of*

Abraham Lincoln, edited by Roy P. Basler, 5: 403–4. https://quod.lib.umich.edu/l/lincoln/lincoln5. Accessed January 10, 2018.

———. "Proclamation of Thanksgiving, July 15, 1863." In *The Collected Works of Abraham Lincoln*, edited by Roy P. Basler, 6: 333. New Brunswick, NJ: Rutgers University Press, 1953.

———. "Reply to Emancipation Memorial Presented by Chicago Christians of All Denominations." In *The Collected Works of Abraham Lincoln*, edited by Roy P. Basler, 5:419–21. https://quod.lib.umich.edu/l/lincoln/lincoln5/. Accessed January 10, 2018.

Livingston, Jane. "Reflections on the Art of Gee's Bend." In *Gee's Bend: The Women and Their Quilts*, edited by William Arnett and Paul Arnett, 52–61. Atlanta: Tinwood Books, 2002.

Logan, Shirley Wilson. *We Are Coming: The Persuasive Discourse of Nineteenth-Century Black Women*. Carbondale: Southern Illinois University Press, 1999.

Lu, Min-Zhan, and Bruce Horner. "Introduction: Translingual Work." *College English* 78, no. 3 (2016): 207–18.

———. "Translingual Literacy, Language Difference, and Matters of Agency." *College English* 75, no. 6 (2013): 582–607.

Lunsford, Andrea A., and Lisa Ede. "Representing Audience: 'Successful' Discourse and Disciplinary Critique." *College Composition and Communication* 47, no. 2 (1996): 167–79.

MacDowell, Marsha. "Native Quiltmaking: History, Traditions, and Studies." In *Women and the Material Culture of Needlework and Textiles, 1750–1950*, edited by Maureen Daly Goggin and Beth Fowkes Tobin, 129–46. Burlington, VT: Ashgate, 2009.

Mao, LuMing. "Introduction: Searching for the Way: Between the Whats and Wheres of Chinese Rhetoric." *College English* 72, no. 4 (2010): 329–49.

———. "Re-Clustering Traditional Academic Discourse." In *ALT DiS: Alternative Discourses and the Academy*, edited by Christopher Schroeder, Helen Fox, and Patricia Bizzell, 112–25. Portsmouth, NH: Boynton/Cook-Heinemann, 2002.

Martinez, Aja Y. "A Plea for Critical Race Theory Counterstory: Stock Story versus Counterstory: Dialogues concerning Alejandra's 'Fit' in the Academy." *Composition Studies* 42, no. 2 (2014): 33–55.

Marzio, Peter. "Foreword." In *Gee's Bend: The Women and Their Quilts*, edited by William Arnett and Paul Arnett, 7–9. Atlanta: Tinwood Books, 2002.

Mathieu, Paula, and Diana George. "*Not* Going It Alone: Public Writing, Independent Media, and the Circulation of Homeless Advocacy." *College Composition and Communication* 61, no. 1 (2009): 130–49.

Mattingly, Carol. *Appropriate[ing] Dress: Women's Rhetorical Style in Nineteenth-Century America*. Carbondale: Southern Illinois University Press, 2002.

———. "Telling Evidence: Rethinking What Counts in Rhetoric." *Rhetoric Society Quarterly* 32, no. 1 (2002): 99–108.

"May." Cambridge Dictionary English Grammar Today. http://dictionary.cambridge.org/grammar/british-grammar/modals-and-modality/may. Accessed October 30, 2017.

May, Isaac. "The President's Friends and Foes: The Effect of the Nixon Presidency on the Divisions of American Quakerism." *Quaker History* 102, no. 1 (2013): 17–38. https://doi.org/10.1353/qkh.2013.0000.

McNatt, Glenn. "Controversy Blankets Gee's Bend Community." *Chicago Tribune*, June 29, 2007. http://articles.chicagotribune.com/2007-07-29/news/0707260758_1_william-arnett-mr-arnett-quilts. Accessed May 15, 2011.

Miller, Carolyn R. "Foreword." In *Rhetoric and Kairos: Essays in History, Theory, and Praxis*, edited by Phillip Sipiora and James S. Baumlin, xi–xiii. Albany: State University of New York Press, 2002.

———. "Genre as Social Action." *Quarterly Journal of Speech* 70 (1984): 151–67.

Mott, Richard, ed. *Memoir and Correspondence of Eliza P. Gurney*. Philadelphia: J. B. Lippincott & Co., 1884.

Murray, Jesse George, ed. *New Horizons (An Autobiography) by Dr. Francis E. Townsend*. Chicago: J. L. Stewart Publishing Co., 1943.

NeCamp, Samantha. *Adult Literacy and American Identity: The Moonlight Schools and Americanization Programs*. Carbondale: Southern Illinois University Press, 2014.

Nelson, Julie. "'Out of the Mountain of Despair a Stone of Hope': Black Twitter and Rhetorics of Hope." Presentation. Rhetoric Society of America Conference, May 30–June 3, 2018.

Neuberger, Richard L., and Kelley Loe. *An Army of the Aged: A History and Analysis of the Townsend Old Age Pension Plan*. Caldwell, ID: Caxton Printers, 1936; rpt., New York: DaCapo Press, 1973.

Obama, Barack, and David Letterman. "My Next Guest Needs No Introduction with David Letterman." Interview. Netflix. Accessed January 14, 2017.

Pennycook, Alastair. *Language as a Local Practice*. New York: Routledge, 2010.

Perelman, Chaïm and Lucy Olbrechts-Tyteca. *The New Rhetoric: A Treatise on Argumentation*. Translated by John Wilkinson and Purcell Weaver. Notre Dame, IN: University of Notre Dame Press, 1969.

Pernot, Laurent. *Epideictic Rhetoric: Questioning the Stakes of Ancient Praise*. Austin: University of Texas Press, 2015.

Pettway, Tinnie. *Gee's Bend Experience: Poems and Tidbits about Life by Quilter Tinnie Pettway*. Alberta, AL: That's Sew Gee's Bend, 2008.

Pezzullo, Phaedra C., and Ted Striphas. "Resistance: Taking a Stand, Struggling to Matter." *Rhetoric Society Quarterly* 48, no. 3: 306–14. Special issue: *Keywords: A Glossary of the Pasts and Futures of the Rhetoric Society of America*.

Powell, Malea. "Listening to Ghosts: An Alternative (Non)Argument." In *ALT DiS: Alternative Discourses and the Academy*, edited by Christopher Schroeder, Helen Fox, and Patricia Bizzell, 11–22. Portsmouth, NH: Boynton/Cook, 2002.

Prior, Paul, and Jody Shipka. "Chronotopic Lamination: Tracing the Contours of Literate Activity." In *Writing Selves / Writing Societies: Research from Activity Perspectives*, edited by Charles Bazerman and David R. Russell, n.p. Fort Collins, CO: WAC Clearinghouse, 2003.

Pristash, Heather, Inez Schaechterle, and Sue Carter Wood. "The Needle as the Pen: Intentionality, Needlework, and the Production of Alternate Discourses of Power." In *Women and the Material Culture of Needlework and Textiles, 1750–1950*, edited by Maureen Daly Goggin and Beth Fowkes Tobin, 13–29. Burlington, VT: Ashgate, 2009.

"The Proclamation." *National Republican*, September 30, 1862. Primary Documents of American History, Library of Congress Chronicling America: Historic American Newspapers. http://www.loc.gov/rr/program/bib/ourdocs/EmanProc.html. Accessed October 10, 2017.

Propen, Amy. *Locating Visual-Material Rhetorics: The Map, the Mill, the GPS*. Anderson, SC: Parlor Press, 2012.

"Quilts from Gee's Bend." CraftBanter.com, Jelsoft Enterprises. Updated December 31, 2004. http://www.craftbanter.com/showthread.php?t=36051. Accessed May 15, 2011.

Raines, Ben. "Gee's Bend: A Fight for Rights." *Mobile Register* (Alabama), June 15, 2007.

Rao, Sameer. "This 'Black-ish' Scene Perfectly Captures Many Black Americans' Reaction to the Election." *Colorlines*, January 12, 2017. https://www.colorlines.com/articles/black-ish-scene-perfectly-captures-many-black-americans-reaction-election.

Ratcliffe, Krista. *Rhetorical Listening: Identification, Gender, Whiteness*. Carbondale: Southern Illinois University Press, 2005.

"Read Oprah Winfrey's Rousing Golden Globes Speech." *CNN*, January 10, 2018. https://www.cnn.com/2018/01/08/entertainment/oprah-globes-speech-transcript/index.html.

Reynolds, Nedra. "Ethos as Location: New Sites for Understanding Discursive Authority." *Rhetoric Review* 11, no. 2 (1993): 325–38.

———. *Geographies of Writing: Inhabiting Places and Encountering Difference*. Carbondale: Southern Illinois University Press, 1997.

Rhodan, Maya. "Transcript: Read Full Text of President Barack Obama's Speech in Selma." *Time*, March 7, 2015. http://time.com/3736357/barack-obama-selma-speech-transcript/.

Richardson, Elaine. "'To Protect and Serve': African American Female Literacies." *College Composition and Communication* 53, no. 4 (2002): 675–704.

Rietveld, Ronald D. "Reviewed Work: *Essays on Lincoln's Faith and Politics* by Hans J. Morgenthau, David Hein." *Illinois Historical Journal* 78, no. 1 (1985): 78–80. www.jstor.org/stable/40191830.

Ritchie, Joy S., and Kate Ronald, eds. *Available Means: An Anthology of Women's Rhetoric(s)*. Pittsburgh: University of Pittsburgh Press, 2001.

———. "Introduction: A Gathering of Rhetorics." In *Available Means: An Anthology of Women's Rhetoric(s)*, edited by Joy S. Ritchie and Kate Ronald, xv–xxx. Pittsburgh: University of Pittsburgh Press, 2001.

Rivers, Nathaniel. "Tracing the Missing Masses: Vibrancy, Symmetry, and Public Rhetoric Pedagogy." *Enculturation* 17 (2014). http://enculturation.net/missingmasses.

Robinson, William, ed. *The Annual Monitor for 1883 or Obituary of the Members of the Society of Friends in Great Britain and Ireland for the Year 1882*. London: Barrett Sons & Co., 1882.

Rohan, Liz. "I Remember Mama: Material Rhetoric, Mnemonic Activity, and One Woman's Turn-of-the-Twentieth-Century Quilt." *Rhetoric Review* 23, no. 4 (2004): 368–87.

Royster, Jacqueline Jones. "Academic Discourses or Small Boats on a Big Sea." In *ALT DiS: Alternative Discourse and the Academy*, edited by Christopher Schroeder, Helen Fox, and Patricia Bizzell, 23–30. Portsmouth, NH: Boynton/Cook, 2002.

———. *Traces of a Stream: Literacy and Social Change among African American Women*. Pittsburgh: University of Pittsburgh Press, 2000.

———. "When the First Voice You Hear Is Not Your Own." *College Composition and Communication* 47, no. 1 (1996): 29–40.

Royster, Jacqueline Jones, and Gesa E. Kirsch, eds. *Feminist Rhetorical Practices: New*

Horizons for Rhetoric, Composition, and Literacy Studies. Carbondale: Southern Illinois University Press, 2012.

Russell, Heather D. "Quilted Discourse: Writing and Resistance in African Atlantic Narratives." In *Stitching Resistance: Women, Creativity, and Fiber Arts*, edited by Marjorie Agosín, 201–11. Kent, UK: Solis Press, 2014.

Ryan, Kathleen J., Nancy Myers, and Rebecca Jones. "Introduction: Identifying Feminist Ecological *Ethē*." In *Rethinking Ethos: A Feminist Ecological Approach to Rhetoric*, edited by Kathleen J. Ryan, Nancy Myers, and Rebecca Jones, 1–22. Carbondale: Southern Illinois University Press, 2016.

———, eds. *Rethinking Ethos: A Feminist Ecological Approach to Rhetoric*. Carbondale: Southern Illinois University Press, 2016.

Sanchez-Eppler, Karen. "Then When We Clutch Hardest: On the Death of a Child and the Replication of an Image." In *Sentimental Men: Masculinity and the Politics of Affect in American Culture*, edited by Mary Chapman and Glenn Hendler, 64–85. Oakland: University of California Press, 1999.

Schlesinger, Arthur. *The Age of Roosevelt: The Politics of Upheaval*. Boston: Houghton Mifflin, 1960.

Schneider, Stephen A. *You Can't Padlock an Idea: Rhetorical Education at the Highlander Folk School, 1932–1961*. Columbia: University of South Carolina Press, 2014.

Schroeder, Christopher, Helen Fox, and Patricia Bizzell, eds. *ALT DiS: Alternative Discourses and the Academy*. Portsmouth, NH: Boynton/Cook-Heinemann, 2002.

Schulz, Kathryn. "What Calling Congress Achieves." *New Yorker*, March 6, 2017. https://www.newyorker.com/magazine/2017/03/06/what-calling-congress-achieves. Accessed June 6, 2017.

Seaton, Tony. "Travel and Touring in England by Elite Quaker, Industrial Families in the Long Century: The Journeys of Mary-Anne Schimmelpenninck (Née Galton) of Birmingham (1778–1856)." *Quaker Studies* 20, no. 1 (2015): 117–44.

Selzer, Jack, and Sharon Crowley. *Rhetorical Bodies*. Madison: University of Wisconsin Press, 1999.

Sheard, Cynthia Miecznikowski. "The Public Value of Epideictic Rhetoric." *College English* 58, no. 7 (1996): 765–94.

Shipka, Jody. "Including, But Not Limited to, the Digital: Composing Multimedia Texts." In *Multimodal Literacies and Emerging Genres*, edited by Tracey Bowen and Carl Whithaus, 73–89. Pittsburgh: University of Pittsburgh Press, 2013.

———. *Toward a Composition Made Whole*. Pittsburgh: University of Pittsburgh Press, 2011.

———. "Transmodality in/and Processes of Making: Changing Dispositions and Practice." *College English* 78, no. 3 (2016): 250–57.

Showalter, Elaine. *Sister's Choice: Tradition and Change in American Women's Writing*. Oxford: Clarendon Press, 1991.

Sinor, Jennifer. *The Extraordinary Work of Ordinary Writing: Annie Ray's Diary*. Iowa City: University of Iowa Press, 2002.

Sipiora, Phillip. "Introduction: The Ancient Concept of *Kairos*." In *Rhetoric and Kairos: Essays in History, Theory, and Praxis*, edited by Phillip Sipiora and James S. Baumlin, 1–22. Albany: State University of New York Press, 2002.

Skinner, Carolyn. *Women Physicians and Professional Ethos in Nineteenth-Century America*. Carbondale: Southern Illinois University Press, 2014.

Smitherman, Geneva. *Word from the Mother: Language and African Americans*. New York: Routledge, 2006.

Sohan, Vanessa Kraemer. "'But a Quilt Is More': Recontextualizing the Discourse(s) of the Gee's Bend Quilts." *College English* 77, no. 4 (2015): 294–316.

———. "Relocalized Listening: Responding to All Student Texts from a Translingual Starting Point." In *Reworking English in Rhetoric and Composition: Global Discussion of Interrogations, Local Interventions*, edited by Bruce Horner and Karen Kopelson, 191–206. Carbondale: Southern Illinois University Press, 2014.

———. "Thinking Differently about Language Difference: Relocalized Listening." PhD diss., University of Louisville, 2011.

———. "Working English(es) as Rhetoric(s) of Disruption." *JAC: A Journal of Composition Theory* 29, nos. 1–2 (2009): 270–76.

Solomon, Martha, and Lucy Hogan. "Extending the Conversation: Sharing the Inner Light." *Rhetoric Society Quarterly* 25 (1995): 32–46.

Sullivan, Dale L. "The Ethos of Epideictic Encounter." *Philosophy and Rhetoric* 26 (1993): 113–33.

Sullivan, Patricia. *Experimental Writing in Composition: Aesthetics and Pedagogies*. Pittsburgh: University of Pittsburgh Press, 2012.

"Sympathy, n." Oxford English Dictionary Online. Florida International University Libraries. http://www.oed.com/view/Entry/196271.

Timmerman, David M. "Epideictic Oratory." In *Encyclopedia of Rhetoric: Communication from Ancient Times to the Information Age*, edited by Theresa Enos, 228–31. New York: Routledge, 1996.

Tobin, Jacqueline L., and Raymond G. Dobard. *Hidden in Plain View: A Secret Story of Quilts and the Underground Railroad*. Columbia: University of Missouri Press, 1994.

"Topic: Gee's Bend Quilts in Smithsonian." Artisan's Square, Simple Machines Forum. Updated October 17, 2006. http://artisanssquare.com/sg_classic/index.php?topic=916.0. Accessed May 15, 2011.

Torsney, Cheryl B., and Judy Elsley. "Introduction." In *Quilt Culture: Tracing the Pattern*, edited by Cheryl B. Torsney and Judy Elsley, 1–10. Columbia: University of Missouri Press, 1994.

Trapani, William C., and Chandra A. Maldonado. "*Kairos*: On the Limits to Our (Rhetorical) Situation." *Rhetoric Society Quarterly* 48, no. 3 (2018): 278–86.

Trueblood, David Elton. *Abraham Lincoln: Theologian of American Anguish*. New York: Harper & Row, 1973.

Turkle, Sherry, ed. *Evocative Objects: Things We Think With*. Cambridge, MA: MIT Press, 2007.

Villanueva, Victor. *Bootstraps*. Urbana, IL: NCTE, 1993.

———. "*Memoria* Is a Friend of Ours: On the Discourse of Color." *College English* 67, no. 1 (2004): 9–19.

Wahlman, Maude Southwell. *Signs and Symbols: African Images in African-American Quilts*. New York: Studio Books, 1993.

Wallace, David. *Compelled to Write: Alternative Rhetoric in Theory and Practice*. Logan: Utah State University Press, 2011.

Walzer, Arthur. "*Epideictic Rhetoric: Questioning the Stakes of Ancient Praise*, by Laurent Pernot." *Rhetoric Society Quarterly* 46, no. 5 (2016): 1–5.

Wardlaw, Alvia. "Introduction: The Quilts of Gee's Bend." In *Gee's Bend: The Women and Their Quilts*, edited by William Arnett and Paul Arnett, 10–21. Atlanta: Tinwood Books, 2002.

Watson, Missy, and Rachel Shapiro. "Clarifying the Multiple Dimensions of Monolingualism: Keeping Our Sights on Language Politics." *Composition Forum* 38 (2018). http://compositionforum.com/issue/38/monolingualism.php#note1.

Weathers, Winston. *An Alternate Style: Options in Composition*. Rochelle Park, NJ: Hayden Book Co., 1980.

Weaver, Stephanie. "An Activist Rhetorician Joins Indivisible: Extracurricular Rhetorical Education in the Trump Era." Presentation for Rhetoric Society of America, May 2018.

Welch, Nancy. "Living Room: Teaching Public Writing in a Post-Publicity Era." *College Composition and Communication* 56, no. 3 (2005): 470–92.

Welsh, Teresa. "A Forgotten Era of Activism." *U.S. News and World Report*, November 21, 2013. https://www.usnews.com/opinion/articles/2013/11/21/the-forgotten-era-of-grassroots-american-activism-in-the-70s-and-80s.

Wenger, Etienne. *Communities of Practice: Learning, Meaning, and Identity*. Cambridge: Cambridge University Press, 1998.

Whipp, Glenn. "MacGyver's Pop Cultural Hold on Us." *LA Times*, May 16, 2010. http://articles.latimes.com/2010/may/16/entertainment/la-ca-macgyver-20100516.

Why Quilts Matter: History, Art & Politics. DVD. The Kentucky Quilt Project, 2011.

Williams, Mary Rose. "A Reconceptualization of Protest Rhetoric: Women's Quilts as Rhetorical Forms." *Women's Studies in Communication* 17, no. 2 (1994): 20–44.

Willis, Owen. "The Most Important Bulletin Ever Issued to Townsendites." *TNW*, n.d., n.p.

Winger, Stewart. *Lincoln, Religion, and Romantic Cultural Politics*. Dekalb: Northern Illinois University Press, 2003.

"With Malice toward None: The Abraham Lincoln Bicentennial Exhibition: Frederick Douglass Describing Lincoln." Library of Congress. https://www.loc.gov/exhibits/lincoln/ext/al0177.html?loclr=blogtea. Accessed December 1, 2017.

Wolfshank, Joshua. "Lincoln's Great Depression." *The Atlantic*, October 2005. https://www.theatlantic.com/magazine/archive/2005/10/lincolns-great-depression/304247/. Accessed September 9, 2017.

Wright, Sheila. "Gaining a Voice: An Interpretation of Quaker Women's Writing, 1740–1850." *Quaker Studies* 8, no. 1 (2003): 36–50.

Young, Vershawn Ashanti. *Your Average Nigga: Performing Race, Literacy, and Masculinity*. Detroit: Wayne State University Press, 2007.

Young, Vershawn Ashanti, and Aja Y. Martinez, with Julie Anne Naviaux. "Introduction: Code-Meshing as World English." In *Code-Meshing as World English: Pedagogy, Policy, Performance*, edited by Vershawn Ashanti Young and Aja Y. Martinez, with Julie Anne Naviaux, xix–xxxi. Urbana, IL: NCTE, 2011.

Zacharek, Stephanie, Eliana Dockterman, and Haley Sweetland Edwards. "Person of the Year: The Silence Breakers." *Time*, December 18, 2017.

Zegart, Shelly. "Myth and Methodology: Shelly Zegart Unpicks African-American Quilt Scholarship." *Selvedge* 21 (2008): 48–56.

Zulick, Margaret D., and Michael Leff. "Time and the 'True Light' in Lucretia Mott's 'Discourse on Woman.'" *Rhetoric Society Quarterly* 25 (1995): 20–31.

Index

Page numbers in italics refer to illustrations.